How to
Read the Bible in
Changing Times

How to
Read the Bible in
Changing Times

Understanding and
Applying God's Word Today

Mark L. Strauss

BakerBooks
a division of Baker Publishing Group
Grand Rapids, Michigan

Published by Baker Books
a division of Baker Publishing Group
P.O. Box 6287, Grand Rapids, MI 49516-6287
www.bakerbooks.com

Printed in the United States of America

Library of Congress Cataloging-in-Publication Data
Strauss, Mark L.
    How to read the Bible in changing times : understanding and applying God's word today / Mark L. Strauss.
        p.   cm.
    Includes bibliographical references and index.
    ISBN 978-0-8010-7283-3 (pbk.)
    1. Bible—Hermeneutics. I. Title.
BS476.S79 2011
220.601—dc22   2011013439

Contents

Preface

THE IDEAS INTRODUCED IN THIS BOOK HAVE BEEN DEVELOPING over the past twenty years, as I have taught principles for reading and applying the Bible ("hermeneutics") to students in undergraduate, graduate, and church settings. Yet the immediate circumstances arose when Jack Kuhatschek, Executive Vice President and Publisher for Baker Publishing Group, approached me a few years back about writing it. Jack, a close friend (and frequent theology dialogue partner), has a long history of work on this topic, including his immensely practical volume on the application of Scripture, *Taking the Guesswork Out of Applying the Bible* (InterVarsity, 1990). For years Jack wanted someone to take the subject further. I am honored that he approached me for this task. The title of the book was his idea, and it sums up beautifully the challenge of determining how a collection of ancient books written to God's people millennia ago can be relevant to us today in our rapidly changing world.

I am grateful to Jack for his input along the way, and also to my project editor at Baker, Amy Donaldson, both for her expertise as an editor and for her exceptional scholarship. Her careful eye and sharp mind greatly improved the volume.

The book is dedicated to Jack, but also to the many students who have engaged, questioned, challenged, developed, and utilized practically the ideas that are presented here. This book is for them; but ultimately, I pray, it is for the glory of God.

Mark Strauss
March 2011

vii

1

Introduction

The Unchanging Word in a Changing World

FIRST MET JOHN WHEN HE SHOWED UP AT THE COLLEGE MIN-
istry in the church where I was serving as a college intern. John, a
diesel mechanic, had come from a very tough background and was a
recovering alcoholic and drug abuser. He had recently made a decision to follow Jesus Christ and was anxious to find fellowship with
other Christians. I had some doubts about his potential, considering
his rough exterior, but we started meeting together regularly in a discipleship relationship. Someone had given him a Bible, and he began
to read it voraciously. We decided to do a Bible study together, and I
asked him which book of the Bible he wanted to study. "Romans!"
he said. He had heard this was the apostle Paul's greatest theological
work and wanted to go deep into "hard-core" Bible study. I had my
doubts, unsure he could handle such a challenging book, but we
began meeting at his apartment, drinking coffee and discussing the
passage we'd read that week.

As the months went by, I was constantly amazed at John's growing
insight into the text. He would make a profound comment about the
meaning of this or that passage, or about how a passage connected to

Paul's larger thought in the letter. I would ask him, "Who taught you that?" or "Did you hear that from a preacher somewhere?" His answer was always the same: "No, that's what the text says! Remember, you told me to read it in context." (That statement warms the heart of a Bible professor!) Not only did I see John's knowledge of the Bible grow, but I saw his life transformed, as he began to be shaped into a man of God. I witnessed before my eyes the transforming power of the Word of God.

The Transforming Power of the Word of God

The Bible is the best-selling book of all time. More Bibles are published each year than any other book. The Bible is also the most revered book of all time. Christians affirm that the Bible is the "Word of God"—his message to us and our guidebook for life. Countless generations can testify how the Bible has transformed their lives, turning sinners into saints, giving meaning to life, and providing strength and guidance through life's most difficult circumstances.

In *How Christianity Changed the World*, Alvin J. Schmidt documents the profound impact that the Bible and Christianity have had on the world.[1] Biblical teaching and values have been the impetus behind many of the world's great social and ethical movements. These include the abolition of infanticide and advocacy for the value of human life, raising the status and dignity of women, building hospitals and promoting health care, establishing schools and broadening education, defending the rights of workers, feeding the poor and combating poverty, sponsoring the arts and sciences, and working for justice for all.

On a more personal level, the Bible provides guidance and comfort in the lives of individuals. I remember sitting beside the bed of a dear friend who was dying of cancer. She had dropped into a coma, the last stage of her disease, and the family had asked me to come by. They gathered around the bed, and I opened my Bible and read Psalm 23. We reflected together that even when we pass through life's darkest valleys we have nothing to fear, because the Lord is with us. We have hope, knowing that we will "dwell in the house of the LORD forever" (Ps. 23:6).

Even more personally, I remember standing at my father's grave shortly after his death in 1993, with my mother and three brothers beside me. One of my brothers opened his Bible and read 1 Thessalonians 4:13–18. This great passage reminded us that this was not the end. One day graves would be opened and all who had died in Christ would rise to meet the Lord in the air—a great reunion that would last forever.

Transforming experiences like these have confirmed for countless generations that the Bible is God's Word—a message from God of comfort, instruction, and guidance.

Message from God or Tool of Manipulation?

While the Bible is the most revered book of all time, it may also be the most misunderstood and misused, a tool of manipulation, evil, injustice, and even genocide. In the 2010 movie *The Book of Eli*, Denzel Washington plays a character named Eli, who has in his possession the last copy of the Bible in a postapocalyptic world. His mission is to get this Bible—the book of ultimate answers—to a safe haven where it can be copied, read, and passed down for posterity. His nemesis is a man named Carnegie, who desperately wants to get the book for himself. Carnegie's motives, however, are more sinister. He knows that the book has extraordinary power to control people and wants that power for himself. Though the movie is disturbing in many respects, it is a fascinating allegory about the power and potential of the Bible for good or for evil. For one man, the Bible has the answers to the ultimate questions in life and the power to redeem humanity. For another, it is a manipulative tool for self-promotion and power.

Throughout history, misuse of the Bible has had sometimes tragic results. William Miller (1782–1849), a Baptist preacher and a student of Bible prophecy, developed a system of biblical interpretation that he claimed could determine the time of the second coming of Jesus Christ. Drawing especially from Daniel 8–9, he predicted that Christ would return during the year 1844. One of his followers, Samuel S. Snow, refined Miller's method and identified an even more specific date, October 22, 1844. Miller's followers, known as Millerites, anxiously awaited that day; some even sold their possessions in anticipation of the coming millennial kingdom. The day came and went without incident, resulting in disappointment, disillusionment, and for some, loss of faith. It became known in history as the "Great Disappointment."[2]

Sadly, such end-time prognostication continues today in best-selling books written by "experts" on Bible prophecy. Some of them set dates, either general or specific; others point to contemporary persons or events as "signs" of the end times. Amazingly, despite the consistent and repeated failure of such books to accurately predict times, persons, or events, the Christian public seems to have an insatiable appetite for these works, which continue to sell briskly.

While such prophetic gurus may seem harmless and even entertaining, some end-time interpretations of the Bible have led to catastrophic results. In the early 1990s, a man named Vernon Howell assumed leadership of an end-time sect known as the Branch Davidians.[3] The group was established in the 1930s by Victor Houteff (1886–1955), who had broken away from the Seventh-Day Adventists to form his own group. Houteff developed an elaborate system of interpretation for the end times based on the seven seals of the book of Revelation (Revelation 6–8). After Houteff died, a series of leaders succeeded him, and the group gradually grew. Howell joined the sect in 1981 and, through his charismatic personality and vast biblical knowledge, gradually usurped the leadership and gained authority over the group. Howell changed his name to David Koresh—"David" because he considered the group to be the reestablishment of Israel's Davidic dynasty, and "Koresh" from the name of the Persian king Cyrus, who was appointed by God to restore Israel as a nation after the Babylonian exile (Isa. 45:1).

Koresh convinced his followers that the prophecy of the seven seals of the book of Revelation was soon coming to fulfillment in their little group. Living in a compound near Waco, Texas, they sought to become self-sufficient, farming the land and stockpiling food and weapons in preparation for the coming apocalypse. On February 28, 1993, dozens of heavily armed federal agents raided the compound in search of illegal weapons. Koresh and his followers were convinced that the end of the world was at hand. In the shootout that resulted, four agents and six members of the group were killed. Koresh was seriously wounded, and a standoff ensued. In the following weeks, federal agents negotiated with Koresh, who claimed he would end the siege once he had decoded the seven seals of Revelation. After fifty-one days, the government's frustration reached a breaking point, and Attorney General Janet Reno ordered an assault on the compound. The raid ended in tragedy as the compound caught fire and burned. Eighty-six members of the group died in the assault, including many women and children. Controversy has raged for years over the proportion of blame for the tragedy and whether the government overreacted. One thing is certain, however: Koresh's misrepresentation of prophetic Scriptures had tragic results.

Prophets of the end time are not the only ones who misuse the Bible. It is quoted by all kinds of people—politicians, social commentators, religious leaders—to promote a bewildering array of agendas. A yoga master and swami cites Jesus's words, "Blessed are the pure in heart, for they shall see God," and then explains that the blessed are those "who purify their consciousness, for they shall see themselves as God."[4] The original intent of the passage is ignored, and the text is read through a pantheistic worldview where the interpreter sees himself as God. Mormons identify the prophecy of two sticks in Ezekiel 37:15–23 as a prediction for the emergence of the *Book of Mormon* as an authoritative revelation from God beside the Bible (the passage actually refers to the reunification of the northern and southern kingdoms of Israel).[5] Jehovah's Witnesses identify themselves as the 144,000 special servants "sealed" with the name of God in the book of Revelation (Rev. 7:3–8; 14:1–4) and so as the only true believers in the end times. The Bible can be used to justify almost any agenda or doctrine, if the original intent of the biblical authors is misunderstood or distorted.

The Bible has been used to promote crusades of conquest, riots and pogroms against Jews and other minorities, and even the subjugation of whole people groups. In the years leading up to the Nazi Holocaust, some German theologians reinterpreted the New Testament to distance Jesus and his followers from their Jewish roots.[6] Many claimed that the region of Galilee was populated by non-Jews and that Jesus came from Aryan rather than Jewish ancestry. Jesus's goal, it was argued, was to abolish Judaism, a violent religion that threatened all Christians. In this literature, "Jesus was transformed

5

from a Jew prefigured by the Old Testament into an anti-Semite and proto-Nazi."[7] This Aryan Jesus became part of the justification for the genocide of millions of Jews during the Holocaust.

While the Nazi justification of the Holocaust was certainly the most destructive misuse of the Bible, the most tragic misuse in American history was the defense of African slavery. Advocates of slavery asserted that the distinction of races arose from Noah's three sons—Ham, Shem, and Japheth—and that the so-called Hamitic curse of Genesis 9:25 relegated Africans to an inferior status as slaves.[8] Benjamin M. Palmer, a New Orleans clergyman and leading proponent of slavery, wrote in 1858:

> the race of Shem [from whom the Jews arose] was providentially selected as the channel for transmitting religion and worship; . . . Japhet and his race . . . seemed designated to be the organ of human civilization, in cultivating the intellectual powers. . . . The Japhetic whites, spreading over the diversified continent of Europe, through a protracted discipline develope [sic] the higher powers of the soul in politics, jurisprudence, science and art: while the Asiatic Japhetites dispersed over a more monotonous continent, embark in those pursuits of industry fitted to the lower capacities of our nature. The descendants of Ham, on the contrary, in whom the sensual and corporeal appetites predominate, are driven like an infected race beyond the deserts of Sahara, where under a glowing sky nature harmonizes with their brutal and savage disposition.[9]

Today we are shocked at such outrageous and absurd stereotyping: religious Semites, intellectual and creative whites, industrious Asians, and brutal and savage blacks. But it is also tragic that people have used the Bible to justify such stereotypes. Advocates of slavery further claimed that God has sanctioned slavery in the Old Testament (Lev. 25:44) and that the Bible never calls for its abolition. Indeed, they argued, Peter commands slaves to submit "in reverent fear of God" to their masters, "not only to those who are good and considerate, but also to those who are harsh" (1 Pet. 2:18). Paul, too, repeatedly calls for slaves to submit to their masters (Eph. 6:5–6; Col. 3:22; Titus 2:9).

There were contrary voices in this debate, who also quoted the Bible.[10] Those working for the abolition of slavery countered the pro-slavery arguments with biblical texts of their own, pointing out that the dignity of human beings created in God's image (Gen. 1:26) demanded the abolition of slavery. No human being should own another. Paul himself says that in Christ "there is neither Jew nor Gentile, neither slave nor free, nor is there male and female" (Gal. 3:28). Paul also encourages slaves to gain their freedom if they are able (1 Cor. 7:21), and asserts the essential equality before God of slave and master (Eph. 6:8; Col. 3:24; Philem. 16–17).

In short, the Bible was used to support both agendas. So what does the Bible teach about slavery? Is there an authentic message from God in the text, or can people make the Bible mean whatever they want it to mean? For Christians who believe in the authority of Scripture, this is a critical and urgent question. In a world of constantly changing agendas and ideas, can we hear in the Bible a consistent and authoritative message from God?

Finding a Verse to Fit Your Agenda

While the two issues discussed above—human slavery and geno-cide—are egregious examples of the misuse of Scripture, throughout history people have used the Bible to support every conceivable agenda. Consider the following hot-button topics in our society today.

1. *War and killing.* Pacifists claim the Bible calls for peace and non-resistance. Jesus says to turn the other cheek when someone strikes you and, when a burden is forced upon you, to carry it for an extra mile. If someone sues you and takes your shirt, you should give them your coat as well (Matt. 5:38–42). In a world of hate and retribution, he calls for people to love even their enemies (Matt. 5:43–44). The apostle Paul affirms the same thing. He writes not to take revenge and never to repay evil with evil. We are not to be overcome by evil, but to overcome evil with good (Rom. 12:17–21). Advocates of just war, on the other hand, assert that war and killing are sometimes justified. God himself has called for war and even the slaughter of entire populations (Josh. 6:21; 8:24–27). Capital punishment is repeatedly mandated in the Old Testament: "Whoever sheds human blood, by humans shall their blood be shed; for in the image of God has God made mankind" (Gen. 9:6). The New Testament affirms

that God has established human governments to promote justice and to punish evil (Romans 13), and this often involves war and killing. What is God's will when it comes to killing other human beings?

2. *Socialism versus capitalism.* Socialists point out that the Bible calls for social justice and the need to share resources within the larger community (Matt. 5:42; Acts 2:44–45; 4:32). The accumulation of wealth holds great danger (Luke 3:11; 6:24–26; 12:13–21; 16:19–31; 18:18–30; 1 Tim. 6:10), and it is more blessed to give than to receive (Acts 20:35; 2 Corinthians 8–9). The Old Testament Jubilee year required the redistribution of land every fifty years to its original family allotments (Leviticus 25). Capitalists counter that these are misunderstandings of Scripture. The Jubilee year is a command distinctly for the twelve tribes of Israel, and the call to share possessions is always voluntary, never demanded (Acts 4:34–37; 5:4). How can you share freely with others unless you have private property to share? The original creation mandate calls for people to subdue the earth and exercise dominion over it (Gen. 1:28), an implicit recognition of private property and personal freedom. Again, appeal is made to Scripture to support both agendas.

3. *Roles of women and men.* One of the most divisive issues among evangelicals over the last fifty years has been the role of men and women in the church and the home, with both sides appealing to Scripture as their authority. Complementarians argue the Bible teaches that men and women have different, but complementary, roles. Men are to be leaders in the church and the home, while women are to fulfill supportive roles (1 Tim. 2:11–15; 3:2, 12), submitting to their husbands' authority (Eph. 5:22–24; Col. 3:18; 1 Pet. 3:1–6). Egalitarians counter that these commands arose within specific cultural contexts restricted to the first century and that God's design is for full equality between the sexes (Gal. 3:28). The subordination of women is a part of the fall (Gen. 3:16), and believers should work to restore the equality ordained by God at creation. How is Scripture to be read and applied in this case?

4. *Homosexuality.* Perhaps the most controversial and emotional of the issues debated in the church relates to homosexual relationships. Opponents of homosexuality argue that same-sex relationships are clearly rejected in Scripture. The Old Testament law forbids a man to have sexual relations with another man (Lev. 18:22; 20:13),

and the apostle Paul points to male and female homosexual behavior as a distortion of human sexuality resulting from our fallen human nature (Rom. 1:26–27; 1 Cor. 6:9; 1 Tim. 1:9–10). Pro-gay activists counter that these commands relate to practices such as male prostitution and pederasty (sex with children) and have no bearing on modern monogamous and loving homosexual relationships. The ancients had no concept of homosexual orientation and so these commands are not relevant for the church today.

Some readers will be shocked that anyone could possibly read the Bible and still affirm same-sex partnerships. Others will be shocked that anyone could read the Bible and not believe that God's love for people trumps culturally embedded commands against homosexual relationships. So who is right? The problem is that all of us come to the Bible with our own agendas, our own backgrounds, and our own perspectives. How do we look past these differences and determine *God's will in Scripture*?

Random Picking and Choosing?

In the face of so many different interpretations, some people default to the idea that you can make the Bible mean whatever you want. This, in turn, can produce cynicism concerning the Bible's authority. Consider this tongue-in-cheek letter that appeared a few years back on the internet. It is written as though from an adoring fan of radio talk show host Dr. Laura Schlessinger, because of her strong stand against homosexual behavior.

> Dear Dr. Laura,
>
> Thank you for doing so much to educate people regarding God's law. I have learned a great deal from you, and I try to share that knowledge with as many people as I can. When someone tries to defend the homosexual lifestyle, for example, I simply remind him that Leviticus 18:22 clearly states it to be an abomination. End of debate. I do need some advice from you, however, regarding some of the specific laws and how to best follow them.
>
> • When I burn a bull on the altar as a sacrifice, I know it creates a pleasing odor for the Lord (Lev. 1:9). The problem is my neighbors.

They claim the odor is not pleasing to them. How should I deal with this?

- I would like to sell my daughter into slavery, as it suggests in Exodus 21:7. In this day and age, what do you think would be a fair price for her?
- I know that I am allowed no contact with a woman while she is in her period of menstrual uncleanliness (Lev. 15:19–24). The problem is, how do I tell? I have tried asking, but most women take offense.
- Lev. 25:44 states that I may buy slaves from the nations that are around us. A friend of mine claims that this applies to Mexicans but not Canadians. Can you clarify?
- I have a neighbor who insists on working on the Sabbath. Exodus 35:2 clearly states he should be put to death. Am I morally obligated to kill him myself?
- A friend of mine feels that even though eating shellfish is an abomination (Lev. 11:10), it is a lesser abomination than homosexuality. I don't agree. Can you settle this?
- Lev. 21:20 states that I may not approach the altar of God if I have a defect in my sight. I have to admit that I wear reading glasses. Does my vision have to be 20/20, or is there some wiggle room here?

I know you have studied these things extensively, so I am confident you can help. Thank you again for reminding us that God's word is eternal and unchanging.

Kent Ashcraft[11]

The author of this satire is obviously mocking Christians for picking and choosing which commands to obey and which to ignore. But does the author have a point? How can Christians condemn homosexuals yet ignore other commands in Scripture, such as those forbidding the eating of shellfish? We might respond that those are Old Testament commands meant for the nation Israel under the old covenant. True; but Christians apparently pick and choose among New Testament commands as well. Most Christians, for example, do not greet each other with a kiss, even though this is explicitly commanded five times in the New Testament (Rom. 16:16; 1 Cor. 16:20; 2 Cor. 13:12; 1 Thess. 5:26; 1 Pet. 5:14). Nor do they require women to cover their heads in worship, despite Paul's injunction to do so in 1 Corinthians 11:5.

A Static Word in a Dynamic World?

These issues remind us that the Bible was written in a world very different from our own. How do we take a book that was written thousands of years ago, to people in a different culture facing different problems, and find meaning in it for our own time and circumstances? The people in the Bible could never have dreamed of airplanes, or televisions, or satellites, or cell phones, or the internet, or global media. Their world was changing at a snail's pace compared to today's blinding pace of change. We are facing issues that they could not have envisioned, such as genetic manipulation, stem-cell research, sex-change operations, or global terrorism. Can a Bible written so long ago and under such different circumstances have relevance for us in the present day and age?

To respond to these concerns, this book addresses the interpretation and application of Scripture in our changing times. We begin with the assumption that the Bible is God's inspired and authoritative Word, his message for the present day. We believe God has spoken, and we are to *hear* and *heed* his message. But how do we take a message that was written to other people in a different time and place and find meaning and application for us today? In other words, how does God continue to speak through words first spoken to others in ancient times? The goal presented here is to develop a model and framework for reading God's Word that enables us to formulate theological truth, answer ethical questions, and walk with God in our daily lives.

It is *not* a question of discerning which parts of the Bible are applicable to us and which are not. The Bible itself claims that it is *all* relevant. Consider 2 Timothy 3:16–17, perhaps the most important passage in the Bible concerning its own authority and inspiration: "All Scripture is God-breathed and is useful for teaching, rebuking, correcting and training in righteousness, so that the servant of God may be thoroughly equipped for every good work." If all Scripture is inspired and useful for teaching, rebuking, correcting, and training in righteousness, then all Scripture ought to be heard and applied. The question becomes not *whether* a passage of Scripture applies to us, but *how*.

Before we can determine how to apply the Bible, we must understand what the Bible is and what it is not. The next two chapters concern the nature of the Bible. There are many misconceptions about the Bible—even among Christians. For example, despite what some may think, the Bible is not a "magic-answer" book for decision making in life. Nor, at its heart, is it a list of commands to obey or promises to claim. Rather, the Bible is God's story, the drama of redemption, setting out the fundamental problem and solution to humanity's dilemma. The Bible teaches us who God is, who we are in relationship to him and to one another, and what his purpose is for us and for the world. As we grow in our knowledge of what it means to be part of God's story, we will learn to make good and godly decisions in life.

The chapters that follow will set out a "heart-of-God" approach to the Bible, where the goal of Scripture reading is to discern the heart of God and the mind of Christ. This discernment allows us to think God's thoughts after him and to determine his truth and his purpose in the changing world around us.

Discussion and Reflection Questions

1. Has the Bible had a transforming influence in your life? In what ways? What does the Bible mean to you?

2. How would you define what the Bible is?

3. What are some ways the Bible has been misread and misapplied throughout history?

4. Is it true that the Bible can mean anything you want it to mean? Is there a "correct" meaning in the Bible? If so, how do we discover it?

5. What was your reaction to the "Dr. Laura" letter in this chapter? Were you angry? Offended? Confused? Why?

6. Is every command and promise intended for us today? How can you tell which apply to us and which don't?

2

What the Bible Is Not

THERE IS A LITTLE SONG WE USED TO SING IN SUNDAY SCHOOL when I was a kid. It goes like this:

> Every promise in the Book is mine,
> Every chapter, every verse, every line,
> All the blessings of his love divine,
> Every promise in the Book is mine.

This little ditty is a wonderful celebration of the Bible. It reminds us that we have in our hands God's divine Word—his message to us. What an incredible joy and privilege!

Yet when we look closely at this little rhyme, we see that it is not quite accurate. First of all, the Bible is not a book. It is a library. And that library contains a diverse array of different kinds of literature from many different authors and many different times and places. Calling the Bible a "book" risks obscuring the vast diversity within its pages. Second, not every promise in the Bible is mine. There are many promises in the Bible that were never intended for you or for me. For example, in Genesis 22:17 God promises Abraham, "I will surely bless you and make your descendants as numerous as the stars in the sky and as the sand on the seashore. Your descendants

13

will take possession of the cities of their enemies." Can I claim this promise for myself? I doubt very much that my children's children will number in the millions, or that they will capture cities from their enemies. That promise was given to Abraham and concerns his descendants, not mine. It is not quite correct to say that "every promise in the Book is mine."

What about the next line of our little song: "every chapter, every verse, every line"? The problem here is that originally the Bible had no chapters or verses. These are somewhat artificial divisions introduced for organizational purposes hundreds of years after the Bible was written. The chapter divisions used in most Bibles today were first introduced into the Latin Vulgate by Stephen Langton in the early thirteenth century. Our present verse numbers were developed by Robert Estienne for his Greek-Latin New Testament of 1551.[1] Some of these chapter and verse divisions even wound up in the wrong place. For example, notice how most modern Bible versions connect the first verse of 1 Corinthians 11, "Follow my example, as I follow the example of Christ," with the previous discussion in chapter 10 on glorifying God in all things rather than with the discussion of head coverings that follows in chapter 11. Or notice how in most Bibles 1 Corinthians 12:31b ("And yet I will show you the most excellent way") is linked with the celebration of love in chapter 13 rather than with the discussion of spiritual gifts in chapter 12. These are examples where those who added the chapters and verses missed their best placement.

Of course, chapters and verses are helpful for finding things in the Bible. If I were to say to a group of people, "Please turn in your Bibles to page 979," everyone would be looking at different places in their Bibles, since there are so many different versions and editions. But if I said, "Turn to John 3:16," everyone could find the passage. So chapters and verses are helpful. But they can also distract from the more natural divisions of the text into paragraphs and larger sections.

In this chapter we will look at some of the misconceptions concerning the Bible, that is, what it is *not*. In the next chapter we will try to define what it *is*. By discovering the true nature of the Bible, we can discern how to read it and apply it to our lives. We begin with four things the Bible is not. It is not (1) a magic-answer book, (2) a list of commands to obey, (3) a collection of promises to claim, or (4) a textbook of systematic theology.

The Bible Is Not a Magic-Answer Book

Many people approach the Bible as a kind of crystal ball, looking for specific answers to their questions. This approach, though misguided, is motivated by two positive things. The first is a reverence for the Bible as the Word of God and the belief that God is alive and active and wants to communicate his will to us. This is true! The second positive motivation is the belief that the Bible, though written long ago, is still relevant for our lives today. This is also true! So how do we hear God speak to us? The simplest answer might be to listen for an answer in the Bible.

The problem with the crystal-ball approach is that it treats the Bible as something it is not—a message written directly to us. Many jokes have been made about this approach. A despondent person looking for counsel opens the Bible and randomly points to a verse. His finger falls on Matthew 27:5: "Judas . . . hanged himself." He tries again and his finger falls on Luke 10:37: "Go and do likewise." While we recognize this as silly, there is still a tendency for us as Bible readers to "seek a word from the Lord" in the text. Few of us would search the Bible to decide what to have for lunch, what to wear, or even what career to pursue, but we sometimes look for specific answers in more subtle ways.

Consider a particular book that has made a huge impact on the evangelical world, *Experiencing God*, by Henry T. Blackaby and Claude V. King. I love the book because it calls Christians to know and love God in a deeper and more meaningful way. Its central thesis is that "Knowing God does not come through a program, a study, or a method. Knowing God comes through a relationship with a Person. . . . Through this relationship, God reveals Himself, His purposes, and His ways and He invites you to join Him where He is already at work."[2] This is a great theme. God is at work in the world, and we have the privilege to come alongside him, to know him and participate in his purpose for the world. At the end of the introduction to *Experiencing God*, Blackaby and King describe the role of the Bible: "The Bible is God's Word to you. The Holy Spirit honors and uses God's Word in speaking to you. The Scriptures will be your source of authority for faith and practice. You cannot depend on human traditions, your experience, or the experience of others to be accurate authorities on God's will and ways. Experience and tradition must always be examined against the teaching of Scripture."[3] While some people have criticized Blackaby and King for elevating personal experience above God's Word, this passage makes it clear that their highest authority is the Word of God. But how do we determine God's will from Scripture?

A number of years ago, together with two other leaders I was teaching an adult fellowship at a local church on Sunday mornings. We decided to read through *Experiencing God* as a class, with the three of us taking turns leading the class through different chapters. I suppose it was because I was a Bible professor that they assigned me chapter 12, "God Speaks through the Bible." I was excited both because I love the Bible and because I loved the message of *Experiencing God*. I expected the chapter to talk about God's great plan of salvation set out in the Bible and how to find our place in that great story. Instead, I was surprised to see several examples of the magic-answer book approach.

The chapter recounts, for example, how a particular dentist in Texas began to wonder whether God was calling him to become a pastor. During a prayer retreat in New York, several people encouraged him to move to New York and become their pastor. His wife, Gail, however, did not sense God's call to be a pastor's wife, so they continued to pray and seek God's direction. But then, during an "Experiencing God Weekend" at their church, the Scripture reference Luke 4 kept popping into her head. Gail looked up the passage and found that Jesus had to leave his hometown to "proclaim the good news of the kingdom of God to the other towns also" (Luke 4:43). She sensed the Holy Spirit was saying she should leave the comforts and security of home to move with her husband to a new town.[4]

This kind of approach to Scripture is very common among evangelical Christians. I have heard many people recount how God spoke to them through a particular passage. The problem with this approach is that it violates the most fundamental principle of Bible study: a passage must be understood *in its original context*. In context, Luke

16

4:43 has nothing to do with moving from one town to another to become a pastor's wife. It is about Jesus's mission to preach to the people of Galilee so that all Israel would have a chance to respond to his proclamation of the kingdom of God. Does this mean that whenever Christians read this passage they ought to move to a new town and preach the gospel there? Of course not. (What if Gail had read instead Acts 1:4: "Do not leave Jerusalem, but wait for the gift my Father promised"? Would this mean she should stay put and not move?) Someone might respond that in this passage God was speaking *to Gail*, not to all Christians, and so he wanted only her to move. But if this were the case, then the meaning of the text *for her* had nothing to do with its original meaning *in context*.

To put the matter rather baldly (and boldly), I sometimes ask my students this question: Does God speak to us through random verses taken out of context? I don't want to say no too quickly or to sound too negative. I believe God can speak to us in any way he wants. After all, he is God. God could speak to you through an audible voice or through an angel, as he sometimes does in Scripture. He could speak to you through a friend's counsel, through a book you are reading, or even through the message on a billboard at the side of the road. While most Christians would be cautious or even skeptical about these, there is a tendency to assume that if we find something in the Bible—even if it is taken out of context—it has some special authority to guide us. But a biblical passage taken out of context has no more authority than a billboard on the side of the road. *Could* God communicate in this way? Certainly—he can do whatever he wants. Is it likely that he would? I don't think so.

This is what I mean by a "magic-answer book" approach. It is a mystical or even magical approach to Scripture—little different from using a Ouija board or a Magic 8 Ball (remember those?). It is equivalent to asking a question and then looking in a random place to find God's answer. So back to our question: Does God speak through random verses taken out of context? As a student of the Word, I have to answer no, since to answer yes is to break the most fundamental rule of Bible study: read the Bible *in context*. The application of a text must come from its original meaning. To conclude otherwise removes all controls from Bible study and allows anyone to claim an authoritative message from God. The leader of a pseudo-Christian cult could say, "This passage is telling us to do so-and-so," and I could not object, since the original meaning of the text would no longer be the controlling factor.

Gordon Fee and Douglas Stuart, in their classic volume, *How to Read the Bible for All Its Worth*, state it this way: "*A text cannot mean what it never meant.* Or to put it in a positive way, the true meaning of the biblical text for us is what God originally intended it to mean when it was first spoken."[5] If the passage meant one thing to its original audience, then it should *not* be applied in a different way today. If Luke 4:43 was not telling Christians to pack their bags and move to a new town in Jesus's day, then it should not be applied to our lives in that way now.

Some readers might object at this point, especially those who believe they have heard God speak in this way. This issue is actually very personal for me, since I have a family story based on a similar experience. I was raised in Alabama, where my father was a pastor. At one point he received a call to pastor a church in California and was mulling over whether God wanted him to move. As part of his decision-making process, he went off to a private spiritual retreat at a cabin by a lake. In solitude there, he read Scripture and prayed, asking God for guidance. During his study, he came across a passage in Isaiah, where God said, "Remember ye not the former things, neither consider the things of old. Behold, I will do a new thing. . . . I will even make a way in the wilderness, and rivers in the desert" (Isa. 43:18–19 KJV). Since this was a new ministry and California was a desert region, my father decided that God was speaking to him through that verse, directing him to move to California. In 1972 we packed up and moved to California, where my father had a successful pastoral ministry for twenty-one years.

So did my father hear God speak to him through that verse? I know for certain that this passage in Isaiah was not originally intended to tell God's people to pack their bags and to move from Alabama to California. In context it is a promise that God will deliver Israel from Babylonian captivity and ultimately will restore all of creation from its fallen state. It has nothing to do with moving to a desert region to start a new ministry or pastor a church. I do believe that God was guiding my father to this new church in a variety of ways: through circumstances, through the counsel of others, and especially through my father's desire to walk faithfully with God and to participate in God's purpose for the world. But I don't believe that Isaiah 43:18–19 was a special message sent by God to guide my father.

In chapter 12 of *Experiencing God*, Blackaby and King make an important statement about the nature of the Bible: "The Bible . . . is a record of God's dealings with humanity and His words to them. God speaks to you through the Bible." As we will see in the next chapter, this is exactly right. The Bible is a record of God's dealings with humanity—the drama of redemption. But in the next sentence, they write, "Have you ever been reading the Bible when suddenly you are gripped by a fresh new understanding of the passage? That was God speaking!" Here we must be more cautious. That "fresh new understanding" may be a false impression, a misunderstanding of the text, or an inappropriate application to my life. As we will see in chapters to come, it is the *context* of the passage and the community of faith—guided by the Holy Spirit—that provide us with a fresh and *true* understanding of the text. The Bible is not a magic-answer book providing specific answers for our personal questions and problems.

The Bible Is Not a List of Commands to Obey

I started this chapter with a Sunday school song, "Every Promise in the Book Is Mine." Here's another:

> Trust and obey,
> For there's no other way
> To be happy in Jesus
> But to trust and obey.[6]

Again, I firmly believe this to be true. God is our sovereign Lord, and it is our responsibility to trust him and to obey his commands. Throughout Scripture, obedience is identified as one of the most important responsibilities of God's people. When King Saul disobeys God by keeping the best of the plunder he captured from the Amalekites, the prophet Samuel reminds him that the Lord does not delight in burnt offerings and sacrifices as much as in obedience: "To obey is better than sacrifice, and to heed is better than the fat of rams" (1 Sam. 15:22). Jesus tells his disciples that if they love him, they will keep his commands (John 14:15). Love for God is expressed in obedience to his righteous standards.

But what does it mean to obey God? There are many commands in the Bible that Christians do not obey. There are other commands that some Christians obey but others do not. How do we decide which commands are for us and which aren't? The second thing we have to affirm about the nature of the Bible is that it is not simply a list of commands to obey.

Culture-Specific versus Universal Commands

Consider the following biblical command. "Love the LORD your God with all your heart and with all your soul and with all your strength" (Deut. 6:5). Should we obey this command? I think all Christians would say, "Absolutely!" The most fundamental part of the Christian life is loving and serving God. But consider these other Old Testament commands:

This is what you are to offer on the altar regularly each day: two lambs a year old. (Exod. 29:38)

Of all the creatures living in the water of the seas and the streams you may eat any that have fins and scales. But all creatures in the seas or streams that do not have fins and scales . . . you are to regard as unclean. (Lev. 11:9–10)

Do not mate different kinds of animals. Do not plant your field with two kinds of seed. Do not wear clothing woven of two kinds of material. (Lev. 19:19)

Probably everyone would agree that passages like these do not apply to Christians today. We no longer offer animal sacrifices. Most Christians believe there is nothing wrong with eating shellfish or planting two kinds of seed in a garden or wearing clothes made of more than one kind of material (for example, cotton/polyester blend). The reason, of course, is that these commands were given to the nation Israel in the Old Testament, not to the modern church. But then why do we say that Deuteronomy 6:5 ("Love the LORD

20

your God. . . .") is a command for Christians? It too was given to the nation Israel. Someone might say that this command is repeated in the New Testament and so we are required to obey it. But there are many Old Testament commands we obey that weren't repeated in the New Testament. Furthermore, as noted in the previous chapter, Christians don't obey all New Testament commands either.

Identify which of the following commands you think apply to Christians.

So whether you eat or drink or whatever you do, do it all for the glory of God. (1 Cor. 10:31)

Pursue righteousness, faith, love and peace, along with those who call on the Lord out of a pure heart. (2 Tim. 2:22)

Does not the very nature of things teach you that if a man has long hair, it is a disgrace to him . . . ? (1 Cor. 11:14)

Women should remain silent in the churches. They are not allowed to speak, but must be in submission, as the law says. (1 Cor. 14:34)

Greet one another with a holy kiss. (1 Cor. 16:20)

Are you pledged to a woman? Do not seek to be released. Are you free from such a commitment? Do not look for a wife. (1 Cor. 7:27)

Stop drinking only water, and use a little wine because of your stomach and your frequent illnesses. (1 Tim. 5:23)

I think everyone would agree that 1 Corinthians 10:31 is a command for all believers for all time. Everything we do should bring glory to God. Similarly, 2 Timothy 2:22 surely applies to all believers, who should pursue righteousness, faith, love, and peace. Yet most Christians would not say that it is a disgrace for a man to have long hair (though in the 1960s and '70s many were saying that!), or that women should never speak in church, or that Christians must greet each other with a kiss, or that it is wrong to look for a spouse. And nobody I know considers it a biblical command to drink wine instead of water.

The simple fact is that few, if any, Christians obey *every* command in Scripture—from either the Old or New Testament—because they recognize that these commands were not given to them. The commands about long hair, about women speaking in the church, about greeting one another with a kiss, and about not seeking a wife were given to the church at Corinth in ancient Greece, and they all related to something specific in that cultural or social situation. The command to stop drinking water exclusively was given to Paul's assistant Timothy, because of his special health concerns. Yet we must also acknowledge that the command to glorify God in all things (1 Cor. 10:31) was given to this same Corinthian church in their unique cultural and social context. And the command to pursue righteousness, faith, love, and peace was given to this same individual, Timothy. What makes these commands different? Why do we intuitively know that these relate to us, while the others do not?

I would suggest that we—unconsciously, perhaps—are interpreting and applying these commands from a much larger framework, a framework related to who God is, who we are in relation to him, and the nature of his purpose for the world. We intuitively know that certain commands are universal, because we have come to know the heart of God—not perfectly, but enough to make correct judgments in these cases. This knowledge does not come simply from reading and applying commands from the Bible; it comes also from our understanding of the whole of Scripture, our shared experience as the community of God, our walk with God in the past, and our openness to guidance from the Holy Spirit.

In reality, *none* of the individual commands of Scripture were written *to you*. The commands in the Old Testament were given to the nation Israel. The commands in the New Testament were given to various churches and individuals scattered throughout the Mediterranean region in the first century AD. Discerning when and how these commands apply to us involves discerning the heart of God behind the text.

I tell my students that one reason the Bible can be so hard to understand and apply is because it wasn't written to you.[7] This always causes surprise and some discomfort ("Is our professor . . . [that dreaded word] a *liberal*?"). But then I quickly add, "Though it wasn't written *to* us, it was written *for* us." The Bible is God's Word. It

22

contains a message from God *for* us. But it is not his direct Word *to* us because it was written to a variety of people in a variety of contexts. To whom were the two letters to the Corinthians written? They were written to first-century Christians living in the Greco-Roman city of Corinth. To whom was the letter to Timothy written? It was written to Timothy and the church he was overseeing in Ephesus. To whom were the prophecies of Zechariah written? They were written to the postexilic community of ancient Israel in the fifth century BC. We must first understand the biblical documents in their specific life situations before we can apply them appropriately to our own lives. Learning to apply the Bible means moving from the "to" (them) to the "for" (us). This is the challenge of application.

This conclusion reminds us how important it is to read the Bible in context. We will avoid a world of problems if we first of all interpret the commands of Scripture in context as commands *to them* (the original audience) before we apply these commands to ourselves. While at first sight it might seem perfectly acceptable to say, "Paul tells us to glorify God in all we do" (1 Cor. 10:31), it would be better to say, "Paul tells *the Corinthian believers* to glorify God in all they do." Then we can ask, "How does that apply to us?" We would not want to say, "Paul commands us to drink wine instead of water" (1 Tim. 5:23) or "Peter commands us to greet one another with a kiss" (1 Pet. 5:14), but rather "Paul commands *Timothy* to drink a little wine for the sake of his health" and "Peter encourages *the first-century believers of Asia Minor* to greet one another with a kiss." Then we can ask, "If that was God's word to them, what is God's word for us?" Doing this with all of Scripture's commands prevents inappropriately assuming that every command of Scripture necessarily applies to us. It also forces us back to that critical key to all biblical interpretation: context, context, context.

Of course, there will always be a tendency to pick and choose those commands that fit our own traditions and agendas and to reject those that do not. Consider a series of exhortations given by Paul in 1 Timothy 2:8–12:

> Therefore I want the men everywhere to pray, lifting up holy hands without anger or disputing. I also want the women to dress modestly, with decency and propriety, adorning themselves, not with elaborate

hairstyles or gold or pearls or expensive clothes, but with good deeds, appropriate for women who profess to worship God.

A woman should learn in quietness and full submission. I do not permit a woman to teach or to assume authority over a man; she must be quiet.

In the church tradition in which I was raised, we assumed the first command was cultural: men do not need to lift their hands when they pray. We instead looked for a general principle—in this case, to pray with an attitude of reverent awe toward God. Yet the qualifying phrase, "without anger or disputing," would certainly be a universal command, since prayer should never be done with a spirit of dissension. Similarly, the next sentence begins with a command that is likely for all time. Women (and men) should certainly dress modestly, with decency and propriety. Yet when specific examples of modesty and decency are given in the next sentence—elaborate hairstyles, gold or pearl jewelry, expensive clothes—we did not take these as commands for all time. Modesty, it seems, is culturally determined. Most American Christians would see nothing morally wrong with a particular hairstyle or wearing gold jewelry, a pearl necklace, or expensive clothes (within reason). Immodesty is instead typically connected with how much of the body is revealed—a low-cut blouse or a skirt that is too short or too tight. Yet in a tribe in Irian Jaya (where I have missionary friends), complete or near nudity is not considered immodest, for either men or women. So this command is viewed as culturally conditioned. However, the next phrase in 1 Timothy 2:10, "with good deeds," certainly moves back to a universal command. All women (and men!) should "adorn" themselves with good deeds.

So the passage appears to be moving back and forth fairly randomly between commands that are universal in scope and those that are specific cultural applications. The problem is the next sentence, which is one of the most controversial in the Bible, related as it is to the role of women and men in the church. When Paul says, presumably in a church context, that he does not allow a woman to teach or to assume authority over a man and that she must remain quiet, is he stating a universal principle or a specific cultural application?

Gallons of ink have been spilled over this issue, and entire books have been written promoting one side or the other. Evangelicals are well divided on the subject and have been for decades. I will take up this passage in chapter 8, where—with fear and trembling—I will attempt to apply to this thorny issue the principles introduced in this book. My point here, however, is to stress that this passage, like all biblical passages, must first be understood within its own cultural and historical context. Paul tells *Timothy and the first-century believers in Ephesus* that *he himself* does not allow a woman to teach or assume authority over a man. Paul would not necessarily say the same thing to us. He might, but we cannot assume that he would. This is what we mean that the Bible is not simply a list of commands to obey.

Perplexing Commands

Acknowledging that the Bible is not a list of commands to us also helps us deal with what we might call perplexing commands. These are laws and instructions that we have little or no idea why they were given. Why, for example, were certain foods classified as "clean" and others as "unclean" and so forbidden? Why could Israelites eat fish but not shellfish? Why chicken and beef but not pork? Some interpreters have tried to justify these commands for health reasons, but this is sometimes a stretch from the perspective of health and medical studies (advocates of pork—"The Other White Meat"—would certainly object). Though pork can certainly be dangerous when undercooked, so can chicken and eggs.

It is a fascinating exercise to read through the list of diverse commands in Leviticus 19, trying to figure out the basis for them and their current application. The chapter begins with a summary statement for the purpose of Torah (the law), which is to attain holiness: "The LORD said to Moses, 'Speak to the entire assembly of Israel and say to them: "Be holy because I, the LORD your God, am holy"'" (Lev. 19:1–2). What follows, however, is an odd assortment of laws. Many of these are fundamental moral commands, which can certainly be applied directly today: Respect your parents. Do not worship idols. Do not steal, lie, deceive one another, swear falsely, defraud your neighbors, mistreat the handicapped, pervert justice, slander others, or take revenge. Other commands, however, are far more perplexing. Why, for example, were Israelites not to eat meat with blood still in it (v. 26), or to cut the hair at the sides of their head (v. 27), or to tattoo themselves (v. 28)? While we cannot be sure, these prohibitions likely had to do with avoiding pagan religious practices among Israel's neighbors, since the prohibitions are mentioned near other pagan practices: forbidding divination (v. 26), visiting mediums (v. 31), and turning daughters into (cultic) prostitutes (v. 29).

But what about commands not to mix things that are different? Verse 19 says not to mate different kinds of animals, or plant different kinds of seed in the same field, or wear clothing made of different kinds of material. These likely have to do with symbolic purity. Since God is holy and set apart from all sin and evil, Israel was to practice symbolically certain kinds of ritual separation. But we just don't know for certain. Old Testament scholar R. Laird Harris points to the difficulty of determining the rationale behind these commands:

> The reason for these provisions is not clear. . . . The reference to mixed seeds or cloth is difficult to understand without more background. It might be an effort to reduce adulteration of a good product. Mixing wheat and barley would make harvest difficult because of different times of ripening. Or possibly the prohibition is against using good seed mixed with weed seed. . . . In Deuteronomy the clothing mixtures are specified as wool and linen. Why these should not be mixed is not clear. Flax and wool are spun differently. Whether weaving them together was difficult for people of antiquity we cannot say.[8]

In other words, scholars don't know the reason for these commands, though some guesses might be better than others. Our point here is that we don't need to solve all of these issues to live in obedience to God. These commands were not given to us; they were given to ancient Israel and were one small part of God's much larger revelation of himself and his purpose for the world. We discern the heart of God not from Scripture's isolated and sometimes obscure commands but from its total teaching concerning the nature and purpose of God.

The Bible Is Not a List of Promises to Claim

A third thing the Bible is not is a list of promises to claim. Of course, there are many wonderful promises in the Bible. Take, for example,

Jeremiah 29:11, which many Christians have claimed as their "life verse": "'For I know the plans I have for you,' declares the LORD, 'plans to prosper you and not to harm you, plans to give you hope and a future.'" This promise actually appears in a letter sent by the prophet Jeremiah to the people of Judah who had been exiled by King Nebuchadnezzar of Babylon in the late sixth century BC. We can learn a great deal about the nature of God from this passage. We learn that God is faithful to his covenant promises. We learn that he is a God of second chances, that he forgives his people when they repent and turn to him. We learn that he has the power to turn their lives around and restore their fortunes.

But we also learn that there are serious consequences for people's actions. Judah had been sent into exile because of their injustice, idolatry, unfaithfulness, and unbelief. They had experienced terrible suffering and sorrow because of their sins. They had seen their sons and daughters slaughtered and their property and possessions taken away. They were presently paying the penalty for their sins with seventy years of exile in Babylon. In the midst of this suffering, God makes a promise that one day he will restore them. There is hope because they have a faithful, loving, and forgiving God.

The point is that we must not miss these very important qualifications associated with the promise in Jeremiah. Every promise in the Bible has a context: the specific time and place in which it was given to a specific people. This context must be kept in mind before we can simply "claim" a promise as our own. Indeed, in this same letter in Jeremiah sent to the Babylonian exiles, God makes another promise: "Yes, this is what the LORD Almighty says: 'I will send the sword, famine and plague against them and I will make them like figs that are so bad they cannot be eaten. I will pursue them with the sword, famine and plague and will make them abhorrent to all the kingdoms of the earth, a curse and an object of horror, of scorn and reproach, among all the nations where I drive them'" (Jer. 29:17–18). Not surprisingly, I have never heard anyone claim this as their life verse. No one says, "God has promised to send sword and famine and plague against me and to make me a curse and an object of horror. I'm so excited!" Yet this is just as much a promise from God (and in the same context) as Jeremiah 29:11. While the promise in verse 11 was given to the exiles in Babylon, the one in verses 17 and 18 was given to their fellow Jews still living in Jerusalem.

It should be clear from this example that not every promise in the Book is mine. Every biblical promise has a context and a recipient, and that situation must be understood before any application can be made. Don't misunderstand what I am saying. Every promise in the Bible *is* God's Word. It is God's Word to *them* and must first be interpreted in its original context before it can be applied to *us*. Just as the Bible is not a list of commands to obey, so it is not a series of promises to claim.

Here are a few other examples of pairs of promises, one positive and one negative, that demonstrate the danger of taking promises out of context.

- Someone hoping for a long life could claim 1 Kings 3:14: "And if you walk in obedience to me and keep my decrees and commands . . . I will give you a long life." Or, they might resign themselves to 2 Kings 20:1: "This is what the Lord says: Put your house in order, because you are going to die."
- A couple trying to have children could claim Judges 13:3: "You are barren and childless, but you are going to become pregnant and give birth to a son." Or, they might be disappointed to read Jeremiah 22:30: "This is what the Lord says: 'Record this man as if childless, a man who will not prosper in his lifetime.'"
- Someone hoping for financial success may claim Deuteronomy 28:11: "The Lord will grant you abundant prosperity." Or, they might be depressed to come across 2 Kings 21:14: "[The Lord said] I will forsake the remnant of my inheritance and give them into the hands of enemies. They will be looted and plundered by all their enemies."
- A nation preparing for war could claim the promise of Deuteronomy 1:8: "See, I have given you this land. Go in and take possession of the land"; or they could claim the promise of Deuteronomy 1:42: "Do not go up and fight, because I will not be with you. You will be defeated by your enemies."

I am playing with the text here by intentionally taking these passages out of context. The point is that we cannot claim a promise in the

Bible without recognizing its context, purpose, and qualifications. For every positive promise there are negative ones; there are promises of judgment and suffering as well as of success and prosperity. How, then, do we read and apply the promises of the Bible?

The answer is the same as for the Bible's commands. The promises, like the commands, are part of God's self-revelation within the great Story in the Bible. They teach us who God is, who we are in relationship to him, what his purpose for the world is, and how we ought to live in response to that purpose. Here are two key points to consider with reference to biblical promises.

1. *Each biblical promise was given to a specific individual or group and relates first of all to their situation.* I was watching a news program the other day, where a philanthropist announced to a charity, "I'm giving you a million dollars." I immediately ran to my wife and said, "This guy just promised us a million dollars!" This story (which I just made up) is, of course, absurd. We recognize that a promise made to someone else is not a promise for us; it is for those to whom it is made. As we read the Bible, it is critical for us to understand to whom a promise is made and under what circumstances it applies.

The Bible is unique in that, though it was written *to them*, it is also *for us*. The promises of God given in the Bible have significant application for us. One of my favorite letters of Paul is Philippians, partly because of its wonderful encouragements and promises. In this letter Paul expresses his joy in Christ Jesus and his trust that Christ will meet his needs. In Philippians 4:13, for example, Paul says, "I can do all this through him who gives me strength." That is a great promise. In Philippians 4:5–7, Paul says that if we present our needs and requests to God, "the peace of God, which transcends all understanding, will guard your hearts and your minds in Christ Jesus"—another great promise. In Philippians 4:19, he says, "And my God will meet all your needs according to the riches of his glory in Christ Jesus."

Years ago, when I had just begun my teaching career, I had a forty-five-minute commute each day to the college where I was teaching. My wife and I were recently married, and money was very tight as we tried to make ends meet on our part-time salaries and as I prepared for doctoral studies. I was driving an old 1977 Mazda GLC ("Great Little Car") that I had had for years. One day, as I exited the freeway toward the college, I heard a thud and the car ground to a halt. My transmission had completely seized up. This was disastrous for us. A new transmission would cost well over a thousand dollars. We had no money for another car, and we were dependent on my meager teaching salary. I prayed, "Lord, we really need some help here." I hitched a ride to school and arrived late to my class. I explained to my students what had happened. It was a New Testament survey class; ironically, we had been studying Philippians, and I was teaching how we can trust God to meet all our needs. I jokingly said to the class, "Don't teach something unless you expect to live it out!"

After class, one of my students approached me. He said he was a mechanic and might be able to help. Later that day we drove out to a junkyard, found a wrecked Mazda GLC, and removed its transmission. I think I purchased it for $60. We drove the transmission back to the school, where together we installed it right there in the parking lot. The car ran like a top until I sold it a year later and used the money to help pay for my doctoral studies. I also sent a special gift to my mechanic friend who was about to get married at the time. I certainly claimed the promise of Philippians 4:19: "my God will meet all your needs according to the riches of his glory in Christ Jesus."

Based on my earlier comments, you might ask how I could claim that promise. After all, it was given by Paul to the church at Philippi two thousand years ago. It was not given to me. The answer is that the biblical author is not so much making a promise as making a statement about the nature of God. We have a good God who cares for his people and has the desire and resources to meet their needs. I was very grateful to God for that student mechanic. But even if God had not provided that transmission, he would still be a good God who meets our needs. He would have met my needs by teaching me to learn to trust him even more through financial difficulties, or by sending someone to provide my family with food or shelter if we found ourselves in even more dire circumstances, or in some other way.

There is a common formula used in some Christian churches. One person says, "God is good" and the others reply, "all the time." This is something like what Paul is saying here in Philippians 4:19. God is good, because he meets our needs in any and all circumstances. Indeed, Paul says as much in the passage that follows: "I know what it is to be in need, and I know what it is to have plenty. I have learned the secret of being content in any and every situation, whether well fed or hungry, whether living in plenty or in want. I can do all this through him who gives me strength" (Phil. 4:12b–13). Though not stated in the form of a promise, this passage has the same essential message as verse 19. It is a statement about the nature of the God we serve. We claim God's promises, not by demanding something from him, but by learning about his nature and purpose and then living in light of who God is and who we are as his people.

2. *Promises are often conditional and contingent, dependent on circumstances and the response of the recipient.*[9] This is another important clarification related to biblical promises. One of the most interesting passages in the Bible is the account of the illness of King Hezekiah in Isaiah 38 (paralleled in 2 Kings 20:1–11). When Hezekiah becomes ill, God sends Isaiah the prophet to announce to the king, "This is what the LORD says: Put your house in order, because you are going to die; you will not recover" (Isa. 38:1). Hezekiah, however, weeps and begs God to remember Hezekiah's faithfulness to the Lord and all the good he has done. In response, God says that he will add fifteen years to Hezekiah's life (Isa. 38:5–6). The passage teaches not only the reality that God answers prayer but also that God's pronouncements—whether predictions, prophecies, or promises—are often contingent upon the actions and attitudes of his people. God's announcement that Hezekiah is going to die is not an absolute decree but one possible outcome within God's larger plan.

The same is true of many (maybe even most) of God's prophetic announcements in Scripture.[10] God announces that something is going to happen, but it is contingent upon human response. In the book of Jonah, God commands Jonah to go and preach against the city of Nineveh. After Jonah's disobedience and the incident with the great fish, Jonah repents and goes to Nineveh, preaching that God is going to destroy the city in forty days. The Ninevites believe Jonah and repent, so God changes his mind: "When God saw what they did, how they turned from their evil ways, God changed his mind about the calamity that he had said he would bring upon them; and he did not do it" (Jon. 3:10 NRSV).

In Hezekiah's and Jonah's cases, God's actions were contingent upon human response. Sometimes the conditions are explicit ("if you do not repent . . . ," or "if you remain faithful to me . . ."); other times they are implicit. What at first sight may appear to be a prediction of what *must* happen is instead an announcement of what *could* happen, depending on the human response. The classic expression in Scripture of this contingent nature of prophecy is in Jeremiah 18, where God says to the prophet, "If at any time I announce that a nation or kingdom is to be uprooted, torn down and destroyed, and if that nation I warned repents of its evil, then I will relent and not inflict on it the disaster I had planned. And if at another time I announce that a nation or kingdom is to be built up and planted, and if it does evil in my sight and does not obey me, then I will reconsider the good I had intended to do for it" (Jer. 18:7–10).

If a nation against whom God has prophesied destruction repents, God will change his mind and not destroy them. Similarly, if God promises blessings for a nation, but that nation does evil and rejects him, he will send judgment against them. What may appear at first to be a prophetic pronouncement may in fact be contingent upon the response of the recipients. Robert Pratt writes, "Old Testament prophets revealed the word of the unchanging Yahweh, but they spoke for God in space and time, not before the foundations of the world. By definition, therefore, they did not utter immutable *decrees* but providential *declarations*. For this reason, we should not be surprised to find that intervening historical contingencies, especially human reactions, had significant effects on the way predictions were realized."[11] This helps to explain why some prophecies of Scripture seem not to have been fulfilled as they were predicted.

Robert Chisholm points out the difference between performative speech, which performs some nonlinguistic act—such as a judge pronouncing a defendant acquitted—and dynamic speech, which is intended to motivate and change behavior. Many (even most) prophecies are dynamic instead of performative. Chisholm writes,

> Some popular views of prophecy, as well as some higher-critical approaches, assume that all or most predictions (at least those not marked by "if" or the like) are unconditional and therefore performative. However, an examination of the evidence suggests that prophetic predictive discourse is often (usually?) dynamic. It announces God's intentions conditionally and is intended to motivate a positive response to the expository-hortatory discourse it typically accompanies.

In this case the prophecy's predictive element is designed to prevent (in the case of a judgment announcement) or facilitate (in the case of a salvation announcement) its fulfillment.[12]

Someone may counter that while biblical prophecies may be contingent, God's promises cannot fail. They are absolute. The problem is that there is little difference between a promise and a prophecy. Both state what God intends to do. Both may or may not be contingent upon human response. It is certainly true that some promises or prophecies will come true regardless of human action or response. The prophecy that Christ would die for the sins of the world was not dependent on any human action. The promise that he would rise from the dead victorious was an absolute certainty. The future promise (and prophecy) that he will one day return to reward and to judge is not contingent upon any human response. Yet we know that these particular promises are absolute, not because they are different in kind from other promises, but because of what we know about the nature and purpose of God from the whole of Scripture.

Again, applying God's Word is not about trying to determine whether to apply a particular promise to a particular situation in life. It is about growing in our knowledge of the nature and purpose of God *from the whole of Scripture*—whether laws, letters, stories, psalms, promises, or prophecies—and thereby learning what it means to walk with God and to make good and godly decisions.

The Bible Is Not a Textbook of Systematic Theology

When I was a student in college, I used to work on my car a lot. This was in the days before cars were filled with computers that monitored every part. You could actually fix things with screwdrivers and wrenches. I bought a Clymer car-care guide and used it for repairs. When the car had a problem, I would look it up in the index and follow the step-by-step instructions to fix it. I do something similar with the word processing program on my computer. Whenever I have a problem, I go to the Help menu and look up a topic. I don't want to read a story about others who have had this same problem or to hear a poem about the challenges we all face as computer users. I want a quick, simple, step-by-step answer to the question I ask.

While this quick-answer approach may work when repairing cars or solving computer glitches, it does not work when reading and applying the Bible. A fourth way that people can misread the Bible is by treating it as a textbook of systematic theology, or a comprehensive guide to Christian doctrine and practice.

We rightly say that the Bible is the authoritative and inspired Word of God and that it is true in all it says. But this truth comes to us not as a list of propositions or rules but expressed through a variety of literary forms and in diverse and specific cultural and social situations. The Bible is not a Clymer guide for people repair or a Help menu for questions in life.

This is not to suggest that the Bible is not *theological*. It is all theology (= truth about God) in the sense that every verse reveals who God is, who we are, how we ought to live in relationship to him, and his purpose for the world. But this theology is *progressive, contextual*, and *situational*. It is expressed over time, through a variety of literary forms, and in diverse circumstances and contexts. It does not come to us organized and arranged by topics. Most of the truth in the Bible is not, in fact, propositional truth but truth revealed through story, parable, proverb, psalm, law, prophecy, and a variety of other literary forms. To discern and apply this theology, we must comprehend each passage in its own literary and historical context and according to the rules of its particular genre. Here are some key points concerning how theological truth is expressed in Scripture.

1. *The Bible's theology is progressively revealed.* Theologians speak of the "progress of revelation," which means that throughout Scripture God gradually provides greater and greater insight into his nature and his purpose. Later revelation does not contradict earlier revelation but clarifies and expands it. Consider the question of whether animal sacrifices bring forgiveness of sins. From the perspective of the Old Testament law, we would have to say yes. In Numbers 15, for example, God commands certain animal sacrifices to be made for unintentional sins: "The priest is to make atonement before the LORD for the one who erred by sinning unintentionally, and when atonement has been made for them, they will be forgiven" (Num. 15:28). There is no doubt here that from Israel's perspective the animal sacrifice results in God's forgiveness. If we jump forward fifteen hundred years, however, we learn that these sacrifices never

actually accomplished lasting forgiveness. In contrasting the old covenant with the new, the writer of the New Testament letter to the Hebrews says explicitly, "It is impossible for the blood of bulls and goats to take away sins" (Heb. 10:4). Only Christ's once-for-all sacrifice on the cross can accomplish this (Heb. 10:11–14).

So the answer to the theological question of whether animal sacrifices bring forgiveness of sins is yes and no. From the perspective of ancient Israel, the answer is yes. Yet, from the perspective of the fulfillment of the law in Christ, the answer is no. The Old Testament sacrifices were a sign of obedience and a preview of the once-for-all sacrifice of Christ on the cross. The answer to the question depends on where you are standing in the Story, and from what vantage point you are viewing the sacrificial system. As when searching for a good piece of real estate, the key to discerning theological truth in Scripture is *location, location, location*. We must ask, Where are we in redemptive history? Is this the final word on the subject, or do later texts clarify or qualify it?

2. *The Bible's theological statements are contextually located*. Just as it is important to ask where we are in the story of redemption, so it is necessary to ask what cultural or situational factors may come to bear on the text. The reality that all biblical revelation comes to us within human cultures helps explain some of the more difficult ethical statements in the Bible. If polygamy is wrong, why did God allow it in the Old Testament (Genesis 29; cf. Deut. 21:15–17)? If it is evil to own a person as a slave, why didn't God condemn the practice in ancient Israel instead of providing regulations for it (Leviticus 25)? The answers are in part related to the unique social and cultural situations in which God allowed these practices to continue. God revealed his nature and purpose *within* cultural institutions rather than by abolishing those institutions. In such cases we are seeing not *absolute ethics* but culturally mediated ethics for particular times and places.

This contextual nature of theology also helps to explain passages that at first may seem contradictory. Paul says that a person is saved by faith alone, apart from works (Rom. 3:28). James insists that "faith without deeds is dead" (James 2:26), so that faith plus works saves you. These differences can be resolved when we recognize that Paul and James are addressing two different situations. Paul writes against legalists who are claiming that a person can earn salvation by doing good works, or who perhaps are claiming that salvation has come through the "works of the law"—the hallmarks of Judaism such as circumcision, dietary laws, and Sabbath observance.[13] James, on the other hand, is writing against those who are abusing the doctrine of free grace by claiming that once you are saved by faith, you can live any way you want. James rejects such libertarianism and insists that authentic faith will always result in actions, so that the two work hand in hand. Another way to say this is that Paul is referring to the preconversion experience, what brings you into the people of God, while James is referring to postconversion experience, how a life of faith is lived out. Paul uses "faith" in the sense of saving faith, authentic trust in Jesus for salvation. James uses the word in the sense of "professing," or claiming to believe. If this claim is real, James says, it will always be backed up with actions. The key to harmonizing Paul and James is understanding their distinct contexts.

3. *The Bible's theology is selective, not comprehensive.* Just as the Bible is not a systematic or topical presentation of truth, neither is it comprehensive in its scope. While Scripture ultimately provides all we need to live in right relationship with God and with others, it does not deal with every situation or contingency in life. Much of the theology of the Bible is what we could call "task theology." It is theological truth brought to bear on specific life situations. Since biblical authors seldom deal comprehensively with a particular topic, we must be cautious before assuming that we have the whole truth or the last word in any particular passage.

Take, for example, the issue of divorce and remarriage. Much debate in the church focuses on whether the Bible sets out grounds for divorce that would allow a person to remarry without sinning. Some interpreters claim there are no grounds for divorce. Others, noting Jesus's statements in Matthew 5:31–32 and 19:3–9, claim that there is one ground for divorce: adultery. Still others, picking up Paul's discussion in 1 Corinthians 7, see two grounds: adultery and desertion.[14] But it is important to recognize that neither Jesus nor Paul is specifically addressing the grounds for divorce. Jesus is responding against certain "easy-divorce" rabbis of his day, who take the marriage covenant far too lightly. He insists that marriage is a lifelong covenant and commitment and that God has allowed divorce only because of their hard hearts. Paul, for his part, is addressing certain marital issues in the church at Corinth and encourages the Corinthians not to leave their unbelieving spouses so that they can maintain a holy influence in their homes. To say (as I have heard some teachers say), "the Bible allows only two grounds for divorce," is to assume that the purpose of these passages is to set out what are and are not the legitimate grounds for divorce. But this is not the point of either passage.

What if, hypothetically, Paul had addressed the issue of spousal abuse in a third passage? Would he have allowed divorce in the case of such abuse? Although we can't know for sure, I suspect that he would. My point here is that we cannot merely assume that the Bible contains complete or comprehensive teaching on the topic of divorce, especially since (1) neither Paul nor Jesus specifically addresses the issue of grounds for divorce, (2) neither claims to be giving systematic or comprehensive teaching on the matter, and (3) neither lists the other's exception (Jesus does not mention desertion and Paul does not mention adultery). Our conclusion concerning the legitimate grounds for divorce must be based on a broader understanding of God's perspective on marriage, divorce, and human relationships, not on the assumption that the Bible offers comprehensive or complete answers on this issue (or most other issues).

Consider another topic, the gifts of the Spirit, which Paul repeatedly affirms are given by the Spirit to each believer to build up the church. On several occasions, Paul provides lists of spiritual gifts (Rom. 12:6–8; 1 Cor. 12:8–10, 28–30; Eph. 4:11). So how many spiritual gifts are there? Some interpreters limit spiritual gifts to those listed by Paul in these catalogs. Yet whenever Paul provides such a list, he includes at least one or two not mentioned in the other lists. In other words, it seems his purpose is not to list *all* the spiritual gifts but to give a representative sample. We should be cautious, therefore, about assuming we have a complete list of gifts. If Paul had discussed gifts in another letter, would he have mentioned others? Probably.

My point in both of these illustrations is not to reach firm conclusions on divorce or spiritual gifts but to show that the Bible's ethical instructions and theological statements are representative and exemplary rather than comprehensive. They teach us about the nature and purpose of God, enabling us to discern right theology and right behavior in new and changing circumstances.

This conclusion can be applied to many topics. It is often said, "The Bible has the answer." This is certainly true. The problem, however, is that the Bible does not always have the *question*. The Bible does not give a specific answer to the question of whether divorce is allowed in the case of abuse because this question is never raised. A myriad of contemporary social, ethical, and theological questions are not addressed in the Bible, either because they were not part of the world in which the Bible arose or simply because they never come up in biblical contexts. For example, Scripture has little or nothing (specific) to say about a range of contemporary issues, such as abortion, euthanasia, gambling, drug abuse, genetic manipulation, stem-cell research, illegal immigration, socialism, capitalism, war and pacifism, global warming, environmental care, child abuse, birth control, premarital sex, masturbation, pornography, and transsexuality.

The list could go on and on. We live in a constantly changing world. Even when the Bible does address an issue, its context may have little to do with contemporary practice. Leviticus 19:28, for example, expressly forbids marking the skin with tattoos. Does this apply to modern tattoos? If one of my sons or my daughter wanted to get a tattoo, I'd say yes, it does apply—tattoos are forbidden! But this would be based on my personal bias (which is the right one, of course) rather than on sound interpretation. The Old Testament command probably has little to do with modern tattoos, relating instead to skin markings that demonstrated allegiance to a pagan god. Israel was to avoid such pagan religious practices.

How do we as Christians use the Bible to make decisions on issues that the biblical authors never addressed? The answer, as we will see in the following chapters, is by cultivating the heart of God and the mind of Christ. We do this by applying the truths we have learned about God, about human nature, and about God's purpose for the world to the rapidly changing world around us.

Conclusion

In this chapter we have discussed what the Bible is not. It is not a magic-answer book, a list of commands to obey, a list of promises to claim, or a systematic textbook on theology ethics. These negative

38

answers, however, must give way to positive ones. The next chapter will discuss what the Bible is and how God speaks to us through its diverse cultures, contexts, and literary forms.

Discussion and Reflection Questions

1. Do you see any dangers in a "magic-answer book" approach to the Bible? What are they?

2. Have you ever heard a message from the Lord in the Bible? How did you discern whether this was God's will for you?

3. Identify a few commands from the Bible that Christians are bound to obey. Name a few they are not required to obey. How can we tell the difference? (Don't worry if you're not sure of the answer. We will discuss this more in the chapters ahead.)

4. Is every promise in the Bible meant for you? Why or why not? What is the purpose of biblical promises?

5. What does it mean that most biblical "promises" are contingent upon the response of those to whom the promise is given?

6. In what ways are the Bible's theological statements limited by their contexts and situations? What are some examples given in the chapter? Can you think of any others?

3

What the Bible Is

THE LAST CHAPTER POINTED OUT WHAT THE BIBLE IS NOT. Although the Bible provides the answers to life's deepest and most profound questions, it is not a magic-answer book that provides instant answers to our questions. Although the Bible teaches us how to live in obedience to God, it is not merely a list of commands to obey. Many of the commands in the Bible do not in fact apply to Christians today. Although the Bible reveals a God who is always faithful to his people, it is not a list of promises to claim. Finally, although the Bible is theological to the core, revealing on every page the nature and purpose of God, it is not a textbook on systematic theology or a handbook on Christian ethics. If the Bible is none of these things, what is it?

This chapter will discuss the Bible in terms of its nature and its central theme. The *nature* of the Bible is a divine-human convergence—God's Word delivered through human words. The *message* of the Bible is the story of redemption, the divine drama of the creation, fall, and restoration of the people of God. Its purpose is to call people to live in faith, love, and holiness, to submit ourselves to his authority, and to align our lives with his purpose and will.

Unity in Diversity: God's Word through Human Words

Perhaps the best way to describe the nature of the Bible is with two complementary terms: "unity" and "diversity." *Diversity* refers to the human side of revelation, meaning the Bible came to us through human authors in a variety of cultures, contexts, and literary forms (genres). *Unity* refers to the divine side of the Bible. Though written in many times and places, it has a single, unifying message that runs through it from beginning to end. Its many stories together make the one great Story: God's plan of redemption for his creation. Like a great orchestra, the Bible's diverse instruments each play their own notes. But together they play in harmony, so that the result is a unified, true, and authentic revelation from God.

We will misread the Bible if we deny either its diversity or its unity. Those who deny the unity of the Bible treat it like any other book. They say the Bible is not the inspired Word of God but human words about God, a collection of (fallible) human reflections on religious themes. It may be inspiring, but it is not inspired by God. It may be full of insights, but it is not authoritative for faith and practice. This perspective gleans what is good from the Bible but ignores or rejects what is viewed as in error or what conflicts with one's personal feelings or convictions. By contrast, an evangelical view of Scripture holds that God has spoken and that the Bible is an authentic revelation from him. The reader doesn't presume authority over the text but submits to its instruction and conforms to its values. The unity of Scripture reminds us that though God speaks through human instruments, their message represents God's Word for us.

While some deny the unity of the Bible, others neglect its diversity by treating it as a direct and unmediated revelation from God. This approach might say, "God said it. I believe it. That settles it." While this rightly acknowledges the divine side of revelation ("God said it"), it ignores the human side. God spoke through human beings, using human language, adopting literary forms common to their time and place, and addressing specific historical and social situations. To apply the Bible appropriately to our lives, we must first interpret it rightly with reference to its original audience, entering into the very different world of the text. This entails understanding how language works, how various literary forms function (as narrative, prophecy, poetry, proverb, etc.), and how the human authors address specific life situations.

The task of determining the original meaning of the text is known as *exegesis*. The term comes from a Greek word that means to "draw out" and refers to drawing out the original meaning of the text. Exegesis is the careful study of the historical and literary context to determine *the author's intended meaning*. Since the Bible was written by real people in real historical situations, understanding it means using all the tools of historical research available to us: linguistic, geographical, archaeological, social, and cultural.

Two other concepts, inspiration and incarnation, help to unpack the unity and diversity of Scripture. *Inspiration* means that the Bible is an authentic message from God. The term "inspiration" comes from 2 Timothy 3:16: "All scripture is given by inspiration of God" (KJV), where the Greek word translated as "given by inspiration" is *theopneustos*, meaning "God-breathed" (NIV), or "breathed out by God" (ESV). This message is not merely human but divine. It is not merely a message to "them" long ago; it is a message for us today.

Incarnation means that this message has come to us in human form, with all of the limitations inherent in true humanity. There is a helpful parallel here to the person of Jesus Christ. Just as Jesus, the living Word of God, is fully human yet fully divine, so the written Word, the Bible, is fully human and fully divine. John 1:1 says, "In the beginning was the Word, and the Word was with God, and the Word was God." Jesus is the "Word" (Greek: *logos*), God's self-revelation. He is fully divine: "the Word was God." Yet "the Word became flesh and made his dwelling among us" (John 1:14). Jesus became one of us. Through his incarnation, Jesus took on our humanity, our weaknesses, our limitations, so that he could communicate God's will to us and be our representative, dying to pay the penalty for our sins.

Like Jesus, the living Word, the written Word is fully human and fully divine. It is an authentic and true message from God, but it comes to us through weak human subjects, using imperfect human language, copied and passed down by fallible human beings, and subject to the limitations of human culture and experience. While these limitations mean the message does not reach us in perfect or pristine form, it reaches us as *the true and authentic Word of God*, a trustworthy message from him. This truth is protected through

God's providence and the guidance and oversight of the Holy Spirit. In the next section, we will explore some of the dimensions of this fully human/fully divine nature of Scripture.

The Diversity of Scripture and the Task of Exegesis

The diversity of Scripture reminds us of the need for careful reading, or exegesis, of the text. Some readers say, "I don't interpret the Bible, I just read it." But what they don't realize is that every act of reading is an act of interpretation. Nobody reads anything without interpreting it. Suppose you see a sign next to the sidewalk that says, "Stay off the grass." You have not merely read this; you have interpreted it. You have understood that the sentence is a command because of the form of the verb "stay." You have recognized that "stay off" is an idiom that means not to step on. You have interpreted the word "grass" as that green stuff growing beside the sidewalk. We do all this interpretation immediately and unconsciously, because we speak the language and know the culture in which this sign appears. But suppose the sign reads, *Manténgase fuera de la hierba.* Unless you know Spanish, you would not be able to understand the sign because you could not interpret its words or idioms. Every act of reading is an act of interpretation.

In the same way, every time you read the Bible you are already interpreting it. The only question is whether you will interpret it well or poorly—that is, whether you will hear the text as the author intended it to be heard, or whether you will impose your own ideas onto the text. Exegesis means *drawing out* the author's original meaning. "Eisegesis" refers to the opposite: misinterpreting the text by *reading into* it your own assumptions and meaning.

Of course, these definitions need to be qualified. After all, no one comes to the Bible with a clean slate. We all bring our backgrounds to the text and so by necessity read it through our own worldviews and life experiences. But by acknowledging the diversity or "otherness" of the text, we take a first step toward understanding. We bring our worldview within the purview of the worldview of the text. Anthony Thiselton speaks of two "horizons," or boundaries—the horizon of the text and the horizon of our subjective experience in the world.[1] Though these horizons can never become one, they can touch each other significantly enough to create *true* understanding. In our exegesis of the text, we must take into account the diversity of Scripture in five areas: authors, languages, literary forms, social and cultural contexts, and purposes in writing.

Diverse Human Authors

Contrary to the view of some people, the Bible did not drop out of the sky from heaven. It came to us through human authors in real-life situations. In the controversial novel *The Da Vinci Code*, the character Leigh Teabing, a British Royal Historian, mocks those who revere the Bible as the Word of God: "The Bible did not arrive by fax from heaven. . . . The Bible is the product of *man* . . . not God. The Bible did not fall magically from the clouds. Man created it as a historical record of tumultuous times." While most of what *The Da Vinci Code* says about the Bible is utter nonsense, this point about the Bible not falling from heaven is certainly true. The Bible came to us through real human authors and arose in the crucible of human experience. It is a very human book. To deny this human side of the Bible is to misread the text.

The nature of the process of revelation is certainly a mystery. How did human authors communicate *God's* message? While 2 Timothy 3:16 speaks about Scripture being "inspired" or "breathed out" by God, this does not tell us a great deal about the actual process. Second Peter 1:21 says prophets spoke for God as they were "carried along" (NIV) or "moved" (NRSV) by the Holy Spirit. But, again, exactly how the Holy Spirit guided them is unclear.

We know the Bible was not simply dictated by God. The Holy Spirit did not whisper in the ears of Jeremiah, or David, or James, who then wrote down his exact words. This is clear from the fact that different biblical authors have different styles of writing. Compare, for example, the authors of two of the Gospels. Luke writes in a fine literary Greek style. He is obviously an educated person with a mastery of the Greek language. Mark's Gospel, on the other hand, has a much rougher, Semitic literary style, suggesting that the author speaks Greek as a second language. The letters of the New Testament also reveal diverse styles. The apostle Paul was certainly fluent in Greek, but he writes in an emotional, energetic, staccato style. The unknown author of the letter to the Hebrews writes on a higher literary plane, with carefully crafted sentences structured for rhetorical impact and a rich, sophisticated vocabulary. It is clear that these writers are composing their works using their own minds and drawing on their unique educational backgrounds and life experiences.

We also see authors' personalities emerging through their writings. Jeremiah has been called the "weeping prophet" because of his emotional outbursts of anger, frustration, and anguish (Jer. 9:1; 10:19–20; 23:9). He is prone to self-criticism (10:24) and rails against his enemies, calling for their punishment (12:1–3; 15:15; 17:18; 18:19–23). The apostle Paul, too, often writes from a deep well of emotion. He expresses great love and affection for his churches, his spiritual children, and is fiercely protective of their well-being (1 Thess. 2:1–3:13; Phil. 1:3–7). He pleads with his followers to remain faithful to him and to the Lord (1 Cor. 4:14–16; 2 Corinthians 10–13) and at times threatens them with disciplinary action. "What do you prefer?" he writes to the Corinthians, "Shall I come to you with a rod of discipline, or shall I come in love and with a gentle spirit?" (1 Cor. 4:21; see also 2 Cor. 10:11). He is not above sarcasm (2 Cor. 10:1; 11:19; 12:16), and he chides his opponents for their arrogance and impotence (2 Cor. 11:13–23). These authors are not robots, delivering a message verbatim from God, but rather God's spokespeople, who discern God's purpose and will and then speak authoritatively for him.

A classic example of this human side of biblical revelation appears in 1 Corinthians 1. Paul is responding to the disunity in the church at Corinth, and especially to the reality that the church is breaking into factions around their support for human leaders. Some of the Corinthians are saying, "I follow Paul," "I follow Apollos," "I follow Cephas," or even "I follow Christ." Paul is disgusted with such divisions and responds, "Is Christ divided? Was Paul crucified for you? Were you baptized into the name of Paul?" He then says that he is glad that he did not baptize many of them, since baptisms can create these kinds of human divisions and alliances. Paul writes, "I thank God that I did not baptize any of you except Crispus and Gaius, so no one can say that you were baptized in my name. (Yes, I also baptized the household of Stephanas; beyond that, I don't remember if I baptized anyone else.) For Christ did not send me to baptize, but to preach the gospel" (1 Cor. 1:14–17).

This is a wonderful passage to remind us that the Christian life is not about gaining prestige or followers; it is about glorifying Christ. But the passage also demonstrates something about the nature of biblical revelation. Notice that Paul first says he only baptized two of the Corinthians, Crispus and Gaius. Then he stops and realizes he is mistaken, because he also baptized the household of Stephanas. Finally, he stops again, because he might be mistaken again, so he adds that he can't remember exactly how many he has baptized.

The point is that the Holy Spirit is communicating here through Paul's normal experiences, his personality, and even his forgetfulness! Someone reading the Bible in an overly literal way might say, "The Bible is in error, since Paul says he only baptized two of the Corinthians, when in fact he baptized more." But if we acknowledge the human side of revelation, we realize that this is a normal pattern of human discourse. Paul's message comes through, despite—or even because of—his misstatement. Indeed, his own forgetfulness makes the point even stronger. Paul was so uninterested in gaining the support of those he baptized that he forgot how many he baptized. Furthermore Paul's own forgetfulness reveals his human frailty and so reiterates that this is not about Paul's prestige but about God's glory. To read the Bible well we have to take into account how language functions in normal human discourse and literature.

Diverse Languages

A second key aspect of the Bible's diversity is the fact that it came to us in the limitations of human language, and in languages different from our own. To properly exegete the Bible—in other words, to do exegesis—these languages must be translated and interpreted. This task always involves a measure of ambiguity and imprecision. Indeed, all communication through language entails a degree of imprecision. Yet while communication through language is never perfect, it can be effective and reliable, and the message conveyed can be accurately received.

The year 2011 marks the 400th anniversary of the original publication of the "Authorized" or King James Version of the Bible

(1611). The King James Version (KJV) has had a profound impact throughout the world. For three and a half centuries it was the Bible of choice for most English-speaking Christians, shaping the language, literature, and culture of the Western world. I grew up reading it, hearing it in church, and memorizing large sections of it. Many Bible verses still sound "wrong" to me if they don't imitate the style and cadence of the KJV. Some people still view the KJV as the only "real" Bible. I've heard the joke many times that if the King James Version was good enough for the apostle Paul, it should be good enough for us. Of course, the joke is funny because the KJV was not Paul's Bible; it was published over fifteen hundred years after he died. Paul didn't speak Elizabethan English (the language of the KJV), which wasn't around in his day; he read his Bible (the Hebrew Scriptures, our Old Testament) in Hebrew, Aramaic, and Greek and wrote his letters in Greek.

The Old Testament was originally written in Hebrew, with a few sections in Aramaic. The New Testament was written in Hellenistic or Koine ("common") Greek, which was the common trade language spoken throughout the eastern Mediterranean region in the first century AD. Most people in the world today must therefore read the Bible in translation. Even most modern Greeks read the Bible in a contemporary Greek version, because the Greek language has changed greatly since the first century. All Bible study therefore involves translation, done either by the reader, if they know Hebrew and Greek, or by someone who has translated the text for them.

Not only does all Bible reading involve translation, but all translation involves interpretation. Anyone who has ever learned a second language recognizes that translation is an inexact science and that a passage can be translated in various ways and still communicate the meaning accurately. I preach regularly to several Chinese churches in the San Diego area. Often there will be someone present to translate my message into Chinese for those who do not speak English. Suppose there were two translators doing the work simultaneously. Even if both were equally skilled, they would not translate my words in exactly the same way. This is because all translation involves interpretation and no two languages are the same in terms of word meanings, grammar, or idioms. The translator must first comprehend the meaning of the text in their own language and then determine the best way to communicate that message in the target language.

Even a fledgling translator soon learns that a literal or word-for-word translation is not an accurate one, because languages say the same things in different ways. Consider the Spanish phrase *Tengo hambre*. Translated literally, the sentence reads, "I have hunger." But no English speaker would say that. They would say, "I'm hungry." Literal translation does not work. The translator must first ask, What does this Spanish sentence *mean*? and then, How do we say this in English? Consider another Spanish example: *Me gusta la sopa* means, literally, "The soup pleases me." But in English, we would say, "I like the soup." The Spanish *¿Cuántos años tienes?* translated literally would be, "How many years have you?" In English, we say, "How old are you?" An accurate translation is not a literal one. All good translation involves, first, interpreting the *meaning* of the text, and second, finding an equivalent expression in the target language. The best Bible translation is one that uses clear, accurate, and natural-sounding English.[2]

An important corollary is that the authority and inspiration of the Bible relate to the *meaning* of the text as a whole, not to its individual *words*. This is because meaning is communicated not through words in isolation but through words in dynamic interaction with other words. While individual words are certainly important as part of a larger act of communication (hence the need for word studies), the goal of language is not to reproduce words on a page but to communicate a *message* from one person to another. A Bible translation is successful when the reader hears the message of the text in the way that the original author intended it to be heard. This involves finding the best way to reproduce the text's message, not just mimicking its form.

In summary, the diversity of the Bible reminds us that we have to cross a language barrier to hear God's Word. Fortunately for English readers, much of the hard work has already been done. There are dozens of excellent English versions of the Bible, produced by scholars who are experts in the language and culture of the Bible. Readers should get in the habit of using more than one Bible version, since no translation is perfect and since different translations bring out different aspects of the text's meaning.[3] Readers should also learn to consult good Bible commentaries and other study tools when the meaning of the text is difficult. Again, exegesis is a critical first step in our application of the Word.

Diverse Literary Forms or Genres

Just as the Bible comes to us in different languages, so it comes to us in a variety of genres, or literary forms. The diversity of the Bible teaches us that we must learn the "rules" for each of these literary forms. Chapters 6 and 7 will discuss specific principles and cautions related to the application of different literary forms. Here the point is simply the importance of genre identification.

Different literary genres must be interpreted differently. Historical narrative can generally be taken at face value, that is, as describing historical events. But poetry tends to use more symbolic language. When we read in 1 Samuel 16 that the prophet Samuel went to the home of Jesse in Bethlehem and there anointed David to be the next king of Israel, we assume that the author intends readers to understand this as an actual historical event. On the other hand, in Psalm 22:12–13 David says, "Many bulls surround me; strong bulls of Bashan encircle me. Roaring lions that tear their prey open their mouths wide against me." Here we recognize that David is not recounting a terrible accident at the zoo; rather, he is poetically describing his human enemies as vicious beasts. David continues in the next verse: "I am poured out like water, and all my bones are out of joint. My heart has turned to wax; it has melted within me" (Ps. 22:14). Again we recognize that David's body has not actually dissolved like water nor has his heart melted like the Nazi soldiers in *Raiders of the Lost Ark*. These are symbolic and poetic descriptions of intense emotional and physical distress. Identifying the genre in each case is critical to understanding the author's meaning and drawing legitimate application.

Genre identification can make or break the proper interpretation of a biblical book or passage. Enormous controversy surrounds the opening chapters of Genesis concerning whether the heavens and the earth literally were created in six days or whether the creation took place over a much longer period. This is not so much a debate between those who take the Bible seriously and those who don't but rather a question of genre identification. What literary genre is the author of Genesis using to describe creation? Is this meant to be a historical and chronological account of the timeline of creation, or is it a poetic presentation about the nature of God and his relationship to the world? Or is it some combination of these? The genre question must be answered first before we can raise historical or scientific questions.

Similar questions of genre relate to the Song of Songs. Is this an allegory symbolically depicting God's love for his people, as the book has often been interpreted throughout church history? Or is it an ancient love song, celebrating sexual love between a man and a woman? Most contemporary scholars would say it is a love song. It is essential for us to answer this question about literary form before we can properly interpret the Song of Songs. Each of the Bible's literary forms—whether narrative, poetry, psalm, proverb, law, prophecy, letter, or apocalypse—has its own rules of interpretation. In chapters 6 and 7 we will look more closely at the various literary forms of the Old and New Testament.

Diverse Social and Cultural Contexts

Just as the genre or literary form determines the manner in which a text expresses truth, so the social context in which the author writes impacts the text's meaning and application. A good example of this appears in 1 Corinthians 8–10. Paul begins chapter 8 with the statement, "Now about food sacrificed to idols . . ." (8:1). Immediately we are brought into a world very different from modern Western civilization. Food sacrificed to idols? What we need to understand is that in the Greco-Roman world most meat sold in the marketplace had first been offered as a sacrifice to a pagan god. Of course, the god did not eat much, so the meat could then be used for various purposes. The person who initially purchased the offering and the priest who sacrificed it could each get a portion; the temple where it was offered might then sell the rest in the marketplace for profit. This meat sold in the marketplace is what Paul refers to as "food sacrificed to idols."

Jews refused to eat such meat, viewing it as idolatrous, so they set up their own butcher shops, where "kosher" or ritually undefiled

51

food would be sold. The question the Corinthians were asking Paul was, Should Christians do the same? Paul's detailed response takes into account a variety of social factors. He affirms, first of all, that idols are nothing but wood and stone, with no life of their own. To eat meat offered to such lifeless objects is therefore of no religious significance (8:4–6). However, some believers are former idolaters and, for them, to eat would be to participate in pagan worship. For their sake, Paul says, you should refrain from eating so as not to cause them to fall into sin (8:7–13).

In 1 Corinthians 10 Paul returns to the issue of idol meat and addresses more specific social contexts. He first tells the Corinthians to avoid eating meat that is part of a celebration in a pagan temple.[4] To participate in such ceremonies is to join in pagan worship, which is the same as worshiping demons (10:14–22). A second context relates to marketplace meat. Paul says the Corinthians can buy any food in the marketplace to eat at home without raising questions, since "the earth is the Lord's, and everything in it" (10:23–26, quoting Ps. 24:1). Finally, Paul discusses a case where an unbeliever invites a Christian to their house, and food sacrificed to an idol is served (10:27–30). Here Paul gives his most nuanced answer. If nothing is said about the food, he instructs, go ahead and eat it. But if the host points out it has been offered to an idol, you should refuse. Paul's point is that if the host places no spiritual significance on the meat, go ahead and eat. But if the host makes the meat a test of whether you are willing to participate in pagan worship, you must refuse. Christians worship the one true God, and to give the impression that you are willing to worship an idol would be sin.

This passage illustrates the diverse social, cultural, and religious contexts in which the Bible arose. It also reminds us of the need for careful exegesis. Understanding the ancient marketplace and the religious milieu of the Greco-Roman world is essential to comprehending Paul's argument. Finally, the passage provides an example of how to apply God's Word in a constantly changing world. When faced with a new ethical question, Paul reaches a conclusion not by quoting a single Old Testament command but by drawing on broader truths related to the nature of God, who we are as his people, and how we accomplish his purpose in the world. It is significant that Paul concludes this passage with an overarching principle for dealing with difficult ethical questions: "So whether you eat or drink or whatever you do, do it all for the glory of God" (1 Cor. 10:31).

Interestingly, as our world shrinks and diverse cultures come into closer contact with one another, our ability to understand the cultures of the Bible can expand. Several years ago I was teaching 1 Corinthians 8–10 in a course on Paul. I mentioned how alien this passage was to Western culture, since we know nothing of food sacrificed to idols. One of my students raised his hand and said that earlier that day he had gone into a doughnut shop to pick up a dozen doughnuts for a Bible study he was leading. The owner of the shop, a recent immigrant from Southeast Asia, said the doughnuts were not quite ready yet because he had not offered them to his god. When the owner emerged smiling a few minutes later and handed my student the box of doughnuts, the student had a funny feeling in his stomach. Should he eat the doughnuts and share them with the members of his Bible study, or were they now equivalent to a pagan sacrifice? Paul's principles about food sacrificed to idols suddenly came alive in a new way.

If the issue of food sacrificed to idols provides a glimpse into the social and cultural diversity of the biblical world, certain Old Testament passages may take us even farther from our own cultural context. Many modern readers are horrified to read in Exodus 21:7 stipulations related to a man selling his daughter into slavery: "If a man sells his daughter as a female slave, she is not to go free as the male slaves do" (NASB). How, we might ask, could any father sell his own daughter into slavery? Worse yet, why would God allow this?

To understand this passage, we have to enter the social and economic world of the ancient Near East. Families in these cultures lived together in clans or tribal units that provided social stability and protection. A man who became destitute might need to sell himself or his family into indentured service to a fellow countryman.[5] This could be a matter of survival during times of famine or severe economic decline. By becoming an indentured servant, the man could survive and work off his debt. To avoid exploitation of the poor, the law placed a limit of six years on the length of this servitude (Exod. 21:2). The work counted as payment of the debt, so in the seventh year the man would go free.[6] Such a system was necessary to avoid destitution and starvation in a society that lacked other social welfare structures.

Exodus 21:7–11 picks up the situation of a daughter sold into this kind of indentured service. In this case, she is sold with the intention of becoming the master's wife or concubine. (A concubine was a "secondary wife," one of lower social status in the household than the man's first wife.) Again, in the Western world we may view this as terrible exploitation of women. But in that cultural context a woman outside the protection of a household could not survive. Allowing multiple wives (or concubines) enabled additional women to come under the provision and protection of a single household.

Verse 7 says that unlike the indentured man, the woman is not to be set free after six years. The reason is that as a wife or concubine, she is now viewed as part of this new family and remains under their authority. If the master decides not to take her as his concubine, he may *not* sell her outside the clan but must allow her to be redeemed (purchased back) by her original family (v. 8). If he takes another woman (presumably another concubine), he must not deprive the first wife of her marital rights in any way, or else she is allowed to go free (presumably to return to her family) without any payment. If she marries the man's son, the master must grant her the full rights of a daughter, not treat her as a servant.

What may seem at first like cruel and barbaric treatment is in fact part of a complex economic and social system that was meant to provide a measure of social stability, on the one hand to avoid destitution, and on the other, to avoid exploitation of the poor. Difficult questions certainly remain. To modern Western sensibilities, the system may still seem unfair and oppressive, because women were not viewed as equals in society and did not have the freedom to chart their own course in life.

We may draw two conclusions from this passage in Exodus. First, exegesis is essential. To comprehend the reason for these laws we must seek to understand the social situation in which the text arose, a setting often very different from our own. If we view such commands solely through our own cultural lens, we will inevitably misunderstand and misrepresent them. Second, we see that all of God's commands are given *within* human culture and are shaped and adapted to fit the structures in place within that culture. They represent what we might call "contextualized ethics," ethical mandates set within a particular social and cultural context. Behind them lies a God of absolute righteousness and justice. But he is accommodating in order to affirm and advance his values *within the limitations and weaknesses of human culture.* While cultural features like indentured servitude and polygamy do not represent the ideal ethics of the kingdom of God, God is willing to work within these institutions—rather than simply to abolish them—to accomplish his greater purpose for the world.[7]

Diverse Purposes in Writing

We have seen the Bible's diversity in terms of authors, language, genres, and social and cultural contexts. Finally, we should note its diversity in terms of an author's purpose in writing and the audiences addressed. In all communication, identifying the purpose of an author or speaker is essential for proper understanding. When I open the mail, my first goal is to determine who sent each letter and their purpose in writing. Is this an advertisement trying to sell me something? A bill requesting payment? A check reimbursing me? A thank-you note expressing appreciation? At times I have opened a letter and a check has fallen out. My first inclination is to cash the check, until I read the small print saying that cashing it automatically enrolls me in a credit card protection plan. What is masquerading as a check is in fact a solicitation for my business. Determining the purpose of the letter is essential for both interpretation and application. (In this case my application is to send the check through the paper shredder.)

We need to read biblical literature with the same goal in mind—to determine the author's purpose in writing. Paul's letters are written to various churches and individuals in the first century AD. The purpose of each letter is to address issues peculiar to that church or person. Paul's first letter to the Thessalonians, for example, is written to praise the church located in Thessalonica (in Macedonia, northern Greece) for their faith and endurance in the face of suffering and persecution and to encourage them toward even greater faith and love. The letter to the Philippians is intended to inform the church at Philippi of Paul's current situation, to thank them for the gifts they have sent, and to encourage them to a greater unity and dependence on God.

Purpose is closely related to genre. The purpose of the Old Testament prophetic books is to call the people of Israel to faith and obedience and to warn them of the consequences of unfaithfulness. The purpose of the proverbs is to instruct God's people in wise and godly living. The purpose of biblical narrative is to describe God's redemptive acts in history and how people have responded to those actions in the past. Our present application must arise from the author's original purpose.

All these aspects of the Bible's diversity—author, language, genre, culture, and purpose—confirm the need for careful exegesis, entering the world of the text to hear its message as it was originally heard. From the nature of the Bible as God's Word in human words, we turn next to the central message of the Bible: *the story of redemption*.

The Bible as Story: From Creation to New Creation

If the diversity of the Bible teaches that we need to read it with eyes focused and ears attuned to the diverse human voices, the unity of the Bible reminds us that the message we hear will be consistent and true. But how do more than forty authors writing sixty-six books over a period of fifteen hundred years produce a unified message? The answer is that the Bible is not just a library of religious books; it is the inspired and authoritative Word, a unified message *from God to us*.

Perhaps the best way to characterize the Bible and its message is as a story or a drama. Stories by their very nature have a beginning, a middle, and an end. They progress through a plot or story line. This plot includes conflicts between opposing forces, a crisis where the conflict reaches its highest point, and ultimately a resolution. Stories contain characters—protagonists ("good guys"), antagonists ("bad guys"), and others. They have settings, the world in which the characters interact and the plot runs its course. The Bible, seen as a unified whole, has all of these features. Its plot is the actions of God in human history, the record of the human race from creation to catastrophe to new creation. Its protagonist and hero is God, along with those who align with him. Its antagonists include Satan, demons, and those who reject God's sovereignty. Its setting is the cosmos that God has created—a world that is fallen, yet in the process of being restored. By immersing ourselves in the Story, we are able to identify our place in it and then live out the role God has planned for us. In the Bible we learn about who God is, who we are, and what it means to walk with him and to live as his people in the world. We learn to discern his purpose and will. We learn to identify the heart of God.

The Power of Story in Our Lives

When I was in junior high school, my English literature teacher required us to read the little western novel *Shane*, by Jack Schaefer. The book is a young person's classic, with the traditional theme of the lowly homesteaders against the powerful rancher. Joe Starrett and his family have settled in the Wyoming wilderness, where they are trying to make a life for themselves by working the land. The big-time rancher Fletcher hates the homesteaders and is doing everything he can to drive them out. A mysterious stranger named Shane arrives on the scene and takes a job working for the Starretts. Shane is quickly drawn into the feud between the homesteaders and Fletcher and takes on the cattleman's bullying ranch hands in several fistfights. Fletcher eventually brings in a hired gun named Stark Wilson to eliminate Shane and force the homesteaders out. The story is told from the perspective of Joe's young son, Bob, who idolizes Shane. In the boy's eyes, the former gunfighter becomes a mythic character who has come to save the family. I won't spoil the ending, but the climax of the story reveals honor, courage, sacrifice, and redemption.

As a kid, I was drawn into the book. I especially remember its protagonist and main character. Although a skilled gunfighter, Shane has become a man of peace who now turns to violence only as a last resort. He is a man of justice. His violent past haunts him, but he will not walk away from those who are harassed and oppressed. He is a man of compassion who shows touching care for an enemy, a young ranch hand named Chris, who picks a fight with him. Though he could easily have killed Chris, Shane sees his own younger self in the man and shows him mercy. Shane is a man of character. When Joe's wife, Marian, begins to fall in love with Shane, he cares too much for the family to act on his own feelings for her. Although it seems a bit silly now, as a kid I found myself emulating Shane, trying to act with the same kind of courage, honor, and justice. When I entered a room, I would look for the best vantage point to sit, so as to be ready for any danger, just as he did in the book. When I saw another kid being bullied, I would try to stand up for the weak. The protagonist of the book became a model for me of authentic character and courage.

This is the power of story. We relate to the characters we see in movies or read about in books. We are drawn into the plot and experience the conflict, climax, and resolution. We root for the protagonist and envision ourselves in the same situations. We experience the joys and sorrows of the characters, and our lives are shaped by their actions and attitudes. We learn how to live as we find our place in the story.

This is not just a picture of the books we read and the stories we hear. It is a picture of life. Life is living out our story in relationship to the stories of those around us. We grow up with parents, family members, teachers, and peers, and our lives are shaped through our interaction with them. We emulate and follow the example of some and seek to avoid the failings of others. We find our place and our role in various stories—those of family, peers, school, work, and larger society. Relationships within these stories can be positive or negative, places of growth and fulfillment or of conflict and dysfunction.

Living "biblically," I would suggest, means recognizing our place in God's story and living in such a way that we reflect his nature and purpose in the world.

God's Story: The Metanarrative of Scripture

Postmodernism has made much of this idea of our lives as story. Each of us has our own story, and life consists of living out our stories in interaction with the stories of others. This emphasis on life as many interrelated stories is a helpful one, reminding us of our subjective perspectives, personal biases, and limited viewpoints. Each of us sees life from within the limited horizons of our own story. We grow and mature by hearing, experiencing, and learning from others.

Yet where postmodernism has gone wrong is in its denial of the reality of a larger *metanarrative*, a great unifying Story that makes all of our individual stories part of God's story.[8] The Bible may best be described as the authorized and definitive metanarrative—the story of the creation, fall, and redemption of the world in relation to its Creator. It is *authorized* because it is a message approved by God himself, his authoritative Word. It is *definitive* because it is true and complete, providing all we need in order to be restored to a right relationship with God and to live rightly with him and with others.

The Plot of the Story: From Creation to New Creation

If we are going to find our place in the Bible's story, we have to know the plot: how the story moves from introduction to crisis to climax to resolution. The next few pages will summarize the Bible's story, giving a bird's-eye view of the drama of redemption. Various interpreters have introduced this idea of the Bible as story, or as a drama divided into acts.[9] N. T. Wright identifies five acts in this grand drama of redemption: creation, the fall, Israel, Jesus, and the church.[10] Craig Bartholomew and Michael W. Goheen helpfully expand with a sixth act, ending not with the church but with new creation.[11] It is this six-act drama that best represents the biblical narrative.

Act 1. Creation. The drama begins with a lone character on the stage: "In the beginning *God* . . ." (Gen. 1:1). The Bible begins not with the origin of God or with arguments for his existence but rather with the assumption that he is the one true God who created all things. God is the main character and hero, but it is not really *his* story. After all, God is infinite and eternal, existing long before this drama begins and continuing long after it ends. The Bible is not a biography of God. It is rather *our* story, the narrative of God's relationship with human beings. It was written to guide us and to teach us the ways of God.

Genesis 1 recounts how God speaks and the heavens and the earth come into existence. His word alone is efficacious. The pinnacle of his creation is not the awesome stars and the galaxies, the majestic seas or continents, but lowly human beings, male and female, whom God creates in his own image (Gen. 1:27). What it means to be created in God's image is a mystery, but it certainly means that we, like God, are creative, spiritual beings who are capable of having a meaningful relationship with him. The reason for our creation is to bear God's image, to be in relationship with him, to walk with him, and to bring him glory. We do these things not in isolation but in relationship with other people. When Adam is created he is incomplete. So God creates Eve, the woman, to complete his humanity (Genesis 2). Together, man and woman bear the image of God and find their fulfillment in him. As God himself is community (the Trinity), so human beings were created to live in loving relationship with one another and with God.

God places Adam and Eve in the garden of Eden, an idyllic place where they can be caretakers of the earth and live in perfect relationship with each other and with God. Though created for relationship with God, they are not his equals. Humanity's purpose is to know God, to serve him, and to bring him glory. To test their fidelity, God places the tree of the knowledge of good and evil in the garden and forbids them to eat its fruit. Disobedience to this command will result in death (Gen. 2:16–17). Obedience would result in a "graduation" from their present state of innocence to one of maturity, or to perfect humanity (we can assume this from later in the Story: Heb. 2:10; Rom. 8:30; 1 John 3:2).[12]

Act 2. The fall. The story has barely begun, however, when disaster strikes. Tempted by the crafty serpent, Eve eats the fruit and gives some to Adam, who also eats. Desiring to be like God, they claim his authority as their own and so fail the test. Though they do not die physically right away, they die spiritually and will one day return to the dust from which they were created. God judges not only Adam and Eve but the whole creation, which now stands under a curse. The world becomes a broken place. All that is wrong today—all evil, conflict, disease, suffering, natural disasters, and death—has resulted from the fall of humanity.

But as a loving father, God refuses to give up on his creation. Though we have called the first three chapters of Genesis Acts 1 and 2, because of their profound significance for the story as a whole these chapters may also be called our drama's "prologue"; the rest of the story is about God's plan of redemption, how he will restore humanity to a right relationship with himself. All of the individual stories, laws, prophecies, parables, psalms, proverbs, and letters are woven into this grand narrative of redemption.

Act 3. Israel: Redemption initiated through covenant. Since relationships have been broken, relationships must be restored. The key Old Testament word for relationship is "covenant." God's rescue plan for humanity centers on a series of covenants, or binding obligations, that he establishes with his people. As his part of each covenant, God promises provision, protection, and salvation for his people. The people, in turn, are called to love, obey, and serve God. Obedience to the covenant results in peace (Hebrew: *shalom*), a right relationship with God, and security in the land. Disobedience results in judgment, suffering, and exile. It is through the promises contained in these covenants that God carries forward his plan of salvation.

To launch his rescue operation, God chooses one family to be his special people and to mediate his presence to the world. He calls Abraham from his clan and country and makes a covenant with him, promising to create through him a great nation (Israel), to give him the Promised Land (Canaan), and to bless all nations through his descendants (Genesis 12; 15; 17). In response, Abraham owes God obedience and faithfulness. Abraham answers God's call and becomes a model for what it means to walk with God and to live a life of faith before him (Romans 4; James 2:20–24).

God renews this covenant with Abraham's son Isaac and grandson Jacob, whom he renames "Israel." Enslaved in Egypt, the "children of Israel" grow into a great nation, until God through Moses leads them to freedom (Exodus 1–15). The exodus from Egypt represents God's great act of redemption in the Old Testament and is repeatedly recalled by the prophets to demonstrate God's power and faithfulness. It is also the prototype and foreshadowing of ultimate redemption in the New Testament, the cross of Christ. Just as in the exodus the blood of the Passover lamb protected the Israelite children and allowed the nation to escape from slavery in Egypt, so in the New Testament the blood of Christ, the final Passover lamb, allows the children of God to escape from slavery to sin, Satan, and death (1 Cor. 5:7).

But this is getting ahead of our story. The exodus results in the birth of the nation Israel, God's chosen people. God reveals himself to Israel by his covenant name, YHWH, or Yahweh (translated in most English Bibles as "the LORD"). At Mount Sinai the LORD makes a covenant with Israel (Exodus 19–31). As long as the people remain faithful to this covenant and its stipulations (the law, or *torah*, a Hebrew term meaning "instruction"), he will bless them and establish them in their land. Disobedience will result in judgment and exile. A tabernacle is established (replaced later by a temple), representing the presence of God among his people. Israel's role is to be a light to the nations, to draw other people back to the presence of God and to model what it means to be righteous—a right relationship with him. A system of sacrifices provides atonement and forgiveness of sins for the restoration of broken fellowship. Running side by side with the theme of covenant is the theme of God's love and justice. Fallen human beings are marred by sin and so fail to live rightly before God. In his justice, God punishes sin, but he offers mercy and forgiveness to those who humbly repent.

After Israel enters the Promised Land, the nation's subsequent history becomes a cycle of disobedience, judgment, repentance, and deliverance. God raises up first judges and then kings to rule over his people. When the people turn away from God, they suffer judgment and foreign oppression. When they repent, God delivers and restores them. The Old Testament prophets repeatedly call God's people to faithfulness to the covenant and a right relationship with God.

The promises of God in the covenants made with Abraham and with Israel at Mount Sinai are individualized in God's covenant with David, Israel's greatest king. Despite his failings later in life, David is "a man after [God's] own heart" (1 Sam. 13:14), who becomes the model for Israel's subsequent kings and the prototype for the ultimate king—the Messiah ("Anointed One")—who will restore God's righteous reign. In this covenant, God promises that he will raise up one of David's descendants after him to have a father-son relationship with God and to reign on David's throne forever in justice and righteousness (2 Sam. 7:12–17).

The kings after David, however, fail to live up to this ideal, and they continue the cycle of sin and judgment. Their failure to keep the covenant results in a divided kingdom and then in exile. The northern kingdom of Israel is taken into exile by the Assyrians; the southern kingdom of Judah, by the Babylonians. Yet in the midst of destruction and exile, there is hope. The prophets continue to predict the coming of the Messiah, who will establish God's eternal reign in justice and righteousness (Isa. 9:1–7; Jer. 23:5–6; Mic. 5:2), reversing the results of the fall and renewing creation (Isa. 11:1–16). The return from exile is portrayed as a new and greater exodus—a preview of the final restoration of creation (Isa. 11:6–9; 40:3–4). Isaiah also speaks of the Messiah as the Lord's "Servant," who will suffer and die as an atoning sacrifice for the people (Isa. 52:13–53:12). Jeremiah describes a new covenant that God will make with his people, greater than the covenants of old. It will bring true knowledge of God and full and complete forgiveness of sins (Jer. 31:31–34).

Act 4. Jesus: Redemption accomplished and the kingdom inaugurated. The Bible's story reaches its climax in the coming of Jesus the Messiah, whose life, death, and resurrection is the center point not only of the Bible but of all human history (Gal. 4:4–5; 1 Cor. 10:11). Jesus comes on the scene with a message: "the kingdom of God has come near" (Mark 1:15). Though the phrase "kingdom of God" does not appear in the Old Testament, the concept permeates the entire story. The kingdom or "reign" of God refers to his sovereign authority over all things. When Adam and Eve sinned, they challenged that rule and placed themselves on their own throne, seeking to become "like God" (Gen. 3:5). The results were disastrous and the world became a fallen place. Yet God has promised to restore his reign one day, to fix his broken world. When Jesus says, "The time has come. . . . The kingdom of God has come near," he is declaring that this promise is about to be fulfilled. The Story has reached its climax.

The New Testament writers describe Jesus as the fulfillment of all that has come before (Luke 24:27). He is the second Adam, whose faithful obedience to God reverses the effects of Adam's disobedience and brings restoration to a fallen world (Rom. 5:12–21; 1 Cor. 15:21–22). He is the fulfillment of the covenant to Abraham; all nations will be blessed through him (Matt. 1:1; Gal. 3:7–9). He is the new Moses, who leads God's people on a new exodus out of slavery to sin and death and into the freedom of eternal life (Acts 3:22; 7:37). He is the new David, who will reign forever on David's throne with justice and righteousness (Luke 1:32–35; 2:11; Rom. 1:3). He is the final high priest, whose once-for-all sacrifice of himself on the cross has inaugurated the new covenant, brought true knowledge of God, and achieved eternal salvation for those with persevering faith (Heb. 8:7–13; 9:11–15; 1 Cor. 11:23–26). He is the incarnate Son of God, who has come from heaven to bring glory to the Father and eternal life to all who believe (John 1:14; 3:16–18). Ultimately, he is the self-revelation of God, the creator and sustainer of all things, who graciously and sacrificially restores the relationship with his creation (John 1:1–18; 8:58; 20:28; 1 Cor. 8:6; Heb. 1:2–3; Col. 1:15; 2:9).

Act 5. The church: Redemption announced through mission and discipleship. If Jesus's life, death, and resurrection represent the definitive act of salvation, the establishment of the church is the "rest of the story," the spread of that message of salvation to a lost world. The book of Acts describes the coming of the Holy Spirit on the Day of Pentecost, the fulfillment of the promises for an end-time outpouring of the Spirit (Joel 2:28–32). Recognizing that God's salvation has been accomplished in Christ, the early Christians set off as his witnesses to bring the message of salvation to a fallen world (Acts 1:8) and to accomplish Jesus's commission to make disciples of all nations (Matt. 28:18–20). The mission of the church, inaugurated in the book of Acts and illustrated in the New Testament Epistles, carries the story forward into our time and place. The Bible's story here becomes our own.

Act 6. New creation: Redemption complete. The death and resurrection of Christ are the climax of God's story, not the resolution. The salvation accomplished on the cross awaits its consummation with the glorification of God's people and the full restoration of creation. The Bible, which starts "in the beginning" with the creation of the present heaven and earth, ends with a new beginning, the creation of a new heaven and a new earth (Rev. 21:1; cf. Isa. 66:22). In the book of Revelation, Jesus brings the Story to its grand finale. He is "the Alpha and the Omega, the First and the Last, the Beginning and the End" (Rev. 22:13; see also Rev. 1:8, 17; 2:8; 21:6; cf. Isa. 44:6; 48:12). He is the Lamb who was slain to provide salvation for people from every tribe, language, people, and nation (Rev. 5:9–12). At the consummation of history he will return to judge the wicked, to deliver the righteous, and to right every wrong (Revelation 19–22). God's universal reign—the kingdom of God—will again be fully established. As in the garden of Eden, God himself will dwell with his people: "They will be his people, and God himself will be with them and be their God. 'He will wipe every tear from their eyes. There will be no more death' or mourning or crying or pain, for the old order of things has passed away" (Rev. 21:3–4; cf. Isa. 25:8). God's plan for reconciliation will be complete.

The Purpose of the Story: Living out a Christian Worldview

Knowing well the Bible's story provides us with the framework to identify our place in the Story and so to live in light of God's purpose for the world. This is the goal of all biblical application, to walk in step with God and be the people he wants us to be.

Another way to say this is that walking with God means living in light of and in line with a *Christian worldview*. Brian Walsh and Richard Middleton have articulated well the meaning of "worldview." A person's worldview, they suggest, depends on how that person answers four key questions: "(1) *Who am I?* Or, what is the nature, task and purpose of human beings? (2) *Where am I?* Or, what is the nature of the world and universe I live in? (3) *What's wrong?* Or, what is the basic problem or obstacle that keeps me from attaining fulfillment? In other words, how do I understand evil? And (4) *What is the remedy?* Or, how is it possible to overcome this hindrance to my fulfillment? In other words, how do I find salvation?"[13]

The biblical answer to these questions would be something like this: (1) *Who are we?* We are human beings created in the image of God. Our purpose is to be in relationship with the one true creator God, to love and serve him, and to bring him glory. (2) *Where are we?* We live in a universe created perfect by God, who himself is *transcendent* and so separate from that creation, but also *immanent* in that he is actively engaged in the affairs of his creation. He is not one god among many (polytheism), nor identical with the universe he created (pantheism), nor a hands-off God who never intervenes in his creation (deism). The creation is now in a fallen state due to human sin but is in the process of being renewed and restored by God. (3) *What's wrong?* All that is wrong with the world—all evil, suffering, and death—is a result of sin, which is rebellion against God and rejection of his authority. When human beings first sinned, they entered a state of fallenness, resulting in a relationship of conflict with and alienation from God, one another, and creation itself. (4) *What's the remedy?* Salvation is God's act of reconciling with

65

human beings, who were created in his image, and redeeming creation to the perfection he designed for it. This was accomplished because of God's grace and through his power, when he himself took on the punishment for our sin through the sacrificial death of Christ on the cross. People can now be reconciled to God and ultimately achieve full and true humanity by identifying with Christ through faith in his life, death, resurrection, and exaltation. Salvation is not an escape from the material world (which was created "good"), but the world's restoration to a right (= spiritual) relationship with God. While this process of reconciliation and restoration is being accomplished in the present, its consummation awaits God's final intervention in the future. Applying the Bible ultimately means bringing our lives in line with God's worldview, adopting his values and purpose for creation.

Of course, it can be problematic to speak about either a "Christian" worldview or a "biblical" one. The problem with the term "Christian worldview" is that there are as many Christian worldviews as there are Christians, or at least Christian subcultures. An American believer may consider a Christian worldview to include self-reliance, personal freedom, private property, capitalism, American patriotism, and conservative politics. An African Christian may see little that is Christian in these things, instead affirming concern for the poor, sharing of global resources, the creation of Christian community, and victory over spiritual powers. All of us bring our own cultural values to the table, so that it is necessary to be self-analytic, seeking to discern *God's values* over the values of our own culture.

Speaking of a "biblical worldview" can also be problematic, since the Bible's theology is progressive rather than static. The worldview of the Old Testament people of God was clearly deficient in certain ways. Though they worshiped Yahweh, the one true creator God, God had not yet revealed his three-in-one nature, his triunity. Though the people recognized that God's justice demands that sin be atoned for through blood sacrifice, they did not comprehend the preparatory nature of animal sacrifices and that true atonement could be achieved only through the once-for-all sacrifice of God's own Son. Their worldview may have been "true" as far as it went, but it was partial and incomplete (Heb. 1:1–4).

When people speak of a "biblical worldview," they sometimes mean replicating the biblical story at a particular time and place, such as the glories of the Davidic kingdom or the idyllic period of the early church described by Luke (Acts 2:42–47; 4:32–35). But the commands and promises made to the early church are also contextualized for their time, place, unique situations, and cultural limitations, just like the commands given to Israel in the Old Testament. All biblical theology is *contextualized* theology— truth brought to bear in particular times and places to deal with specific issues.

Our goal, therefore, is neither to impose our cultural values on the text nor to replicate exactly the world portrayed by the text. It is rather to discern the heart of God in the text, to see the world as God sees it, to adopt his values and purpose, and to walk with him as his people in his story. We will fully comprehend this worldview only when our salvation is consummated, when we will "know fully" as we are fully known (1 Cor. 13:12).

Conclusion

This chapter has explored the unity and diversity of Scripture. Though the Bible comes to us through many authors over many centuries, it represents one great Story, God's plan to bring humanity back into relationship with him. If the Bible is the story of God's redemptive plan, its purpose is to enable us to enter God's story and live out our own stories in conformity to his. We learn from the Story who God is, who we are as his people, and how we ought to live in relationship to him. This, in turn, provides the framework for us to make good and godly decisions, to draw theological and ethical conclusions in line with the nature and purpose of God. We apply the Bible, therefore, by learning to walk with God, meditating on his purpose and plan, and cultivating the mind of Christ.

This has important implications for how we read and apply the Bible. We do God's will not by claiming every promise or obeying every command but by entering the Story and learning to live in loving and faithful relationship with God and with others. In the next chapter, this approach is described as a "heart-of-God" hermeneutic. We learn the ways of God through the text, through fellowship with his people, and through the guidance and empowering of the Holy

Spirit. This enables us to walk faithfully with him through life's journey and to stay faithful to his will in a constantly changing world.

Discussion and Reflection Questions

1. What do we mean by the unity of Scripture? What do we mean by the diversity of Scripture? Why is acknowledging each of these essential for reading and applying the Bible?

2. What is the goal of exegesis? How does exegesis relate to the diversity of the Bible?

3. God's revelation was given within specific social and cultural contexts of the ancient world. How does this affect the way we read and interpret specific commands?

4. What does it mean that the Bible is God's "metanarrative"?

5. Summarize the story of redemption from creation to fall to new creation. How does the story unfold through the themes of covenant and kingdom of God? Who are the main characters in the story?

4

A Heart-of-God Hermeneutic

Walking with God in His Story

A FEW YEARS BACK, I WAS THE SPEAKER AT A MEN'S RE-treat. I had spoken to the same group a year earlier, and they asked me to return the following year. The first year I had given a series of messages on key disciplines of the Christian life: establishing priorities in our lives, cultivating a prayer life, serving others in relationship, and reading and meditating on God's Word. For the second year they wanted to go deeper into this last topic and spend our sessions on how to read and study the Bible.

I jumped at the chance to speak on this topic, because it is my great passion. I love studying the Bible and teaching others how to read it. This is due, in part, to other passions in my life. I love literature and history, and the Bible is full of great literature and great history. (The joke around our house is that Dad prefers boring documentaries to "real" television shows.) I love God and his people, and the message of the Bible is all about God's grace and love for his people.

So when I was asked to teach my favorite topic ("hermeneutics"—the science and art of biblical interpretation), I happily agreed. In these sessions, I gave the men principles on how to read and apply their Bibles. We talked about which translations to use, how to determine the context and background of a passage, how to seek the author's intention, how to draw theology from a text, and how to apply the truths to our lives (all in one weekend!).

This was one of the most engaging church groups I had taught in a long time. They asked questions and raised important issues. In the middle of our sessions, however, one of the guys pulled me aside. He could see the excitement of those around him, but he confessed that he was a terrible Bible reader and had little interest in study. He had tried many times but just could never practice any kind of discipline. He was a contractor and worked with his hands, and he had never been much of a student. When he tried to read his Bible he usually fell asleep or his mind wandered. I responded with my usual encouragement in cases like this: get a simple, easy-to-read translation and use a study Bible with brief, to-the-point notes. I even encouraged him to get an audio Bible so that he could hear the Word while driving or working.

He agreed to try several of these suggestions. What was curious, however, was that as I got to know him and saw him interacting in the group, I realized he was one of the most mature Christians there. He was a man of integrity; he loved his wife and kids; he cared for the needs of others—he practiced everything that we would identify as a mature Christian lifestyle. In other words, though he was a terrible student of the Word, he lived it out faithfully in his life. It became clear to me that applying the Bible is more than just knowing its content.

I have another friend who is a former pastor. He was a very fine student of the Word, a gifted theologian, and an excellent teacher. He did well in seminary and went on to become a successful pastor. I enjoyed having conversations with him because he loved to talk "shop"—key issues in the Bible and theology. Years later, however, I learned that during much of the time I knew him he had been living a double life. Though a pastor and part-time teacher at a Christian college, he had several affairs with women in his church. He and his wife divorced, and he left the ministry. Though he was an excellent student of the Bible, he was not living "biblically."

I've had a number of similar experiences, where one person truly walks with God despite a relative lack of biblical knowledge—they

70

cannot discuss higher-level theology, but they love God and are led by the Holy Spirit—while someone else knows the Bible well but does not live it out. It is clearly not enough to know the Bible or theology, or even *how* to apply it to our lives. Living biblically means having both a *character* that reflects the nature of God and *actions* that reveal a life of obedience to him.

This might seem like a strange point to make in a book about how to read and apply the Bible. But it is an important one. Our *ultimate* goal when reading the Bible is not to exegete or interpret a text well (though that is important). It is not to discern cultural factors in Scripture in order to draw out the kernel of abiding truth (though that too is important). These are means to an end. Our goal is to walk with God, to learn to love him with all our heart, soul, mind, and strength, to love others as ourselves, and to make good and godly decisions in life. It is about comprehending God's purpose for the world and finding our place in his story.

It follows that our passion should not be for Scripture per se but for the One who reveals himself in Scripture. The Christian life is a relationship with a person, not with a book. This in no way diminishes the importance of the Bible, since it is the authorized and definitive self-revelation of that person. We dare not ignore the Bible's message, or we will misunderstand and misrepresent the nature and actions of God. We cannot know and love God without his self-revelation. But the goal remains knowing the person of God and living under his authority.[1]

There is an old hymn called "Break Thou the Bread of Life," which contains these words:

> Beyond the sacred page I seek thee Lord;
> My spirit longs of Thee, O Living Word![2]

The hymn states that the true goal of looking to Scripture is to see "beyond the sacred page" to Christ himself, to have a living encounter with him. Reading the Bible is an important means by which we come to know God and walk with him. But there are other ways as well. People can learn biblical truth (= God's truth) from the family in which they were raised, from following the example of their pastor or other mentors, from Christian (and non-Christian!) friends, from books they read, from prayer and meditation. My friend at that men's retreat had clearly assimilated God's Word into his life in a variety of ways. He may not have known his Bible well, but he was living in light of biblical truth. He was faithfully following his Lord.

Imitatio Christi, or What Would Jesus Do? (WWJD)

Several years ago there was a resurgence of a Christian slogan that originated in the 1890s: "What would Jesus do?"[3] Young people in particular wore wristbands and other paraphernalia imprinted with the abbreviation WWJD, reminding them that in whatever challenges or trials they face they need to ask themselves, "What would Jesus do?" The slogan was taken from Charles Sheldon's 1896 novel, *In His Steps*, which had the question as its subtitle. In the book, Rev. Henry Maxwell encounters a homeless man who challenges him to take seriously the imitation of Christ. Maxwell passes this wisdom on to others, and as various characters encounter crises or difficult decisions, they ask themselves, "What would Jesus do?" In this way, each considers their actions and attitudes and orients their life more closely to the model and example of Jesus.

While WWJD is sometimes viewed as a trite and simplistic slogan that bases behavior more on subjective experience than on biblical truth, in fact the concept behind the slogan has a long and venerable history in the church, especially expressed as *imitatio Christi*, "imitation of Christ," or *imitatio dei*, "imitation of God."[4] In most every area of life, we learn best not by reading instructions or memorizing theoretic principles but by watching others and following their example. Athletes learn to play sports such as golf or tennis by watching others and then practicing what they have seen modeled. A child learns how to love unselfishly by living in a home with parents who love one another and who seek the best for each family member. It is the same in the Christian life. We grow best not by memorizing rules or learning principles but by following in the footsteps of the Master and modeling our life after his example.

Of course, there are cautions and qualifications related to *imitatio dei*. Some characteristics of God we are not called to imitate. God, after all, is the sovereign Lord of the universe, the creator and sustainer of all things. He demands worship from all creation and is the judge of all people. While we are called to imitate God's moral attributes—his love, mercy, kindness, patience, and self-sacrificial love—we do not imitate those attributes that set him apart—his omniscience, omnipresence, and omnipotence.[5] Seeking to imitate these, in fact, is the essence of sin: seeking to *be* God rather than to serve him. *Imitatio dei* therefore means not so much acting like God but being the kind of people he wants us to be.

Some have questioned *imitatio Christi* for other reasons. Martin Luther and other Protestant theologians criticized that the practice leans toward a works-oriented righteousness. The imitation of Christ, Luther believed, "must inevitably involve a denial of grace and conceal an incipient doctrine of works."[6] This, however, is surely an overreaction. The imitation of Christ is not the means of salvation, which is wholly by God's grace. It is rather the manner in which you "work out your salvation with fear and trembling" (Phil. 2:12). Our sanctification, just like our justification, is the work of the Holy Spirit, not something we do in our own power. In the next chapter we will examine the role of the Holy Spirit in the application of Scripture.

The idea of *imitatio Christi* is in fact pervasive throughout the New Testament. When Jesus appoints the Twelve, he calls them first to "be with him," to learn from his example so "that he might send them out to preach and to have authority to drive out demons" (Mark 3:14–15). He repeatedly points to his own life of service and self-sacrifice as a model for them to follow. Those who want to be his disciples must deny themselves, take up their cross, and follow him (Matt. 10:38; Mark 8:34; Luke 9:23). Every student who is fully trained "will be like their teacher" (Luke 6:40). At the Last Supper in John's Gospel, Jesus takes the basin and washes the disciples' feet, pointing out they must follow this example: "Now that I, your Lord and Teacher, have washed your feet, you also should wash one another's feet. I have set you an example that you should do as I have done for you" (John 13:14–15). In his little classic, *The Master Plan of Evangelism*, Robert Coleman describes Jesus's method of training the Twelve: "Jesus had no formal school, no seminaries, no outlined course of study, no periodic membership classes in which he enrolled his followers. . . . Amazing as it may seem, all Jesus did to teach these men his way was to draw them close to himself. He was his own school and curriculum."[7]

The apostles recognized the power of *imitatio Christi*. Paul repeatedly calls on his churches to "Follow my example, as I follow the example of Christ" (1 Cor. 11:1; cf. 1 Cor. 4:16; Phil. 3:17; 4:9; 2 Thess. 3:7). He points to Christ's "emptying" of himself to become a servant and his self-sacrificial death on the cross as the paradigm for all Christian relationships, calling on believers to "have the same mindset as Christ Jesus" (Phil. 2:5; see vv. 6–8). The goal of the Christian life, John says, is to live as Jesus lived (1 John 2:6). Just as Jesus laid down his life for us, so we ought to lay down our lives for others (1 John 3:16). "To this you were called," Peter says, "because Christ suffered for you, leaving you an example, that you should follow in his steps" (1 Pet. 2:21).

The remainder of this chapter presents a heart-of-God approach to biblical application. We live out God's Word not by imitating the world of the Bible in all its details but by imitating Christ himself, bringing our lives into conformity with his values, attitudes, and actions as expressed and illustrated in the biblical text. Our goal is to understand who God is, who we are in relationship to him, and how we ought to live as his people in the world.

We will first examine several metaphors or models that help us to comprehend this heart-of-God hermeneutic. Then we will explore four key questions to ask of any biblical text.

Analogies for Application: Stories, Dramas, and Journeys

The previous chapter introduced the concept of story or narrative as a good way to envision the nature of the Bible and the hermeneutical task. The Bible is the authorized and definitive narrative of redemption. We live out the Christian life by entering the story and adopting the values and purposes of God as presented in the story. Two related models or analogies provide additional insight into the nature of the Bible and the task of interpretation and application. The first builds on the story analogy by specifying the Story as a divine *drama* or play, where the world is the stage and the Bible is the script that guides us through God's will and ways in the world.

The second is the analogy of a *journey*, where the Bible is the travelogue that guides our steps as we walk with God along the road of redemptive history. Both of these metaphors provide helpful insights for envisioning and performing the hermeneutical task.

Performing the Divine Drama

Building on the work of Hans Urs von Balthasar, Kevin Vanhoozer claims that the best model for understanding and applying Scripture is "theodrama."[8] Interpreting and applying the Bible is not simply a matter of reading the text and doing what it says but instead involves "participating in the great drama of redemption of which Scripture is the authoritative testimony and holy script."[9] In this theodramatic model the world is the stage and the Bible is the script that narrates the drama and solicits the church's active participation as performers.

This emphasis on performance and participation is an important one. To live biblically means not just processing the information of the text but "inhabiting" the world it projects. Rather than being an end in itself, theology provides stage direction "for the fitting participation of communities in the drama of redemption."[10]

This drama-of-redemption model has many strengths. Most helpful is that it acknowledges the metanarrative of Scripture and identifies believers as participants in that drama. Whereas a story can be observed without being enacted, a play is *performed* by its actors. We, as God's people, live in God's story and are called to act in accord with his worldview (the stage) and his purpose for the world (the script he has given us).

All analogies, however, break down at a certain point. The comparison of Scripture to a dramatic script is not precise since a script explicitly tells an actor what to say or do. Yet our goal as believers is not to replicate the world of the Bible but to live out in a constantly changing world the values of God exhibited in Scripture. Samuel Wells responds to this concern by pointing to the theatrical concept of improvisation. "When improvisers are trained to work in the theater, they are schooled in a tradition so thoroughly that they learn to act from habit in ways appropriate to the circumstance. This is exactly the goal of theological ethics."[11] Just as actors learn to adapt and respond appropriately to new and unexpected dramatic situations because they have so thoroughly inhabited the world of the drama, so Christians who have become thoroughly immersed in the actions and purpose of God in Scripture will respond appropriately to new and unexpected ethical and theological challenges.

Vanhoozer makes a similar point. Doctrines do not simply tell us what to say and do but "instill in us habits of seeing, judging, and acting in theodramatically appropriate manners."[12] In light of our rapidly changing world and constantly shifting situations, believers improvise the script by "grasping the relationship between what the Bible says about God and what we know about the contemporary situation, and then acting accordingly."[13] The goal is not to strictly replicate a prior pattern or behavior but to "canonically cultivate the mind of Christ" by discovering "the kind of world we live in and the kind of thing God does in the world and the kind of people we are to be in response."[14]

A Journey with God[15]

Another model or analogy that provides insight into the herme-neutical task is a *journey* or *walk with God*. This motif is an ancient one. The early church found it so compelling they adopted it as their name: the "Way," "Path," or "Road" (Greek: *hodos*; Acts 9:2; 18:26; 19:9, 23; 22:4; 24:14, 22). Journeying with Jesus meant following the one who is the way, the truth, and the life (John 14:6). The early Christians did not create this model but drew it from their scriptural heritage. In the Hebrew Scriptures, Adam and Eve walked with God until that fellowship was broken by sin (Gen. 3:8). Enoch "walked with God" so that God took him (Gen. 5:24). Noah (6:9), Abraham (17:1; 24:40), and Isaac (48:15) similarly "walked" with God. The psalmist calls "blessed" those who do not "walk in step with the wicked" but meditate day and night on God's law (Ps. 1:1–2). Jesus calls on his followers to walk with him, even on the path to the cross (Mark 8:34). He encourages them to take the narrow "way" (*hodos*) that leads to life, rather than the broad one that leads to destruction (Matt. 7:13–14). Walking with God is a rich and pervasive biblical image. In this scriptural tradition, John Bunyan's *Pilgrim's Progress* allegorizes the Christian life as a journey by its protagonist, Christian, from the City of Destruction to the Celestial City.

Like the history of redemption, a journey has a beginning, a middle, and an end, in this case moving progressively from creation to new creation. Those who came before walked the same path, but in an earlier time and place, and in different circumstances. The scenery along the road changes but our travel companion—the Creator God—does not. In new situations, he gives different commands and different promises. These may alter and adapt his earlier instructions, but the new commands never contradict the previous ones, since both arise from his unchanging character.

How does Scripture fit into this journey motif? The Bible is our divinely inspired travelogue (travel-*logos*?), the authoritative account (story or script) that we carry with us on the journey, with each generation passing it on to the next. From this divinely inspired record of earlier travelers and past journeys we learn who God is, who we are as his people, and how we ought to live in relationship with him and with others. The biblical covenants are key landmarks along the road, where God sets specific guidelines, conditions, and blessings that enable his people to maintain their walk with him along a particular segment of the road.

This salvation-historical journey divides at the same milestones as the acts of the Story—creation, the fall, Israel, Jesus, the church, and new creation—with the cross of Christ as the great climax and center point. Before the cross, those walking with God trusted in his promise of future salvation. Those walking on this side of the cross experience its salvation blessings and the indwelling presence of the Spirit.

The Bible's diverse genres fit well into this model, since the divine travelogue contains not only the stories of God's people but also their divinely inspired laws, prophecies, psalms, proverbs, and correspondence of pilgrims on the road. Reading the Bible is both a historical and a devotional task. We read the stories of the past in order to live, or walk, in fellowship with God in the present. God speaks to us today because his Spirit is present on the journey, illuminating the message of the text and its significance in new and different circumstances.

How do we apply the Bible's laws, commands, promises, and narratives in contemporary contexts? Like travelers crossing from rural farmland to an urban metropolis, we in the modern world move from the biblical world to our own, encountering new and different opportunities, challenges, and threats. We face these by remembering the ways of God in the past and by experiencing his guidance in the present. Immersing ourselves in Scripture, we come to know who God is (his nature and character), who we are as his people, and what his purposes are in the world. This awareness, together with daily dependence on God's Spirit (Gal. 5:25) and journeying together in a community or caravan of faith, allows us to choose the right path at each crossroads—making good and godly decisions. The Christian life involves not just knowing the Bible's teaching or obeying its commands but walking so close to and so far with God that in each new situation we can identify the heart of God (1 Cor. 2:13–16).

These various metaphors—story, drama, and journey—are not mutually exclusive. Each provides insights into the hermeneutical task. Life may be envisioned as both a journey along the path of life and participation in God's story or drama. Scripture may be viewed as an inspired travelogue from earlier journeys as well as the script that sets the stage for and guides the plot of the divine drama. In each case, however, the purpose remains the same: to equip God's people with the knowledge, wisdom, and insight to live a life of faith, to face new challenges as the people of God, and to pursue God's purpose for the world. This is a heart-of-God hermeneutic—identifying God's values, will, and purpose for the world and orienting our lives in step with these.

Four Questions to Ask of Any Passage of Scripture

Based on the nature of the Bible and the task of application, here are four questions we should ask of any passage of Scripture:

1. Where is this passage in the larger story of Scripture?
2. What is the author's purpose in light of the passage's genre and historical and literary context?
3. How does this passage inform our understanding of the nature of God and his purpose for the world?
4. What does this passage teach us about who we ought to be (attitudes and character) and what we ought to do (goals and

actions) as those seeking to reflect the nature and purpose of God?

Before we discuss these questions, at least three qualifications are in order. First, no single passage of Scripture provides a complete picture of the greater Story or of God's nature and purpose. The answer to each question must therefore build off the teaching of Scripture as a whole. Just as we cannot comprehend the nature of a character in a story by only reading their description on the first page, so we cannot understand the heart of God—his values, will, and purpose for the world—without reading the whole story. This is sometimes called the "analogy of Scripture," which means that Scripture interprets Scripture and that every part is ultimately interpreted by the whole. If the Bible is indeed God's Word, then it will contain an internal unity, with each individual part supplementing and complementing the message as a whole.[16]

A second qualification is that, while each of the four questions builds on the previous one, the four also constantly interact with one another. For example, we can only determine what a passage teaches about the nature and purpose of God (question 3) if we have properly interpreted it in its historical and literary context (question 2). And we can only discern the attitudes and actions God expects of us (question 4) if we comprehend the nature and purpose of God in the world (question 3). At the same time, it is impossible to do sound exegesis (question 2) without a broader understanding of the nature and purpose of God (question 3). And it is impossible to engage in authentic theological reflection (question 3) outside the process of personal transformation (question 4). Just as exegesis is the foundation for our theology, so theology must inform and guide our exegesis. Both the interpretation and application of Scripture are holistic enterprises.

A third qualification is to acknowledge that there are paradigmatic texts that provide important landmarks or milestones in the journey of Scripture, or key headings or call-outs[17] in the divine drama. We have already noted several of these paradigmatic moments. The first line of the Bible is certainly paradigmatic: "In the beginning God created the heavens and the earth" (Gen. 1:1). God as the sovereign Lord of the universe and creator of all things is foundational for the whole story. The creation of human beings in the "image of God" (Gen. 1:27) and as the pinnacle of creation is similarly paradigmatic, explaining humanity's special place in the redemptive plan of God. Many more paradigmatic texts could be cited: the call of Abraham and God's promise to bless all people through him (Gen. 12:3); God's self-revelation to Moses at the burning bush as "I AM WHO I AM"—Yahweh, whose name Israel will call upon from generation to generation (Exod. 3:13–15); the Decalogue (Ten Commandments), the foundation and epitome of the covenant given through Moses (Exodus 20; Deuteronomy 5); the *Shema* ("*Hear*, O Israel . . ."), Israel's monotheistic creed and the command to love God with heart, soul, and strength (Deut. 6:4–6). These paradigmatic texts introduce central themes in the drama and provide a thematic context for the Bible's many genres. The paradigmatic promise to Israel of prosperity, long life, and possession of the land, as long as they "walk in obedience to all that the LORD your God has commanded you" (Deut. 5:33), becomes the lens through which the period of the judges, prophets, and kings may be understood. Israel's failure to live up to its covenant obligation results in foreign oppression, defeat in battle, and exile.

The New Testament is also full of such paradigmatic moments, texts, and themes: Jesus's announcement of the kingdom of God (Mark 1:15), his command to turn the other cheek and to love our enemies, his "fulfillment" of the law in the Sermon on the Mount (Matt. 5:38–48), his role as the Son of Man who has come to serve and to give his life as a "ransom" for many (Mark 10:45), his Great Commission to take the message of salvation to all people everywhere (Matt. 28:18–20; Acts 1:8). Such paradigmatic texts continue in the book of Acts, the Epistles, and Revelation: the coming of the Spirit as a sign of the dawn of the new age (Acts 2; Romans 8); the repeated affirmation that Jews and Gentiles equally are saved by God's grace through faith (Rom. 3:23; Eph. 2:8–9); the equality of all—slave and free, Jew and Gentile, male and female—as recipients of God's salvation (Gal. 3:28); the suffering role of believers as foreigners and sojourners in this world (1 Pet. 1:3–9); the ultimate defeat of sin, Satan, and death and the establishment of the new heaven and the new earth (Revelation 20–22).

Many more such texts and themes could be noted, and we risk oversimplification by citing just these few. The point, however, is that while the individual parts of Scripture must be understood in order to interpret the whole, the whole is also the key to interpreting the parts. When we have grasped the story as a whole, its individual parts come into sharper focus. The more we learn about God and his purpose for the world, the better we will discern his purpose in individual texts. With these qualifications in mind, let us turn to the four questions.

1. Where Is This Passage in the Larger Story of Scripture?

The application of Scripture depends, in large part, on where the passage (a narrative, law, command, promise, etc.) lies in the story of redemption. The Pentateuch (Genesis through Deuteronomy) includes hundreds of commands given by God to Israel as part of his covenant with her. We do not apply these commands directly to the church because they were intended for Israel in its unique social, cultural, and religious situation. Israel's civil laws were contextualized especially for the ancient Near East. The ceremonial laws related to the temple and the sacrificial system point forward to the once-for-all sacrifice of Christ on the cross and the new covenant inaugurated through his life, death, and resurrection. The first step in discerning application of any particular law is to recognize its place in salvation history.

This does not mean that these Old Testament laws have no relevance for today. After all, "All Scripture is God-breathed and is useful . . ." (2 Tim. 3:16). The law is relevant because all Scripture came from God and therefore teaches us something about his nature and his purpose for the world. Chapter 6 will have more to say on the application of Old Testament laws, where we will look more closely at the various genres of the Old Testament.

An illustration from the period of Jesus in the New Testament ("Act 4" of the drama; see chap. 3) further emphasizes this point about the passage's location in the drama of redemption. At one point in Matthew's Gospel, Jesus commands his disciples not to take the gospel message to the Gentiles but to bring it only to the lost sheep of Israel (Matt. 10:5–6). This is part of the redemptive plan of God, where the righteous remnant of Israel is called to repentance and commissioned to be a light of revelation for the nations (cf. Isa.

42:6; 49:6). Paul too acknowledges this redemptive priority when he says the good news is for the Jew first and then for the Gentiles (Rom. 1:16) and when on his missionary endeavors he preaches to the Jews first (Acts 13:46–48). Jesus modifies his command after the resurrection, however, when he tells the new messianic community of disciples to preach the gospel to all nations (Matt. 28:18–20). Should the good news be proclaimed to the Jews only (Matt. 10:5–6), or to both Jews and Gentiles (Matt. 28:18–20)? It depends on where you are in the Story.

2. What Is the Author's Purpose in Light of the Passage's Genre and Historical and Literary Context?

Once we have identified our passage's place in redemptive history, the next question is the crucial one of *exegesis*: determining the author's original message in its historical and literary context. This step is essential to application since, as stated earlier, a text cannot mean what it never meant.[18] Exegesis is the discovery of the *historical meaning of the text*. To deny the importance of the historical meaning is to deny that God's self-revelation in the past has relevance for its application in the present. Such a denial results in an "anything-goes" approach, where no interpretation is better than any other and the meaning of the text becomes whatever it means to me.

It was commonplace in biblical scholarship of a generation ago to deny the possibility (or even desirability) of discovering an author's intended meaning.[19] The text, it was argued, is not simply an object that can be analyzed and interpreted like a specimen on a laboratory table. Rather, once the text has left the author's pen, it achieves a life of its own. Readers, having no direct access to the author or the author's world, bring their own life experiences and background to the text. Each new reading of the text becomes a new "language event," a dialectic (back-and-forth conversation) between text and reader. What emerges is something new, a transformation of both text and reader. Meaning is not static, therefore, but dynamic, changing with each new reading.

There is actually much truth in the previous paragraph. It is certainly true that we all bring our own worldviews and life experiences to everything we read. There is no such thing as a neutral or unbiased observer. This recognition has resulted in a "chastened" or refined view of exegesis and authorial intent. Preferable to the philosophy of naïve realism (the view that we can know things with absolute objectivity) is that of critical realism, the claim that there is indeed real meaning in the text that can be interpreted through "critical" (analytical, scientific) research.[20] Though full objectivity and absolute certainty are never possible, conclusions can be reached with a high degree of probability. We can know something *truly* without knowing it *absolutely*.

In light of this more balanced approach, the "author" has made a comeback in recent hermeneutical discussions. Contemporary communication theories stress that a historical text like the Bible is not simply words on a page, waiting to be refashioned into the image of each new reader. Rather, it is the record of a historical act of communication from one person to another.[21] Like any act of communication—say, a conversation overheard in a coffee shop—that message can be heard clearly or dimly, interpreted well or poorly. How well such a coffee-shop conversation is understood depends on at least four factors: Does the listener know the language being spoken? What is the nature of the conversation? (Is it an argument? a rehearsal for a play? the recounting of a story?) What are the circumstances surrounding the conversation? (Are these friends? enemies? lovers?) What was said before and after the listener showed up? How well these factors are known will determine how well (or poorly) the communicative act is understood, that is, how well each speaker's intention can be determined.

These same four factors are key for the interpretation (exegesis) of written communication, such as that found in the Bible: (1) the *meaning* of the words and *syntax* of the language, (2) the *genre* or literary form of the text, (3) the *historical context* (time and place: geographical, political, religious, social, and cultural contexts); and (4) the *literary context* (the flow of thought; sometimes called the "logical context" or "co-text").

This book is not primarily about exegesis, so it will not discuss each of these in detail; I refer the reader instead to the more detailed works on biblical exegesis.[22] Here, we will look at examples of the exegetical process, one from the Old Testament and one from the New.

Example 1: Isaiah's Song of the Vineyard (Isa. 5:1–7). Consider the famous Song of the Vineyard in Isaiah 5:1–7. In terms of its *genre*, like so much of the prophetic literature of the Old Testament the song is both poetry and prophetic oracle. As poetry it contains rhythm and meter, symbolic language, and evocative imagery. As prophetic oracle it contains a call for repentance and a warning of judgment. The *historical context* of Isaiah's prophecies is the rising power of the Assyrian Empire in the eighth century BC. Because of the unfaithfulness of his people, God will use the Assyrians to judge them, to destroy the northern kingdom of Israel and to devastate the southern kingdom of Judah.

The *literary context* (flow of thought and rhetoric) of the song is powerful because it begins as a love song (vv. 1–2a) but then turns into a judgment oracle (vv. 3–7). Israel is symbolically portrayed as God's precious vineyard, upon which he has lavished his loving care. He chose for his vineyard a fertile hillside, cleared the land of rocks, and planted the choicest vines; he built a wall and a watchtower to protect the vineyard and a winepress to turn its grapes into wine. Yet despite this loving care, the vineyard produced only bad fruit (v. 2).

What follows is a pronouncement of judgment (vv. 3–6). God is going to take away the protective wall from the vineyard, and it will be trampled. It will become a wasteland. Thorns and thistle will grow in its place, and God will command the clouds not to rain on it. The last stanza (v. 7) explains the symbolism. The vineyard represents God's people, the kingdoms of Israel and Judah. When God looked for his people to act with justice, they responded with bloodshed; when he looked for righteousness, he heard from their victims cries of distress (v. 7c). These last two sentences are a play on words, a common feature in Hebrew poetry. The Hebrew word for "justice" is *mishpat*, and the word for "bloodshed" is *mispach*. Similarly, the word for "righteousness" is *tsedaqah*, and "distress" is *tse'aqah*. There is further irony here. Since Israel did not practice justice and righteousness, but instead caused bloodshed and distress, they themselves will experience this same bloodshed and distress.

In this brief summary of Isaiah 5:1–7 we have identified its genre (poetry and prophetic oracle), its historical context (the eighth-century Assyrian threat to Israel and Judah), its literary context (one in a series of prophetic oracles—this one ironically moving from

84

love song to pronouncement of judgment), and we have identified various features of its language and syntax (symbolic imagery, plays on words, etc.). From this exegesis we can establish the purpose of the passage in the context of Isaiah's prophecies: to call God's wayward people back to a life of justice, faithfulness, and trust in him.

Example 2: The call of Levi (Mark 2:13–17). From this Old Testament illustration of exegesis we move to a New Testament one. In terms of its *genre*, the call of Levi is known as a pronouncement story, a short vignette that climaxes in an authoritative statement by Jesus. This mini-genre is part of a larger one—a gospel—which itself has unique literary features. Elsewhere I have referred to the gospel genre as "historical narrative motivated by theological concerns."[23] They are interpretive narratives intended to proclaim the good news of the person and work of Jesus and to call people to faith in him. We expect, therefore, to find in this passage an implicit call to faith.

The *historical context* of the passage is complex, since it involves all we know about the historical, political, and religious situation of first-century Israel. For the purpose of this passage, we need to know that the Pharisees were important religious leaders of Jesus's day who meticulously kept God's law (the Torah) and sought to apply it to every aspect of life. Jesus came into frequent conflict with them, accusing them of pride, hypocrisy, and legalistically raising their human traditions above the true spirit of God's law. We also need to know that tax collectors were hated by most Jews, including the religious leaders, because they were viewed as extortionists in collusion with the Roman government, which ruled Palestine with oppressive power.

The *literary context* of the passage is the first part of Mark's Gospel, where the author presents Jesus as the powerful and wonderworking Messiah and Son of God. Jesus comes on the scene suddenly, announcing the coming of the kingdom of God and performing powerful deeds—healings, exorcisms, miracles of nature—that reveal the transforming power of the kingdom. The call of Levi episode is the second in a series of five controversy stories, where Jesus comes into conflict with the religious leaders over his claims of authority.

At the beginning of the episode, Jesus calls a tax collector named Levi to be his disciple. Levi responds immediately, leaving his tax-collector booth and profession behind (Mark 2:13–14). In gratitude, Levi throws a banquet for Jesus, inviting his tax-collector cronies and other friends to meet Jesus. When the religious leaders see Jesus eating with tax collectors and other sinners, they criticize him for hanging out with such lowlifes (vv. 15–16). Jesus responds with an authoritative pronouncement, beginning with a proverb, "It is not the healthy who need a doctor, but the sick," followed by its application to the present situation, "I have not come to call the righteous, but sinners" (v. 17).

This exegetical summary allows us to determine the purpose of this passage in Mark's Gospel. The gospel genre reminds us that we have here testimony to the salvation-bringing work of Jesus the Messiah. Since this is a pronouncement story, we look to the climactic announcement, "I have not come to call the righteous, but sinners," as the key to the episode. The historical and literary contexts teach us that the religious leaders—traditional "insiders" among God's people—in fact stand in opposition to Jesus, whereas the sinners and tax collectors—traditional "outsiders"—are responding to the invitation to the kingdom of God. Mark's purpose here is to show that the kingdom of God that Jesus has been announcing is not for those who are self-righteous, proud of their own accomplishments, and disdainful of others, but rather those who humbly repent and respond in faith to God's offer of salvation.

These examples from Isaiah and Mark are intended to show that *appropriate application begins with sound exegesis*. Isaiah's Song of the Vineyard should not be used to teach the need to protect our gardens against outside attack from pests or from the trampling of people or animals. This would completely miss the author's meaning in context. Mark's account of the call of Levi is not meant to encourage us to invite IRS agents to dinner or to show disdain for religious leaders. Such (ridiculous) applications have little to do with the *purpose* of these passages in their historical and literary contexts. Our application must be drawn from the author's purpose in context.

A corollary to this point is that the measure of certainty we have in our exegesis should determine the amount of confidence we have in a particular application. Obscure or exegetically disputed passages should not be used to establish firm theological positions or standards for ethical conduct.

A good example of this is in 1 Corinthians 15:29, where, in the course of his discussion of the resurrection, Paul refers to the practice of baptism for the dead: "Now if there is no resurrection, what will those do who are baptized for the dead? If the dead are not raised at all, why are people baptized for them?" There are many theological certainties in the broader context: (1) Jesus rose bodily from the dead and was seen by more than five hundred people; (2) the resurrection is the vindication of all that Jesus said and did; (3) together with his death as payment for our sins, the resurrection is the foundation of the apostolic gospel; (4) the resurrection of Jesus reversed the effect of Adam's fall; and (5) Jesus is the firstfruits of the resurrection, confirming that we too will be raised in glorified bodies.

All of these are truths clearly taught in this passage and affirmed in many other texts in the New Testament. Paul's comment about baptism for the dead, however, is one of the most obscure statements in the Bible. It is nowhere else referred to by Paul or any other New Testament writer. It does not appear elsewhere in the early church. Paul does not explain it or affirm it, but merely uses it as part of his argument for the reality of Christ's resurrection. Is this some kind of proxy baptism for believers who have died before baptism? Is it simply new converts being baptized and so viewed as replacing those who had died? We simply don't know. Such an obscure and disputed passage should never be used to develop a theology of baptism for the dead or to encourage a particular pattern of behavior.[24] Fringe passages like this should not be used to establish core tenets for faith or practice.

The same thing could be said of other passages in the Old and New Testaments. Perplexing Old Testament laws about wearing tattoos and clipping the hair on the sides of your head (Lev. 19:27–28) should not be used to establish ethical standards. Obscure New Testament commands with nearly intractable exegetical difficulties, such as Paul's discussion related to haircuts and head coverings in 1 Corinthians 11:2–16,[25] should not be used as absolute mandates for Christian faith and practice. In our application it is wise to keep what is clear and pervasive in the biblical text central for our theology and ethics, and what is obtuse and obscure on the peripheral.

3. How Does This Passage Inform Our Understanding of the Nature of God and His Purpose for the World?

This third essential question moves us from exegesis to *theology*, from the meaning of the text to the truth it teaches about God and his world. As said above, these four questions cannot be viewed in isolation, nor do they progress only in a linear manner from one to the next. Just as our exegesis provides the building blocks for our theology, so our theology informs our exegesis. To determine what a passage teaches about God we have to determine what it means in context. Yet that contextual understanding is informed by the larger theological landscape.

Example 1: Isaiah's Song of the Vineyard. Just as Isaiah's Song of the Vineyard provides exegetical data to construct a theology of Isaiah and the Prophets in general, so a broader understanding of the theology of Isaiah and of the Old Testament informs our exegesis of the individual passage.

So what do we learn about the nature of God and his purpose for the world from the Song of the Vineyard? The loving care of the owner of the vineyard reminds us that God is the loving father of the nation Israel. He chose them from all the nations of the world to be his special people. His care for them includes both provision and protection. The vineyard owner plants the vineyard on a fertile hillside where it will be nourished by the soil. He clears out the stones to allow its roots to plant themselves securely. He selects for its furrows the finest vines, those with the greatest opportunity to produce plump grapes and sweet wine. He builds a watchtower and a wall to protect it from enemies. These elements reflect key themes of Old Testament theology: God's loving choice of Israel and the abundant grace poured out on the nation. Though Yahweh, the God of Israel, is Lord over all the heavens and the earth, he has chosen this nation to be his special possession. In Deuteronomy 10:14–15, the Lord reminds Moses: "To the LORD your God belong the heavens, even the highest heavens, the earth and everything in it. Yet the LORD set his affection on your ancestors and loved them, and he chose you, their descendants, above all the nations—as it is today."

Being God's special people brings great blessing, but also great responsibility. Though God's love for Israel will never diminish, he will hold the nation responsible for covenant faithfulness. Throughout the Law and the Prophets, God sets out the conditions for blessing and warns against the consequences of unfaithfulness: "So if you faithfully obey the commands I am giving you today—to love the LORD your God and to serve him with all your heart and with all your soul—then I will send rain on your land in its season, both autumn and spring rains, so that you may gather in your grain, new wine and olive oil. I will provide grass in the fields for your cattle, and you will eat and be satisfied" (Deut. 11:13–15). With faithfulness and obedience will come health, prosperity, and fertility (see Deut. 7:12–15), but with disobedience will come judgment and destruction: "Be careful, or you will be enticed to turn away and worship other gods and bow down to them. Then the LORD's anger will burn against you, and he will shut up the heavens so that it will not rain and the ground will yield no produce, and you will soon perish from the good land the LORD is giving you" (Deut. 11:16–17).

The Song of the Vineyard contextualizes this message to Israel for a particular situation, the nation's disobedience during the period of the monarchy leading up to the Assyrian conquest. Israel has failed to live up to her covenant obligations and has turned away to worship idols. God will therefore remove his protection from the Israelites and will allow the Assyrians to crush them.

What do we learn about God's essential nature and purpose for the world from this passage? God is a loving father who freely chooses people to be his children and pours out his love and grace on them. This grace is not based on anything they have done. God delivered Israel from slavery in Egypt *before* they did anything to merit his favor and before he established his covenant with them at Mount Sinai. We also learn that God establishes covenants with those he chooses and that these covenants involve both blessing and responsibility. Love for God and obedience to the covenant result in spiritual prosperity and success. Disobedience and unbelief result in spiritual failure and judgment. Such fundamental attributes of God's nature and purpose certainly do not change and so will enable us to draw relevant application for today.

Example 2: The call of Levi. Returning to our New Testament passage, we ask our third question: How does this passage inform our understanding of the nature of God and his purpose for the world?

Throughout the Gospels, Jesus always represents the evaluative point of view of God.[26] He accomplishes God's will and represents God's nature and purpose for the world. In this regard, we see Jesus constantly reaching out to society's outcasts: the poor, sinners, prostitutes, tax collectors, and Samaritans. This is in line with God's character in the Old Testament, where his love for the lowly and vulnerable is a common theme. He is the defender of the poor, the widow, and the fatherless. Isaiah is characteristic of the Law and the Prophets when he pronounces judgment on those who prey on the weak: "Woe to those who make unjust laws, to those who issue oppressive decrees, to deprive the poor of their rights and withhold justice from the oppressed of my people, making widows their prey and robbing the fatherless" (Isa. 10:1–2). Passages like this confirm that God is a God of mercy and compassion, who cares deeply for those who are most vulnerable. In the same way, Jesus's love for the outcast in the Gospels reflects God's heart of compassion.

But there is more to it than this. It is not just the lowly who are the object of God's favor, but those who humbly acknowledge their need of God and turn to him in faith. When the religious leaders criticize Jesus for associating with sinners and tax collectors (Mark 2:16), he points out he has come not for the "righteous"—that is, those who think they have earned a right standing before God—but rather for sinners who acknowledge their need of him. To receive God's mercy, we have to come to him humbly and in spiritual poverty. Salvation is an offer of undeserved grace to those who do not deserve it and who have not earned it. Paul tells the Corinthians, "For you know the grace of our Lord Jesus Christ, that though he was rich, yet for your sake he became poor, so that you through his poverty might become rich" (2 Cor. 8:9). Salvation comes to those who humbly receive it by faith.

4. What Does This Passage Teach Us about Who We Ought to Be (Attitudes and Character) and What We Ought to Do (Goals and Actions) as the People of God?

Once we have answered the first three questions, this fourth one becomes much easier. This is because our application of any passage of Scripture should be based on the historical meaning of the text in its original context, and on the broader testimony of Scripture concerning the nature and purpose of God. This fourth question then becomes, How do I live in step with God in light of who he is and who we are as his people?

Example 1: Isaiah's Song of the Vineyard. In terms of our Old Testament example, we learn that God provides for the needs of his people Israel and, in response, expects their love, loyalty, and service. Since the church in the New Testament is frequently identified with language reminiscent of God's choice of Israel, we can see that the New Testament people of God have a similar role in the new covenant as the nation Israel did in the old. God has chosen us and poured out his love and grace on us. He calls us to love him and to remain faithful to the covenant he has made with us. With obedience comes blessing and success; with disobedience will come judgment and disaster. The application for us is to remain faithful to him and to "bear fruit," which means living a life of obedience as a light shining in a dark world. The resources to accomplish this are even greater for the church than for Israel in the old covenant, since the new covenant brings with it God's law written on our hearts and the indwelling presence of the Holy Spirit (Jer. 31:31–34; Ezek. 36:26–27; 37:14; 39:29; Joel 2:28–32; Acts 2:17–21).

Example 2: The call of Levi. From our New Testament example, we learn that God resists the proud and self-righteous and reaches out to those in need. The application is that we as believers should reach out to the outsiders in our society, loving all people as God does. It also means we recognize our humble state before God, that all of us are the "sick" in need of the great Physician. This should produce humility as well as an increased awe at the overwhelming grace that God has shown in saving us.

Conclusion

This chapter has introduced a "heart-of-God" approach to biblical application. We live out God's Word not by obeying every imperative of Scripture, or claiming every promise, or seeking to reproduce the world of the Bible. Rather, we adopt the heart of God by daily walking with God, hearing his story, and learning his words and ways. We become so familiar with God's values, attitudes, and actions that we begin to think God's thoughts after him and so can discern his will in new and changing circumstances. This journey with God, however, is not traveled alone. In the following chapter, we will look at our dialogue partners who travel with us along the way: the traditions of the church, the community of faith, and the Spirit of God.

Discussion and Reflection Questions

1. What is the ultimate goal of Bible reading and study? Can someone know biblical knowledge yet not walk with God?

2. In what way is the imitation of Christ the goal of the Christian life? In what ways is it not?

3. Choose one of the metaphors introduced in this chapter—a story, drama, or journey—and explain how it helps us envision the process of biblical interpretation and application.

4. What are the four questions introduced in this chapter that should be asked of any text of Scripture to find appropriate application for today?

5

Seeking the Heart of God in Dialogue

Tradition, Community, and the Spirit

The previous chapter discussed the means by which we determine the heart of God in a text of Scripture. We immerse ourselves in God's story to learn his larger purposes in the world, gradually bringing our worldview in line with God's. As we read, we ask four key questions of the text: (1) Where are we in the story? (2) What is the message of this text in its unique historical and literary context? (3) What do we learn here about the nature and purpose of God? and (4) Who ought we to be and what should we do on the basis of this message?

Even when we ask the right questions, however, errors can creep into our interpretation and flaws into our application. These errors can result from various things: the influence of our own cultural or personal biases, which blind us to something the text is trying to teach us; the presence of sin in our lives, which causes us to rationalize our own attitudes or actions; the power of pride, which prevents us from submitting to God's promptings. How do we avoid these pitfalls? Part of the answer is that we are not in this alone. No one should read the Bible in isolation. Rather, we read the Bible *in dialogue with others*. In this section we will look at three key dialogue partners that guide, sharpen, and correct our reading of Scripture. We need to read the text (1) alongside the Great Tradition, (2) together with the community of faith, and (3) under the guidance of the Holy Spirit.

The Great Tradition and the Heart of God

I began my teaching career almost twenty years ago at a conservative Christian college with deep roots in biblical fundamentalism. The Bible, we strongly affirmed, was the foundation of everything we said and did, the final word for faith and practice. The Reformation cry *sola scriptura* ("Scripture alone") was at the center of our faith. In Bible courses we taught that we find truth not in fallible human places—rationalistic philosophy, personal experience, or church tradition—but in the unchanging Word of God.

At one point two students at the college, both Bible majors, started to have serious questions and doubts during their junior and senior years. They had begun to feel more and more uncomfortable with this perspective on the Bible. Looking around, they saw dozens of Protestant denominations and thousands of evangelical churches, all claiming the Bible was their highest authority, but all reading it and interpreting it in different ways. They saw covenant theologians and dispensationalists fighting over the meaning of the Old Testament and the nature of Israel and the church. They saw charismatics and noncharismatics debating the reality and relevance of spiritual gifts. They saw young-earth and old-earth creationists arguing over the meaning of the Genesis account and whether the earth was created in six days or six billion years. Instead of everyone standing together on the Word of God, it seemed more like everyone was doing what was right in their own eyes (cf. Judg. 17:6). These two students had no desire or intention to go "liberal" or soft on the Bible's authority. What they wanted, rather, was some sense of biblical certainty.

After investigating various church traditions over a period of several years, both students left their Baptist tradition and joined the Eastern Orthodox Church. One even became an Orthodox priest. I had a number of conversations with him over the years both leading up to and after his decision. He explained that he had been desperately searching for three things: deep roots, ecclesiastical unity, and a sense of authority. The Eastern Orthodox Church, he said, had roots that dated back to the first century. The various national branches of the church (Greek Orthodox, Russian Orthodox, Romanian Orthodox, etc.) remained united in fellowship and in their theology. The authority of the Bible in the Orthodox Church resided not in any personal interpretation but in the context of Holy Tradition, that is, in the church's authoritative interpretation of the text (as established through a number of historical "canons," or authoritative decrees by the church).

Over the course of our conversations, I affirmed my friend's quest for truth, but I also pointed out significant problems in Eastern Orthodox history, theology, and practice. I tried to show him that some of the Orthodox Church's theology was actually contrary to what the Bible said and that much of what happened in that church was lifeless ritual rather than a living and dynamic relationship with God. We had a number of fruitful conversations, and we remain friends to this day.

My point here, however, is not to critique the Eastern Orthodox Church. In fact, my intent is just the opposite. It is to critique my own tradition. What these students found lacking in their own Christian experience represents a real and serious gap in evangelical churches, and more specifically in the way we read the Bible. For two thousand years God has been at work in and through his church. We, as the people of God, are part of that Great Tradition, and we need to take advantage of the wisdom and insight of our predecessors. While we must not place ourselves in slavish submission to the traditions of the church, we ignore them at our peril. As the saying goes, those who ignore history are doomed to repeat its failures.

Fortunately, in evangelical circles there has been a recent resurgence of returning to the great traditions of the church.[1] Scot McKnight points out the importance of reading the Bible together with the Great Tradition, the core of Christian truth that has accumulated through the centuries. He notes that the Protestant Reformation's "best and *most dangerous, revolutionary idea* was putting the Bible in the hands of ordinary Christians." One of John Calvin's great passions, for example, was getting the average person to read their

Bible. But he didn't just plop a Bible into everyone's laps and say, "Here, read this! Nothing to it!" He wanted them to learn to read the Bible well, and to do that they would have to learn sound methods of interpretation and a core of biblical theology. So what did Calvin do? "For pastors he wrote his famous *Institutes of the Christian Religion* and his extensive *commentaries on the Bible*, and for laypeople he designed a *catechism* and wrote more lay-level *expositions*."[2] In the same way, Martin Luther was passionate about getting the Scriptures into the hands of ordinary people and so translated the Bible into his vernacular German. But he also knew that bad interpretation would result in schisms and factions, so he required schoolchildren to master his *Catechism* in addition to reading their Bibles.

Tradition can be a very good thing when it draws reflectively on the past, testing it in the light of biblical teaching and human experience, and then adapting it to make decisions in the present. McKnight points to two kinds of tradition, one positive (the Great Tradition) and the other negative (traditionalism).[3] We need to read the Bible in light of the Great Tradition, the body of Christian tradition and theology tested and proven through two thousand years of church history. This includes things like the decisions of the ecumenical councils, the central creeds of the church, and the great theologians of the past. This does not mean that we assume the infallibility of these councils and creeds or place the Bible under their authority or the authority of a church hierarchy or canon law. Rather, we recognize church tradition as the tested and proven wisdom from the past and so an important dialogue partner in our search for biblical truth. We consider new doctrines that are in opposition to this Great Tradition with great caution and return to Scripture to scrutinize their validity. It is certainly possible for church tradition to be wrong. There would have been no Protestant Reformation had Martin Luther not challenged the traditions of the church regarding the sale of indulgences, papal authority, prayers for the dead, and salvation by works.

While we respect and honor the Great Tradition, therefore, we must not let our beliefs and practices become mere *traditionalism*. Traditionalism is elevating human tradition to the level of Scripture (see Mark 7:8), turning cultural applications for one time and place into eternal mandates that we impose on all believers for all time.

Traditionalism is also getting so stuck in *our* way of doing things that we fail to hear God speak in new and refreshing ways through his Word. The Word of God is "living and active and sharper than any two-edged sword" (Heb. 4:12 NASB). We ought to be cut, shaped, and transformed when we read it. Traditionalism changes the Bible from a sharp sword (or scalpel) into a dull shield, defending our traditional interpretations and protecting us from the fresh wind of the Spirit.

The Community of God and the Heart of God

Reading with the Great Tradition means learning from the people of God in the past. But it also means learning from our brothers and sisters in the present.

In my courses I sometimes ask theological questions like, "How many of you believe in infant baptism, and how many believe in believer's baptism?" or, "How many believe someone can lose their salvation, and how many believe that we are 'once saved, always saved'?" After a show of hands, I ask how many of them originally came to that belief through a study of Scripture, as opposed to being taught it by their family or church. The answer is almost always the same, regardless of the theological question. The vast majority of Christians learn their theology and ethics not from the Bible but from their community of faith.

This, of course, can be both bad and good. It can be bad if particular beliefs are based merely on human tradition rather than on God's purpose and will. It is good in the sense that God works with his people and communicates to them *in the context of community*. We as human beings were created to be in community, and it is there we read and apply Scripture. After Adam was created, God pronounced that it was *not good* for the man to be alone and so created the woman as his partner (Genesis 2). God created human beings to be in relationship with one another and with him. We do not exist in isolation. Indeed, the one true God is himself a community, existing as three distinct persons—Father, Son, and Holy Spirit—in perfect fellowship and working in perfect harmony.

Throughout the history of the world, God has worked with his people in the context of community. The assembly or community of Israel was meant to represent God in the world and to reveal his glory to all nations. When individuals sinned against God, the whole community suffered. Achan's sin of disobedience in keeping some of the plunder of Jericho for himself resulted in tragedy for the nation, which suffered defeat in the battle for Ai (Josh. 7:1–5). When Achan's sin was discovered, he and his whole family experienced the tragic consequences of his actions (7:24–26). When Israel's kings turned away from God and worshiped idols, the nation as a whole suffered through famine, disease, and foreign oppression and exile. Just as the actions of a community affect the individual, so the actions of individuals affect the community.

Like the nation Israel, the church (Greek: *ekklēsia*, "assembly") is a community, the new covenant people of God. In 1 Corinthians 5, Paul warns the church at Corinth that the immoral behavior of a single individual is affecting the spiritual state of the whole community. "Don't you know that a little yeast leavens the whole batch of dough?" (1 Cor. 5:6). The community strengthens each individual member, and the individual members strengthen the community as a whole. In his discussion of spiritual gifts in 1 Corinthians 12–14, Paul compares the church to a physical body, where each part is essential to the working of the whole, and no part is unimportant. "Just as a body, though one, has many parts, but all its many parts form one body, so it is with Christ" (1 Cor. 12:12). The gifts and callings given by the Spirit to each member of the body are intended "to equip his people for works of service, so that the body of Christ may be built up until we all reach unity in the faith and in the knowledge of the Son of God and become mature, attaining to the whole measure of the fullness of Christ" (Eph. 4:12–13).

The metaphors used of the church highlight this emphasis on community. Not only is the church the "body of Christ" and the "assembly" of God's people, it is also made up of "fellow citizens" and members of the "household" of faith (Eph. 2:19; 1 Tim. 3:15; Titus 1:7). Believers refer to each other as "brothers and sisters" (Greek: *adelphoi*) because we are family, and the purpose of family is to meet the needs of and to stimulate growth in one another.

Just as the community provides support for individual believers in terms of their physical, social, emotional, and spiritual needs, so the community provides support in the interpretation and application of Scripture. None of us possess sufficient knowledge of the language, culture, and background of the Bible to interpret it perfectly. Similarly, none of us experience the fullness of the Holy Spirit at all times. We need one another. This is a pervasive biblical theme. Ecclesiastes 4:9–12 says, "Two are better than one, because they have a good return for their labor. . . . A cord of three strands is not quickly broken." There is strength in numbers. Proverbs 27:17 says, "As iron sharpens iron, so one person sharpens another." The Jewish Talmud applied this proverb to the study of God's Word: two students sharpen each other in the study of Torah (Babylonian Talmud, *Taanith* 7a).

Reading the Bible in community can provide important checks and balances for application, protecting against the kind of idiosyncratic and self-serving interpretations that are so common. This is because God's Spirit indwells believers both individually and corporately. Our individual bodies are a temple of God, where the Holy Spirit resides (1 Cor. 3:16), but so is the church as a whole (1 Cor. 6:19). Together we have greater wisdom, insight, and experience than we do as individuals. In Matthew 18:20, Jesus says, "For where two or three gather in my name, there am I with them." In context this passage refers to the judicial decisions of the church in the case of a brother or sister who falls into sin. The insight to make such decisions comes from the presence of Jesus in the community, a presence that is magnified when believers gather together.

This community dimension of Bible reading has global implications as well. A group of like-minded people from the same cultural background are likely to see the same things in Scripture, and to *miss* the same things. The diversity of the worldwide church is a great gift from God that is too often ignored by believers in the West. Christians who live in economically underdeveloped countries will be particularly sensitive to the Bible's commands to care for the poor and the oppressed. Believers in countries where the church suffers extreme persecution—such as Sudan, Pakistan, China, Vietnam, Iran, North Korea, or Morocco—can provide greater insight into biblical passages that speak of our responsibility and privilege to suffer for Christ's sake (1 Pet. 1:6–9; 2:21–25; 3:12–18; 4:12–19). In the affluent and powerful West these biblical themes are sometimes spiritualized, downplayed, or ignored.

Though there is still a sad deficiency of interest or engagement from the West in global theology, the situation has improved in recent years. Important works like the *Global Dictionary of Theology*, *Theology in the Context of World Christianity*, *Emerging Voices in Global Theology*, and the *African Bible Commentary* have introduced exegetical perspectives and theological themes that are underdeveloped in Western commentaries and theologies.[4] Theologians from Africa, Asia, and South America, each bringing their own unique perspectives to the global theological dialogue, are also gaining a larger voice in theological circles.[5] Applying God's Word well requires a sensitive ear to the *whole* body of Christ, not just to those members who are like ourselves.

The Holy Spirit and the Heart of God

The third and most important dialogue partner in the heart-of-God hermeneutic is the Spirit of God. This has already been touched on above, since it is impossible to discuss the community of faith without talking about the role of the Spirit that unites and empowers that community.

In John's account of the Last Supper, Jesus promises his disciples that after his departure the Father will send the Holy Spirit, who "will teach you all things and will remind you of everything I have said to you" (John 14:26). This promise is fulfilled on the Day of Pentecost, when the Spirit is poured out in fulfillment of the prophecy of Joel 2:28–32, that in the last days God would pour out his Spirit on all people, providing prophetic insight (Acts 2:17–21; cf. Ezek. 36:26–27; 37:14; 39:29). The new covenant of Jeremiah 31 similarly promises that the dawn of the age of salvation will bring with it a unique and personal knowledge of God: "No longer will they teach their neighbor, or say to one another, 'Know the LORD,' because they will all know me, from the least of them to the greatest" (Jer. 31:34).

All believers today have the Spirit of God dwelling in them, guiding, teaching, and empowering them. Paul affirms this universal reception of the Spirit in 1 Corinthians 12:13: "For we were all baptized by one Spirit so as to form one body—whether Jews or Gentiles, slave or free—and we were all given the one Spirit to drink."

According to Paul, the Spirit's presence in a believer's life is the key to true knowledge of the nature and purpose of God. In 1 Corinthians Paul affirms that "What we have received is not the spirit of the world, but the Spirit who is from God, so that we may understand what God has freely given us" (1 Cor. 2:12). The Holy Spirit living in the believer is the same Spirit who inspired the authors of Scripture so that, essentially, when we are reading Scripture, the Spirit is explaining the Spirit. Those who don't have the Spirit cannot understand the deep things of God, his nature and purpose: "The person without the Spirit does not accept the things that come from the Spirit of God but considers them foolishness, and cannot understand them because they are discerned only through the Spirit" (1 Cor. 2:13–14).

Paul then makes a shocking statement. He first quotes Isaiah 40:13: "Who has known the mind of the Lord so as to instruct him?" (1 Cor. 2:16). This question appears in an amazing oracle on the majesty and sovereignty of God (Isa. 40:12–31). The Lord is the sovereign creator of the heavens and the earth. He sits enthroned above the earth; from his point of view its inhabitants are like tiny grasshoppers. He merely blows on great kings and nations, and they wither like grass and turn to dust. In this context Isaiah 40:13 is rhetorical. Who knows the mind of the Lord? Who can instruct him? The answer is a resounding shout: No one! The mind of God is infinite and eternal. It is utterly unfathomable. But, shockingly, that is not what Paul says. Instead he quotes the passage from Isaiah and then adds, "But we have the mind of Christ" (1 Cor. 2:16). In other words, "Well, actually, we *do* know the mind of the Lord, because we have his Spirit living in us." The Spirit provides supernatural insight into the things of God. We dare not discount this amazing promise as we consider how to read and apply Scripture.

This conclusion, however, raises some challenging questions. If the Spirit provides such profound insight into the things of God, why are there so many different perspectives among Christians? If we have the "mind of Christ," why do we need to study at all? Shouldn't the Spirit just tell us what God wants us to do, instead of requiring the hard work of biblical interpretation?

Reality and personal experience teach us that this is not how God works through Scripture. We have all heard someone explain what a passage of Scripture "means to me" and completely miss its historical meaning. They replace the author's intention with a purely subjective interpretation. In such cases, we cannot simply say, "Well, I guess that's what the Holy Spirit wants us to hear today." The Spirit does not reward shoddy exegesis with spiritual wisdom and insight. We must assume, rather, that the Spirit works *through* rather than *against* the historical particulars of the text. In other words, the Spirit does not overrule the human side of the divine-human convergence of Scripture, but rather guides us and teaches us *through* it. Grammatical and historical exegesis are the conduit through which the Spirit works.

Balance is necessary here, and the study of Scripture must always involve both heart and mind. An emphasis on sound exegesis should not become an excuse for turning our study into a cognitive exercise that superficially acknowledges the work of the Spirit only as an afterthought. But neither should we concede that the Spirit's message to us through the Word will be contrary to the historical meaning of the text or to the testimony of Scripture as a whole.

We can achieve this balance by developing better the art of *listening* to the Word. Listening means, first, hearing the historical meaning of the text, willingly submitting to the Spirit's work through the inspired authors. Rather than coming to the Word of God with our own agenda, we step into the world of the text (the story) and listen for the voices of our brothers and sisters from the past. It is easy to come to the text with our minds set on what we expect it to say. It is much harder to come with open ears and hearts to hear its sometimes foreign message. So, being open to the Spirit's work means first of all listening attentively for the message the Spirit gave to *them* in *their* time and place. But listening also means hearing what God is saying to *us* in *our* time and place. This must not be just a cognitive exercise; like our love for God, it involves heart, mind, soul, and strength.

Some have found help here in the meditative process known as *lectio divina*, a Latin expression meaning "divine reading," or "spiritual reading." It is a traditional practice with roots in the Benedictine Order, involving Scripture reading, prayer, meditation, and contemplation, with a goal of promoting a deeper level of communion with God through the Word. There are four "moments" or steps associated with *lectio divina*, though they are not necessarily or always done in order. The four are *lectio* ("reading"), *meditatio* ("meditation"), *oratio* ("prayer"), and *contemplatio* ("reflection" or "contemplation"). While some have criticized *lectio divina* as too mystical or esoteric (or just too Catholic), I believe that it can provide a framework for a Spirit-guided reading of the Word, especially with the qualifications discussed below.

Lectio involves reading a passage of Scripture slowly and attentively several times over. Reading repeatedly enables us to see things we might normally miss and to overcome the tendency for our minds to wander. This reading, I would add, should be one that takes into account the historical meaning of the text. It is not a naïve reading or overly imaginative, but exegetically informed.

Meditatio takes the passage and ruminates on it, thinking in God's presence about the text. This is not a special revelation from God, but an inward working of the Spirit that enables the believer to grasp a message from God in the text. Here, again, I would add that this kind of meditation should not move too quickly from the meaning *then* to the message *now*. Rather, this is a chance to meditate on how God's Word was originally heard, how our spiritual ancestors needed God to speak to them in their situation, and how they would have responded to this message.

If we are reading the account of the exodus, it is a chance to creatively imagine what the Israelites must have thought when they saw God's awesome power in the ten devastating plagues against the land of Egypt. It means creatively placing ourselves in the story as we walk through the Red Sea on dry land and then join Miriam's choir in a great song celebrating God's triumph and deliverance. It means trembling in terror as the overwhelming presence of God descends on Mount Sinai in fire, darkness, and a cloud.

If we are reading 1 Thessalonians, it means imagining what it was like for Paul, after working "night and day" and pouring his heart and soul into this fledgling church, to be forced to abandon his spiritual children and flee the city because of threats on his life (1 Thess. 2:7–20). It means putting ourselves in the apostle's place as he agonizes over whether his spiritual children might give in to the social, religious, and political pressure to return to the safety and security of their previous life of idol worship. Finally, it means experiencing the joy and exhilaration Paul felt when Timothy returned from the church with the joyous message that these believers were holding fast to their faith despite intense persecution. "For now we really live," Paul says, "since you are standing firm in the Lord" (1 Thess. 3:6–8). Meditation, in other words, means entering the world of the story and dwelling on the reality that *their* story is *our* story. Is it finding our place in the story and then asking, What should I do to live out this common life of faith?

Oratio, the third "moment" of *lectio divina*, is prayer, a conversation with the One who invites us into his presence. Here we allow ourselves to be touched and changed by the Word. As we listen to God speak through the text, we answer and respond, affirming God's divine nature and sovereign purpose and committing ourselves to conform our lives to his. Our listening now becomes a conversation. This conversation may be peaceful and affirming, as we acknowledge and rest in a message of comfort and assurance. Or it may be confrontational and combative, as we wrestle with something in the Word that we don't want to hear or don't want to do. Taking the time to listen and meditate and then respond lets the sword of the Word and the Spirit (Heb. 4:12; Eph. 6:17) do its healing and transforming work in our lives.

The fourth and final moment is *contemplatio*, a simple, loving focus on God that allows us to joyfully rest in his presence. This aspect of *lectio divina* is important because, ultimately, our walk with God is not about doing but about being. It means resting in his loving arms, enjoying his presence, contemplating his perfection. We glorify God by acknowledging who he is as the sovereign God and Lord of all and seeking to bring our lives into conformity to his.

Conclusion

Christian traditions that place a high value on personal Bible study have sometimes been accused of encouraging individualism over community and fracturing the church into a multitude of subjective and idiosyncratic interpretations of the text. As in the days of the Old Testament judges, it seems everyone does what is right in their own eyes when it comes to biblical interpretation. This chapter, however, has suggested that this need not be the case, since biblical interpretation is not an individual but a community endeavor. We read the Bible not in isolation but in conversation with the great traditions of the church, with the broader community of believers, and under the guidance and direction of the Holy Spirit. The Spirit, our ultimate teacher, leads us into all truth, not only by informing our hearts and minds, but also by indwelling individuals and communities of faith from the past and the present.

Discussion and Reflection Questions

1. Who are our essential dialogue partners when we seek to interpret and apply God's Word?

2. What important role does church tradition play in our understanding and application of Scripture?

3. Why is it important to be part of a larger Christian community when we read the Bible?

4. Why is it important to listen to the voices of Christians around the world when we read and apply Scripture?

5. What role does the Holy Spirit play in the application of Scripture? Why is it important to come to the biblical text with open minds and hearts?

6

Finding the Heart of God in the Diverse Genres of the Old Testament

"I<small>T WAS THE BEST OF TIMES, IT WAS THE WORST OF TIMES.</small>" S<small>O</small> begins *A Tale of Two Cities* by Charles Dickens, one of the most famous novels of all time.[1] The book is set in the days of the French Revolution (1789–99) and tells the tragic and heroic story of Charles Darnay and Sydney Carton. Darnay is a French aristocrat who is arrested and sentenced to be executed. Carton, who resembles Darnay, seeks redemption from his own wasted life by exchanging places with Darnay in prison and being executed in his place. The last line of the novel, presenting Carton's final thoughts, is almost as famous as the first: "It is a far, far better thing that I do, than I have ever done; it is a far, far better rest that I go to than I have ever known."

The genre of *A Tale of Two Cities* is historical fiction, meaning that its main characters are fictitious, but it is set in a real time and place. It is not meant to pass on historical material about these characters; it aims to give readers a taste of the *Zeitgeist*—the "spirit of the times"—in which the events purportedly take place. The reader is drawn into the tumultuous world of late eighteenth-century Britain and France. Identifying the genre is essential to understanding the nature of the story and the author's purpose. It would be a mistake, for example, to assume that Darnay and Carton are historical figures and to include their stories in a textbook on the French Revolution.

Genre identification is essential in all areas of life. When I pull a stack of mail from the mailbox, I immediately go into "genre identification mode" (whether I know it or not). I sift through the mail hoping for checks: paychecks, birthday checks, rebate checks—any will do. I cringe when I come across bills, knowing they will negate the benefit of those checks. I pull out the advertisements and discard them. I am most interested in personal correspondence, letters from friends or family (a rarity in the age of email and Facebook). It is also possible to misidentify genre. I opened one letter, and it was a page advertising a product. Apparently handwritten on one side was a note, "Hey, Mark, you've got to try this. It's great! –J." "Hmm," I wondered, "who is 'J'?" I know lots of J's—Jim, John, Jack, Joe, Jane, Joanne, Janice. A closer examination revealed the personal note was a fake, part of a clever advertising technique. Properly identifying a genre allows us to determine the author's purpose and the nature of the communication.

Throughout this book we have discussed the importance of recognizing the Bible's diverse genres when interpreting and applying the Bible. Each genre communicates meaning in a unique way and has its own rules for both interpretation and application. Historical narrative communicates through story, the interaction of characters in the development of a plot. Poetry communicates more emotionally through rhythm and meter and the use of evocative and symbolic language. Law communicates through commands or injunctions mandating certain behavior in certain circumstances. This chapter and the next will survey the Bible's various genres and discuss how they can be lived out in our lives today, that is, how they relate to a heart-of-God hermeneutic.[2]

Old Testament Narrative

Historical narrative is the most common genre in the Bible, making up roughly 40 percent of its content. This makes sense, since the

Bible as a whole is God's great story of redemption. These individual stories tell us how God has worked with his people in the past and so model for us what it means to walk with him in the present.

The Nature and Purpose of Old Testament Narrative

The great majority of Old Testament narrative appears in the Historical Books, Genesis through Esther, the first seventeen books of the Old Testament (in the Protestant canonical order; the Hebrew text is organized differently[3]). When we speak of these portions of Scripture as "story," we are not suggesting that the events did not actually happen. Stories can be either fictional or nonfictional, and we classify these portions of the Bible as *historical* narrative, that is, as nonfiction. Yet the biblical authors are not just historians; they are also purposeful theologians, utilizing narrative techniques to draw readers into their stories and to highlight theological themes. Too often in the past Christians have failed to read the Bible as great literature as well as great history and so miss important literary features of the text.

Though a detailed discussion of the nature of biblical narrative is beyond the scope of this book, a few comments are in order.[4] All narratives have three main features: settings, characters, and plot. Plots progress from introduction to conflict to crisis to resolution. Narratives can be embedded within larger narratives. For example, the account of Moses and the burning bush (Exodus 3) is part of the larger exodus story, which in turn is part of the larger narrative of the story of Israel. As discussed below, identifying a narrative's place in the larger story is one key to appropriate application.

Characters in a narrative can be good (protagonists), bad (antagonists), somewhere in between, neutral, or ambiguous. Of course, good characters can do bad things, and bad characters can sometimes change or act in positive ways. Stories are told by narrators, who can speak in the first ("I") or third ("he"/"she") person. The great majority of Old Testament narrative is third person, though there are occasional first-person narratives. Nehemiah, for example, speaks in the first person throughout his book. Narrators have an "evaluative point of view," which means a perspective and worldview with which the reader is intended to identify. In biblical narratives, where the authors speak the authoritative Word of God, their perspective is assumed to be the same as God's point of view.

Though at times a narrator will make an explicit value judgment about a character's actions, other times such values are taught implicitly. An example of explicit judgment is in the description of the various kings of Israel and Judah in 1 and 2 Kings. The narrator says of King Ahab that he "did more evil in the eyes of the LORD than any of those before him" (1 Kings 16:30). In many other cases, the judgment remains implicit. When Abraham and Sarah cannot have children, Sarah gives her servant Hagar to Abraham to bear him a son (Genesis 16). Although the text does not explicitly say that this was a bad decision, the narrative as a whole makes it clear that God intended to provide a child through Sarah miraculously and that Abraham and Sarah's actions demonstrated a lack of faith. The reader is expected to discern how an action is to be judged based on the larger context and the teaching of Scripture as a whole.

Old Testament narratives serve two main purposes: (1) to chart the ongoing progress of salvation history, and (2) to provide illustrations of God's nature and purpose and the appropriate (and inappropriate) responses of people to God's purpose. New Testament writers often refer to this purpose, pointing out how people of the Old Testament were models for believers to follow or to avoid. In 1 Corinthians 10 Paul points to Israel's wandering in the wilderness as a negative example of how not to respond to God's call. The Israelites experienced God's amazing power and presence in the exodus, crossing the Red Sea, eating manna in the wilderness, and drinking water from the rock. Yet because of their unbelief, God was not pleased with them and "their bodies were scattered in the wilderness" (v. 5). Paul continues, "Now these things occurred as examples to keep us from setting our hearts on evil things as they did" (v. 6). The writer to the Hebrews similarly points to Israel's failures in the wilderness as a warning against falling away (Heb. 3:7–19), as well as to positive examples of those Old Testament saints who demonstrated an enduring faith (Hebrews 11). In Romans 15:4 Paul states: "For everything that was written in the past was written to teach us, so that through the endurance taught in the Scriptures and the encouragement they provide we might have hope."

Reading Old Testament Narrative Today

Here are some important principles to keep in mind when reading and applying Old Testament narrative.

1. *Recognize the three levels at which these narratives function.* The question of location within the greater story is critically important for biblical narrative. Each individual episode is part of a larger narrative, with concentric circles of context moving outward. For Old Testament narratives, three of these concentric circles, or "levels of context," are key: (a) the individual narrative; (b) the place of the narrative in Israel's history; and (c) the place of the narrative in God's plan of salvation (the "metanarrative" of Scripture).[5]

The first level concerns the individual stories of Scripture. In 1 Samuel 16, for example, God tells the prophet Samuel that he has rejected Saul as king of Israel and to go to the home of Jesse and anoint a new king from among Jesse's sons. When Samuel arrives, Jesse brings seven of his sons one by one before Samuel, but in each case God says this is not the one. The Lord tells Samuel not to look on the outward appearance, because "people look at the outward appearance, but the LORD looks at the heart" (1 Sam. 16:7; see also 13:14). Finally, the youngest, David, is brought in from tending the sheep, and God tells Samuel to anoint him. Understood at the level of an individual story, the narrative teaches that David is fit to be king because he has a godly heart. In terms of personal application, it reminds us that God is concerned with a person's heart attitude rather than their outward abilities or appearance.

Yet there is a second level at which the narrative functions—the history of Israel as a nation. This is the beginning of the David narrative in 1 Samuel, which describes the rise of David to the throne of Israel and the establishment of the Davidic dynasty. David will become Israel's greatest king, and every king of Judah and Israel after him will be compared to him either positively or negatively. After David's throne is consolidated, God makes a covenant with him that expands and builds on the covenant God has made with Abraham. God promises to raise up David's offspring after him and to establish the throne of David's kingdom forever (2 Samuel 7). Though Solomon is the initial fulfillment of this promise, Solomon sins and fails to live up to his potential. As the kingdom declines, first through division and then through exile, the prophets of Israel point to a future day when God will fulfill his promise to David, raising up a new anointed one, the Messiah, from David's line (Isa. 9:1–7; 11:1–16; Jer. 23:5–6; Mic. 5:2). Israel's Messiah, it is predicted, will reign in justice and righteousness, reversing the results of the fall, renewing creation, and bringing in an unprecedented era of peace and prosperity. For centuries to follow, Israel will long for the days of the glories of the Davidic reign. The story of David's anointing thus plays a key role in the story of Israel, with reference to both the establishment of the monarchy and the origin of the messianic idea.

The third level at which this narrative functions is the overall drama of redemption. The New Testament points to the coming of Jesus as the fulfillment of the promise made to David (Matt. 1:1; Luke 1:32–35; Rom. 1:3–4). He is the "son of David," born in Bethlehem, David's hometown (Matt. 2:1, 5–6; Luke 2:11), to a legitimate heir of the Davidic throne (Matt. 1:16; Luke 3:23). Through Jesus's death and resurrection, he inaugurates the kingdom of God, conquering sin, Satan, and death. At his ascension he is exalted to the right hand of God, where he assumes his reign on David's throne (Acts 2:29–35). Through this Davidic Messiah, God has accomplished salvation and will eventually restore all of creation from its fallen state. In the book of Revelation, the narrative of the climax of God's universal plan of salvation, Jesus is identified as both "the Lion of the tribe of Judah, the Root of David" and the lamb who was slain (Rev. 5:5–6). As the new Jerusalem descends from heaven and Eden is restored, Jesus is called "the Root and the Offspring of David, the bright Morning Star" (Rev. 22:16).

The Old Testament narrative of the anointing of David therefore functions simultaneously at three narrative levels: (a) the individual story of God's choice of David, a man after God's own heart (see 1 Sam. 13:14); (b) the establishment of the Davidic dynasty and the messianic idea in Israel's history; and (c) the carrying forward of God's universal plan to raise up a Savior who would restore all of creation. Every Old Testament narrative can be read with these three levels in mind. The negative tendency in much application is to focus only on the first level of the individual story. Moral lessons are drawn from David's character, but the story is not seen in its larger context. We can avoid this tendency by adopting the principles that follow.

2. *Keep the focus on God and his purpose for the world.* The identification of the top (third) level of biblical narrative reminds us of perhaps the most important principle to keep in mind when reading Old Testament stories: *God, not any human being, is the main character and hero.*[6] All the narratives of Scripture are ultimately about God and his purpose for the world. Though the passage discussed above concerns the anointing of David, it is ultimately about God's plan to establish a king for Israel and his purpose in bringing the Messiah, who will save his people from their sins and restore creation.

3. *Avoid moralizing biblical narratives.* Recognizing the three levels of narrative and keeping our focus on God and his purpose helps us to avoid one of the most common errors Christians make when reading Old Testament narratives: the tendency to *moralize,* or to seek a lesson for life in every action of the human characters. This begins early in life, in Sunday school lessons for children, and continues in many sermons for adults. We read an event from the life of Moses or Gideon or Daniel and naturally want to draw an immediate application. The problem with moralizing is that not everything that biblical characters do—even the "good" characters—is meant to be an example to follow. For example, when Solomon becomes king after David, he does many good things, including asking for wisdom from God, a request that greatly pleases the Lord (1 Kings 3). But he also consolidates his throne by killing a number of his rivals and settling some old scores (1 Kings 2:13–46). The text makes no explicit verdict on this latter action. This is what kings did in those days. That, of course, does not make it right. What about Jesus's teaching about loving one's enemies (Matt. 5:44)? Did that not apply to Solomon? The point is that not every action in the Bible, even those done by its "heroes," is meant to provide us with moral guidance.

The classic example of this is the story of Gideon's fleece in Judges 6. God calls on Gideon to lead the Israelites in battle against their oppressors, the Midianites. Gideon expresses doubts about this calling and repeatedly asks God for a sign proving that he will indeed save Israel. God patiently gives Gideon the signs he asks for, a wool fleece that is made first wet, then dry, in contrast to the ground around it. The biblical text provides no judgment concerning Gideon's action, and people today sometimes seek God's will by "setting out their fleece," that is, asking God for some specific sign to confirm a decision they have to make. Yet there is no biblical approval for this kind of thing, and much in the Bible would caution against it. We are to live a life of obedience to God, not to test him in trivial ways. We make decisions based on God's values and his greater purposes in the world, not by demanding signs from him. We are not to test the Lord our God (Deut. 6:16; Matt. 4:7; Luke 4:12). Applying Scripture means bringing our lives in line with God's purpose for the world.

4. *Follow the example of biblical characters as they follow God.* One qualification is important with reference to this moralizing tendency. Keeping the focus on God as the central figure and his purpose for the world as the primary theme does not mean that characters in the Bible should *never* be viewed as examples to follow. They often are! The key is to recognize that characters serve as models to be followed *when they act in line with God's character and purpose.* As Paul says in 1 Corinthians 11:1, "Follow my example, as I follow the example of Christ." As characters practice *imitatio dei*, the imitation of God, they become models for us to follow. When they act contrary to God's values and purposes, they become examples to avoid. Paul reminds the Corinthians that the failures of the Israelites in the wilderness should serve as a warning to heed: "Now these things occurred as examples to keep us from setting our hearts on evil things as they did" (1 Cor. 10:6; cf. Rom. 15:4).

In our example text, the anointing of David in 1 Samuel 16, the character and purpose of God is evident: while people look at the outward appearance, God looks at the heart. The heart attitude he desires is one of love, loyalty, and obedience to his commands. Saul has consistently demonstrated a heart of disobedience and rebellion, ignoring God's commands. Samuel, by contrast, demonstrates obedience by going to the home of Jesse despite the possible reprisal from Saul (1 Sam. 16:2). David meets God's approval because his heart is right with God (1 Sam. 13:14). This divine approval is evident in the fact that "from that day on the Spirit of the LORD came powerfully upon David" (1 Sam. 16:13).

5. *Avoid allegorizing the meaning of the text.* Allegorizing means finding spiritual significance behind the many details of an Old Testament narrative. Someone teaching the story of David and Goliath, for example, might say that Goliath represents the giants

114

in our lives, like the temptation to sin, and David's sling represents the Word of God, with which we battle sin. The problem with allegorization is that it can steer us away from the central message of the text, which in this case is David's affirmation that victory will be won not by any human power but by God, because "the battle is the LORD's" (1 Sam. 17:47). We avoid allegorizing texts by asking the exegetical question, *Is this interpretation part of the original meaning of the narrative?* The answer in most cases is no. If it was not part of the original meaning, then it should not be part of the application.

In general, an allegorical interpretation should be followed in two cases. (1) The first is when the original author is *intending* to relate an allegory. We earlier discussed Isaiah's Song of the Vineyard (Isaiah 5), where the vineyard is an allegorical representation of the nation Israel and her failure to produce spiritual fruit. Identifying this as an allegory is simply good exegesis, determining the author's intended meaning. (2) The second reason to consider an allegorical interpretation is when a New Testament writer interprets an Old Testament passage allegorically. When Paul refers to the negative example of Israel in the wilderness in 1 Corinthians 10:1–6, he mentions the rock that supplied water to Israel in the wilderness (Exod. 17:6; Num. 20:7–13) and then adds, "and that rock was Christ" (1 Cor. 10:4). Scholars debate what Paul means here, whether he is saying that Christ was actually accompanying Israel in the wilderness or whether he is simply drawing an analogy—Christ, like the rock, provides life-giving sustenance ("living water").[7] The use of the Old Testament by New Testament writers is a major area of study, and beyond our scope here.[8] But what we can say is that Paul is writing as an inspired author and so we recognize this as an authoritative interpretation of the Old Testament text, or perhaps better, a legitimate analogy drawn from it.

Answering the Four Questions for Old Testament Narrative

Here we take the passage introduced above—the anointing of David in 1 Samuel 16—to illustrate how to apply biblical narratives. We will move through our four essential questions introduced in chapter 4.

1. *Where is this narrative in the larger story of Scripture?* The question of location has largely been answered in our discussion of the three levels of biblical narrative. The anointing of David is part of the story of Israel; more specifically, it begins the account of the origin of the Davidic reign and the Davidic dynasty, that line of kings who would reign in Judah after David. As such the passage establishes the model and standard for kingship in Israel. God's vice-regent is to be "a man after [God's] own heart" (1 Sam. 13:14), who will love God and do his will. To reject this model is to invite judgment and exile. The anointing of David also sets the stage for the promises and prophecies concerning the coming Messiah, the Savior who will one day restore creation to a right relationship with God. This narrative thus has a critical place in the full drama of redemption.

2. *What is the author's purpose in light of the narrative's genre and historical and literary context?* The answer to this question has also been mostly answered in the discussion above. At the first level of biblical narrative (the individual narrative), the author's purpose in 1 Samuel 16 is to show that in choosing a king over Israel, God was looking for someone "after his own heart," who desired to please and obey God. Though King Saul was a mighty warrior, head and shoulders above his fellow countrymen, he repeatedly disobeyed God and pursued his own purposes instead of God's. David, by contrast, was devoted to the Lord and trusted him for the victory (as illustrated in the Goliath narrative, which follows in the next chapter [1 Samuel 17]). At the second level of the narrative (the story of Israel), the author of 1 Samuel intends to show how David came to be king and how through him God would establish the Davidic dynasty. The third level moves beyond this author's perspective to the broader teaching of Scripture, where Jesus will fulfill the promises for the coming of the Davidic Messiah.

3. *How does this narrative inform our understanding of the nature of God and his purpose for the world?* We learn from this narrative that God is the sovereign Lord, who demands obedience from his human subjects. Saul was disobedient and so fell out of favor with God. David is a man after God's own heart, who will do his bidding (1 Sam. 13:14; 16:1). We also learn that sin has consequences. If Saul had been obedient, God would have established his kingdom forever (see 1 Sam. 13:13). Saul's repeated failures means the kingdom will

be ripped from his hands and given to another. Yet this is not simply blind obedience. God is not seeking automatons who simply respond to commands; he desires loving and faithful relationships with the children he has created.

We also learn from this narrative that God accomplishes his purposes through the smallest and most insignificant of his servants. David is the youngest son of Jesse and the least likely, from a human perspective, to be chosen king. Yet the Lord "does not look at the things people look at. People look at the outward appearance, but the LORD looks at the heart" (1 Sam. 16:7). God is looking not for people with great abilities or power but for those who are willing to faithfully serve him. It is only in *God's power* that his servants accomplish his purpose in the world (2 Cor. 12:10; Phil. 4:13).

4. *What does this passage teach us about who we ought to be (attitudes and character) and what we ought to do (goals and actions) as those seeking to reflect the nature and purpose of God?* When we have identified the actions and attitudes of God in the biblical narrative, it is a natural step to answer this final question of application. God found in David a person after his own heart, that is, one whose attitudes, actions, and goals were in line with God's purposes in the world. Our goal should be the same, to bring our lives in line with what God is doing. We should also seek this trait in others, following leaders who pursue God's purpose and his kingdom (Matt. 6:33) rather than their own interests. In the end it is not about the great things we do for God but about God accomplishing great things through those who faithfully love and serve him.

Old Testament Law

Perhaps the most perplexing part of the Bible for many Christians is the Old Testament law, that body of sometimes strange and bizarre regulations governing a wide range of issues in life—things like what foods to eat, what clothes to wear, how to diagnose and quarantine certain skin diseases, who you can and can't marry, and the identification of cities of refuge to escape to in case you accidently kill someone. The most difficult question for believers is how these laws relate to us. Are we supposed to obey them, ignore them, or do something in between? We have already touched on this issue at various places in this book. Here we will discuss the nature and purpose of the Old Testament law and principles for their contemporary application. We will then illustrate these principles by asking our four key questions.

The Nature and Purpose of Old Testament Law

The term "the law" can be used in a variety of ways with reference to the Old Testament. It can refer to the first five books of the Old Testament, Genesis through Deuteronomy, also called the *Pentateuch* (Greek for "five books") or the *Torah* (Hebrew for "law" or "instruction"). When New Testament writers refer to the Old Testament as "the Law and the Prophets" (Matt. 7:12; Acts 13:15), the "Law" is the Pentateuch. The Pentateuch contains a great deal of legal material but also narrative, poetry, genealogies, and other literary forms. The term "law" (Torah) also refers to the legal material itself, both the individual laws or regulations and the collection as a whole. It is these latter two senses that are our present concern; both refer to the law as a literary form or genre.

The fundamental purpose of the law was to maintain Israel's covenant relationship with Yahweh. It is essential to understand Israel's laws as inextricably linked to the covenant that God made with the nation at Mount Sinai. In the early chapters of Exodus, God raises up Moses as a leader over Israel and delivers the nation from slavery in Egypt, triumphantly bringing them through the Red Sea and to Mount Sinai. There he establishes a covenant, or binding agreement, with them. This covenant is in many ways parallel to other suzerainty covenants of the ancient Near East. Such covenants were between a superior ruler (a suzerain) and a weaker subject nation (a vassal). The suzerain decreed that he would provide for and protect his vassal. The vassal, in turn, must give the ruler obedience and loyalty. Many examples of these kinds of treaties have been found. The covenant or treaty set out the specific requirements of the subject nation and the consequences of either obedience or disobedience. It is clear that God uses this ancient covenant form when he establishes the covenant with Israel at Mount Sinai. God promises provision and protection if Israel will abide by the covenant stipulations. The law represents these stipulations, setting out both the requirements and the consequences. Obedience will result in blessings, including security in the land and material bounty. Disobedience will result in foreign oppression, devastation to the land, military defeat, and exile.

So the primary purpose of the law was to maintain this covenant relationship with God, both for individual Israelites and for the nation corporately. A false view of the purpose of the Old Testament law, sometimes taught in the history of the church, is that the law was the means of salvation for Jews in the Old Testament. This view teaches that while new covenant believers are saved by grace through faith, old covenant believers were saved by works, that is, by keeping the law. This is wrong. Salvation in the Old Testament came through God's grace alone, not through works, and was received by faith (Rom. 3:20–22; 4:2). God's covenant was a gracious gift from God, which Israel received by faith. That covenant relationship was then maintained through obedience to the law.

In addition, the law also served a second purpose: to bring order to Israel's community life—its civil, social, and religious institutions. Israel's laws maintained social justice, punished evildoers, and generally ordered society. A third purpose, which is not so explicitly stated in the Old Testament but becomes clear in the New, is that the law was also meant to show people their sin, that is, to reveal their desperate need of God's grace.

Reading Old Testament Law Today

As noted above, the most difficult and pressing issue for Christians with reference to the Old Testament law is how these laws apply to us today. There are two extremes that we can rule out from the start. The first is that Christians ought to follow the Old Testament law exactly. This is both impossible practically and inappropriate theologically. It is impossible to offer sacrifices as mandated in the Old Testament since there is no longer a temple in Jerusalem. Theologically, to offer such sacrifices is inappropriate since the New Testament affirms that Jesus is the once-for-all sacrifice for sins who rendered the Old Testament sacrificial system complete and obsolete.

The opposite extreme is to dismiss the law completely as irrelevant. This approach, which was adopted by the early-church heretic

Marcion, is contrary to the biblical model. Jesus did not consider these commands to be irrelevant, since in the Sermon on the Mount he said he came to fulfill the law, not to abolish it (Matt. 5:17). He actually intensified the law in several respects (5:22, 28, 32, 34) and told his disciples their righteousness should *exceed* that of the Pharisees and experts in the law (5:20). Paul too affirms that "all Scripture is . . . useful for teaching, rebuking, correcting and training in righteousness" (2 Tim. 3:16). For Paul, "Scripture" would include the whole of the Old Testament: the Law, the Prophets, and the Writings.

A modified version of this approach is to claim that the *only purpose* of the law for Christians is to show us our sin and so confirm the impossibility of being saved by works. While this was certainly a part of the law's purpose, it cannot be its primary role. This would ignore the testimony throughout the Old Testament that the law played a positive role in Israel's community life. The people of Israel were not just given the law to be frustrated by their own inadequacies. Throughout the Old Testament, keeping the law is described as a joyful privilege. Read through Psalm 119 (the longest psalm in the Psalter!) to see the exuberant joy the psalmist finds in living in the light of God's laws, statutes, and commandments.

Applying the law. So how do we find application for the law for today? One traditional approach, adopted especially by the Protestant Reformers, was to separate the Old Testament law into three categories: moral, civil, and ceremonial laws. Moral laws reflect fundamental issues of right and wrong and so are eternally binding for all believers for all time. The Ten Commandments would be the epitome of the moral law. Civil laws are uniquely related to Israel's community life in the ancient Near East and so no longer apply to the church. Examples would include dietary laws, laws related to agriculture, and those concerning the management of households and slaves. Ceremonial laws are related to Israel's religious life, including ceremonial purity, temple worship, and the sacrificial system. These laws were fulfilled in the person and work of Christ and so are no longer binding on Christians.

This traditional approach, though helpful in some respects, is inadequate.[9] For one thing, these distinctions are not made in the Old Testament, and laws from different categories appear side by side in Old Testament lists. Read through Leviticus 19, and you will see laws that appear to be moral ("do not steal"; v. 11), civil ("when you enter the land and plant any kind of fruit tree . . ."; v. 23), and ceremonial ("With the ram of the guilt offering the priest is to make atonement"; v. 22). These are introduced side by side and without any apparent distinction. Similarly, individual laws themselves are not easily categorized. Is the command not to wear clothing made of different kinds of material a moral, civil, or ceremonial issue? Most scholars see such commands as symbolic, intended to point to the holiness of God and to call Israel to be separate from the nations around her. If this is the case, the law has moral, civil, and ceremonial dimensions. Similarly, is the Sabbath command moral, civil, or ceremonial? A case could be made for each. Like moral laws, it is part of the Ten Commandments (Exod. 20:8; Deut. 5:12); like civil laws, it was a key aspect of Israel's national identity; and like ceremonial laws, it finds its ultimate fulfillment in Christ (Hebrews 4; Rom. 14:5). Old Testament scholar Peter Vogt points to these and other problems with this approach, noting that such distinctions were also foreign to the ancient Near East, where all of life was seen to have religious significance.[10] God was interested in every aspect of life, not just the (so-called) moral parts.

A *paradigmatic approach.* Drawing especially on the work of Christopher Wright,[11] Vogt and others have suggested instead a paradigmatic approach to the law. A paradigm is "a model or pattern that enables you to explain or critique many different and varying situations by means of some single concept or set of governing principles."[12] In grammar, a verb paradigm uses a model verb to show the pattern by which you can parse many other verbs. Israel as a nation was meant to be a paradigm, a model for other nations to follow, and its laws were meant to be paradigmatic, shaping the nation into the kind of society God desired and one that revealed God's righteous standards to the surrounding peoples. This is why God describes Israel as a "kingdom of priests": after delivering Israel from slavery in Egypt, the Lord says, "You yourselves have seen what I did to Egypt, and how I carried you on eagles' wings and brought you to myself. Now if you obey me fully and keep my covenant, then out of all nations you will be my treasured possession. Although the whole earth is mine, you will be for me a kingdom of priests and a holy nation" (Exod. 19:4–6). A priest's role is to mediate God's presence and his salvation to others. This was Israel's role, to be a light to the world, to reveal God's nature and purpose to the nations.[13]

A paradigmatic approach to the *whole* law avoids the problems noted above of trying to distinguish different kinds of laws. When we read one of Israel's laws, we don't ask whether it is moral, and so binding for all time, or civil, and so irrelevant for today. Rather, we ask how it functioned in Israel's national life, how it was intended to shape Israel into the kind of people God wanted them to be—a society of freedom, justice, love, and compassion that would be God's priesthood among the nations (Deut. 4:5–8).

This concept of Israel as a paradigm fits well with the method and framework for application outlined in this volume. For one thing, it grounds biblical law in God's redemptive plan and identifies Israel's law as part of the story of redemption. In addition, it elevates the divine function or purpose of the law over the specific mandate. By asking and answering the question, How was this passage intended to guide God's people in their unique social, cultural, and religious situation? we can creatively imagine ways to reproduce this same purpose and live out these same values in our own culture.

Answering the Four Questions for Old Testament Law

1. *Where is this law in the larger story of Scripture?* The question of location is crucial when interpreting and applying the law. First, we must recognize that this is Israel's law, meant to enable the nation to function as the paradigmatic people of God in their own unique historical and cultural context. These commands were not given to the church. This is obvious when we read the detailed description in the law concerning how to build the tabernacle or the guidelines associated with various offerings and sacrifices to the Lord. But even the Ten Commandments were part of *Israel's* law, the foundation of God's covenant with them. This does not mean that the Ten Commandments have no application for us now; but it does mean that they were not given *to us*.

Second, we need to recognize that any particular command is not necessarily the last word on the subject. In light of the progress of revelation, a fuller, more complete answer may be coming later in the biblical text. Old Testament commands related to divorce, polygamy, and slavery are clearly not God's last word on these subjects.

Third, the location of a law must be seen in terms of not only its place in the history of redemption but also its location in the ancient Near East. Commands that may seem harsh or unjust to us may in fact be a significant advance in their cultural context. A classic example of this is the "law of retaliation" (*lex talionis*): "eye for eye, tooth for tooth" (Exod. 21:24; Lev. 24:20; Deut. 19:21). We may view this as harsh and severe punishment. In context, however, it is a call for fair and proportional judgment. Someone who is wounded might be tempted to kill the person who did it, but the Bible commands that the punishment fit the crime—no more than "an eye for an eye."

It is certainly true that Jesus takes this law and "corrects" it, calling for acts of love instead of retribution (Matt. 5:38–48). What Jesus is doing here, however, is getting at the true essence of the law, which is to love our neighbors as ourselves. The law of retaliation was never meant to be a means of personal vengeance; it was intended to bring societal justice. Jesus corrects the abusive use of this law as an excuse for revenge. Jesus calls us to break this cycle of violence by loving instead of hating, and repaying evil with good. Here is an example where the Old Testament revelation is incomplete without its fuller explication in the New.

2. *What is the purpose of this law in its historical and literary context?* This example of the *lex talionis* brings up the need for sound exegesis, our second step of application. Before we can find application for today, we must seek to understand the nature of the law in its social and cultural context.

Consider, again, the difficult topic of slavery. As discussed in chapter 3, sound exegesis reveals that indentured servitude in Israel was an institution very different from slavery in the American South. Such servitude was usually a means to escape crushing debt and guarantee survival for an individual and their family. Debt slavery was also of limited duration, lasting six years. When released, freed slaves were to be sent away with liberal gifts of grain, flocks, and wine (Deut. 15:12–15). The law even discusses the (evidently common) situation where a slave's status was so favorable that he would voluntarily choose to stay with the master, "because he loves you and your family" (Deut. 15:16–17; cf. Exod. 21:5–6).

While slaves in other ancient Near Eastern cultures were regarded as mere property to be bought, sold, and disposed of at will, in Israel they were viewed as people with legitimate rights. Slaves were to be included in the weekly Sabbath rest (Exod. 20:10; 23:12), to partake of the annual Passover (Exod. 12:44), and to join in the festivals (Deut. 16:11–14). A slave who was beaten by an owner and lost an eye or a tooth must be set free. If an owner beat a slave and the slave died, the owner would be punished (presumably with death; Exod. 21:20). Slaves were clearly seen as human beings of value created in the image of God.

These texts are by no means the last word on slavery, which is clearly not God's ultimate ethic for human relationships (see Gal. 3:28; Eph. 6:9; Philem. 16–17). But proper exegesis allows us to understand these laws in their unique cultural contexts and so discover the circumstances that motivated them.

3. *How does this law inform our understanding of the nature of God and his purpose for the world?* All of the Old Testament laws come from the heart of God and so reveal his nature, values, and purpose. Even texts on slavery teach us about who God is and who we are as his people. God repeatedly reminds Israel that they were slaves in Egypt and that he delivered them (Deut. 15:15). The redemption of slaves reflects God's fundamental nature as the One who redeems. His demand for provision and protection for the weak shows that he is an impartial God, who demands justice for all. Throughout Scripture God says he is on the side of the humble and lowly and warns people to treat kindly the lowliest members of society.

4. *What does this passage teach us about who we ought to be (attitudes and character) and what we ought to do (goals and actions) as those seeking to reflect the nature and purpose of God?* Discerning the nature and purpose of God in an Old Testament command allows us to apply it appropriately in our own lives. In general we can say that commands that directly reflect the nature of God should be applied directly, while those that indirectly (or symbolically) reflect the nature of God may be applied indirectly or at the level of principle.

The Ten Commandments stand at the head of the law and were foundational for Israel, because they represented God's essential nature (Exod. 20:1–17). God is the one true God of the universe and so idolatry of any kind is forbidden (vv. 2–3). God's "name" represents who he is in all his holiness and righteousness, so the misuse of his name is an affront to his glory (v. 7). Murder is forbidden because

124

human beings are created in God's image and so have inherent value (v. 13). Adultery is always wrong because God is faithful to his covenant relationships and expects the same from his people (v. 14). We don't obey these commands because they are "moral" per se but because they directly reflect the nature of God. To disobey or ignore these commands is to contradict God's nature and so live in defiance of him. Though the Ten Commandments were not given to us as Christians, those that directly reflect the character of God remain mandates for us. (The one possible exception is the Sabbath command, which will serve as a case study in chap. 8.)

In contrast to the Ten Commandments, Israel's laws of separation and purity indirectly and symbolically reveal God's attributes. The purpose of not wearing clothing made of different kinds of material was not, it seems clear, because such mixing was inherently evil or contrary to God's nature, but because God wanted Israel to *symbolically* demonstrate the nation's status as a people set apart to the Lord. These commands were given directly to the people of Israel, so to ignore them would have been to disobey God's command, a willful act of defiance.

Since these commands were not given to us, and since they do not *directly* relate to the nature of God, we are not obligated to obey them directly. We *are* obliged, however, to discover God's values behind them and live according to those standards. We live out the commands related to purity and separation by setting ourselves apart from the sinful and defiling qualities of the world. This would mean avoiding idols such as selfishness, materialism, greed, dishonesty, and lust.

An important conclusion that arises from this discussion is that the *purpose* of the law is more important than the command itself, because that purpose reveals the heart of God. While it would be wrong to disobey any command given directly by God, none of Israel's commands were given directly to the church. All were given to the nation Israel in its covenant context. As with all the biblical genres, we live a life of obedience to God by seeking the heart of God behind the text.

Old Testament Prophecy

Prophecy is one of the most misunderstood genres in the Bible. When people today think of prophecy, most think of predictions about the future, especially the future related to the end times and the events leading up to the return of Christ. Yet prophecies of this sort represent a very small percentage of Old Testament prophecy. Prophecy has often been described as two things: *foretelling* and *forthtelling*. Foretelling is predicting the future. Forthtelling is pronouncing a message from God to his people. By far the primary and most important purpose of prophecy is forthtelling. The role of the prophets was not to tickle the ears of their listeners with tantalizing predictions about the future but to proclaim God's message to God's people for the present, calling them to repent and return to a right relationship with him. Even when the prophets predict the future, the great majority of this foretelling relates to events that are future to the original hearers but are in the past from our perspective. It is essential to keep this historical context in mind as we read and apply this important biblical genre.

The Nature and Purpose of Old Testament Prophecy

In Protestant English Bibles, the books of the prophets comprise the last seventeen books of the Old Testament: Isaiah through Malachi. They are divided between the *Major Prophets* (Isaiah, Jeremiah [and Lamentations], Ezekiel, and Daniel) and the *Minor Prophets* (Hosea through Malachi). "Minor" does not mean less important but refers only to length. The Hebrew Bible has the same books as our Old Testament, but they are arranged differently, with the Prophets comprising a large middle section (between the Law and the Writings). They are divided into the Former Prophets (Joshua, Judges, Samuel, Kings) and the Latter Prophets (Isaiah, Jeremiah, Ezekiel, and "The Twelve" [= the Minor Prophets]; Daniel was part of the Writings). The Former Prophets—Joshua through Kings— are so called because they take the same prophetic perspective as the writing prophets and likely arose from similar circles (that is, they were written by prophets). Their (narrative) purpose is to call the nation Israel back to its covenant relationship with God, as established in the Law (Torah). But since these books are primarily historical narrative, we have treated them above under that genre. Here we are concerned with the writing prophets, Isaiah through Malachi.

The prophets were God's spokespeople, and their primary purpose was to announce God's message to his people (forthtelling). More specifically, the prophet's role was to call the nation Israel to *faithfulness to the covenant*. If the Pentateuch (Genesis–Deuteronomy) represents the establishment and explanation of the covenant, and the Former Prophets (Joshua, Judges, Samuel, Kings) narrate the consequences when Israel either keeps or fails to keep the covenant, the Latter Prophets represent the repeated call through God's spokespeople to covenant faithfulness.

The key themes found in the prophets all revolve around this central theme of covenant faithfulness. Such themes include (1) the glory and majesty of the Lord as the one true God of Israel and of the universe; (2) the worthlessness and impotence of the idols of the nations in contrast to the omnipotence of the God of Israel; (3) coming judgment against Israel for her covenant unfaithfulness, idolatry, injustice, and evil deeds; (4) coming judgment against the nations for their evil ways and their treatment of God's people; (5) the blessings Israel will receive if she repents and changes her evil ways; (6) the ultimate hope of restoration and renewal for all of creation, which God will one day accomplish.

Several structural features stand out when reading through the prophets. First, much of the prophetic material is in poetic form. (We will discuss Hebrew poetry later in this chapter.) This poetic genre means that much of the language of the prophets is metaphorical, affective, hyperbolic, and intended for rhetorical effect. Interpreting the prophets accurately means learning to identify the nature of the metaphors and the historical references behind this poetic language.

A second feature of the prophets is that there is not a clear chronological or topical order. Rather, the books are arranged as a series of independent or semi-independent units or oracles. The reason is that these oracles were prophetic messages received from God and delivered to the people, probably orally, on separate occasions. Identifying the historical context of the book in general, and then each oracle in particular, is important for proper interpretation. What is the general historical setting? Is the nation under threat? By whom? Whom is the prophet addressing? What problems is he addressing? What are the consequences of not responding? Sometimes groups of oracles are related (for example, a series of judgment oracles against the nations; see Isaiah 13–21), but other times the presentation seems odd and disjointed. The oracles sometimes change subjects abruptly and return again and again to similar themes.

The "Fulfillment" of Old Testament Prophecy

Beyond the difficult issues of determining the meaning of prophetic oracles is the challenging question of how these prophecies are fulfilled. As pointed out above, people often misread prophecy by assuming that it is only about predicting the future rather than being God's call to respond in the present. More specifically, they assume that a prophecy has a single, specific fulfillment in the future. Here are some important qualifications concerning the nature of prophetic fulfillment.

1. *Contingent prophecies*. The first qualification, discussed already in chapter 2, is the contingent nature of much Old Testament prophecy. Many, if not most, of the prophecies of judgment and blessing in the Old Testament are not predictions of a definite future event but rather warnings of judgment and promises of blessing, which are dependent on the response of the hearers. This is forthtelling rather than foretelling. In the case of Jonah, for example, when the people of Nineveh repent and turn from their sins, God relents and does not send the judgment he has promised. Contingent prophecies are not necessarily what *must* happen, but what *will* happen if the prophecy is not heeded (cf. Jer. 18:5–10).

2. *Two-stage fulfillment*. A second important qualification concerning the fulfillment of prophecy relates to the progress of revelation, the fact that not every passage of Scripture tells the whole story. Though the Old Testament prophets receive their message from God, they do not necessarily comprehend the details of how that prophecy will come to pass. For example, although Isaiah predicts that the coming "Servant of the LORD" will suffer and die as an atonement for his people Israel (Isa. 52:13–53:12), he surely does not understand that the Messiah will be crucified during the Roman occupation of Palestine. The prophet's vision is true, but not complete.

This point about partial understanding is especially true with reference to prophecies that have a two-stage fulfillment with reference to Jesus's first and second coming. An example of this is the prophecy in Isaiah 11:1–9, where the coming Messiah is described as a "shoot" from the root of Jesse (David's father), upon whom the Spirit of God will rest (vv. 1–2). This prophecy was fulfilled in the coming of Jesus the Messiah, who was born of a descendant of David (Matt. 1:1) and upon whom the Spirit descended at his baptism (Matt. 3:16). Yet the prophecy goes on to say that he will "strike the earth with the rod of his mouth" and slay the wicked "with the breath of his lips" (Isa. 11:4). At that time, "the wolf will live with the lamb," there will be perfect peace, and "the earth will be filled with the knowledge of the Lord" (Isa. 11:6–9). While the first part of this prophecy has been fulfilled in Christ's first coming, the second part awaits his second, when he will return to consummate the kingdom. The prophet provides a clear picture of what the Messiah will accomplish, but he does not envision its fulfillment in two stages.

An analogy has often been drawn to someone looking at two mountains in a distant mountain range. From the person's limited perspective, the two mountains appear to be side by side. In fact they are many miles apart. In the same way, the prophet sees these events from a distance and they appear to be side by side, when in fact they are separated by a long period of time.

3. *Typological fulfillment.* Another example where the Old Testament prophecy alone doesn't give us the full story is in the case of typology. A *type* is a person or event in biblical history that is a model or prefigurement of what would come later (known as the *antitype*). David is a type of Christ in that, as the Lord's anointed one and a man after God's own heart, he is a model for the coming Messiah. Moses, too, is a type of Christ, since he is the mediator of the covenant at Mount Sinai just as Jesus is the mediator of the new covenant (Acts 3:22; 7:37).

Events too can be typological. The exodus from Egypt and the return from Babylonian exile are both viewed in the New Testament as typifying the deliverance Jesus has accomplished through his life, death, and resurrection. In Isaiah 40:1–5, the prophet predicts that though Israel is in exile in Babylon, the Lord will one day come and restore the nation. While in context this passage clearly refers to the return of the Jewish exiles from Babylon in the sixth century BC, it ultimately points to the salvation God will accomplish through the coming of the Messiah. All four Gospels refer to this passage and

129

identify John the Baptist as the "voice . . . calling in the wilderness" (Matt. 3:3; Mark 1:3; Luke 3:4; John 1:23).

The key to interpreting prophecies that are fulfilled in two stages or typologically is to view them through the lenses of the New Testament authors, who were inspired by the Holy Spirit. We could not discern by reading Isaiah 11 alone that its fulfillment would take place in two stages, or that Isaiah 40 would find its ultimate fulfillment in the coming of John the Baptist and Jesus. We are dependent in such cases on the Holy Spirit's guidance through the New Testament documents. As in the case of allegorical interpretation of narrative, it seems best to avoid typological interpretations except in cases where the Bible itself points in this direction.

4. *Messianic prophecies: unique or typological fulfillment?* A discussion of typology in prophecy raises the question of the nature of fulfillment of messianic prophecies. I always get a little uncomfortable when hearing someone defending the Christian faith by claiming that there are four hundred plus messianic prophecies uniquely fulfilled in Christ. It is usually argued that the odds of this happening by chance are astronomical, and that this is certain proof that Jesus was who he said he was.

Please don't get me wrong. There are many remarkable prophecies fulfilled by Christ, such as the prophecies concerning the Messiah's birth in Bethlehem (Mic. 5:2), his endowment with the Holy Spirit (Isa. 11:2; 42:1), his ministry in the region of Galilee (Isa. 9:1), his entrance into Jerusalem riding on a donkey (Zech. 9:9), and—most remarkably—his suffering and atoning death for the sins of his people (Isa. 52:13–53:12). No one expected the Messiah to come first to Galilee, as Jesus did, and as far as we can tell, nobody was looking for a suffering Messiah. These are amazing prophecies that should be more than enough evidence for the skeptic.

My concern, however, is that the great majority of these four hundred plus prophecies are typologically rather than uniquely fulfilled in Christ, so that they do not have the apologetic value that is sometimes claimed. To say they are fulfilled typologically means that their original referent is to an event, person, or class of persons in the past, rather than uniquely to the Messiah. The prophecy of Isaiah 7:14, for example, in context clearly refers to a child born in Isaiah's day (see Isa. 7:13–17). Similarly, Psalm 34:20 is identified in John 19:36 as a prophecy fulfilled when Jesus's bones were not broken on the cross. But in context, Psalm 34 is about a righteous sufferer in David's day (possibly David himself). The same is true of the prophecy of casting lots for Jesus's clothes (Ps. 22:18; John 19:24). These and many other passages are *typologically* rather than *uniquely* fulfilled in Christ.

This does not make these passages any less important. Jesus is the ultimate "Immanuel" of Isaiah 7:14, since he is truly "God with us." He is the true fulfillment of Psalm 34:20, since he is the ultimate righteous sufferer. From the perspective of the New Testament writers, all of history, not just individual texts, has come to fulfillment in Christ. Unlike people in the Western world, the early Christians were not desperate for empirical "proof" through fulfilled prophecy that the supernatural existed or that Jesus was who he said he was. They knew who he was. They had seen his miracles, been transformed by his presence, witnessed his resurrection, experienced the empowerment of his Holy Spirit. This was their reality. They were more interested in the fact that Jesus was the culmination of the Story, that all the Hebrew Scriptures came to fulfillment in him (Luke 24:27). A typological fulfillment was just as powerful for them, or even more so, since it confirmed that salvation history was coming to its climax in Jesus.

Answering the Four Questions for Old Testament Prophecy

Applying the Old Testament prophets means keeping their nature and purpose in mind. Our four questions provide an appropriate framework to illustrate this.

1. *Where is this prophecy in the larger story of Scripture?* Understanding the message of the prophets means recognizing their place in Israel's history and in the Bible as a whole. The time of the prophets spanned the period from the eighth century BC (the 700s) to the middle of fifth century BC (about 430). This period can be divided into three parts: preexilic (before the Babylonian exile), exilic, and postexilic. Most of the prophets prophesied in the preexilic period, during the time of the monarchy. After the reign of King Solomon, David's son, civil war broke out and the united kingdom divided into the northern kingdom of Israel and the southern kingdom of

Judah. Some of the prophets prophesied in the north, and some in the south. The historical backdrop to the prophets can be found in the narrative books of 1–2 Kings, 1–2 Chronicles, Ezra, and Nehemiah. Each king is rated according to whether he has done good or evil in the sight of the Lord. All the kings of the northern kingdom of Israel are identified as evil, while the southern kings are mixed.

The northern kingdom of Israel was destroyed and taken into captivity in 722 BC by the Assyrian Empire. The southern kingdom of Judah was taken into exile by the Babylonian Empire starting in 605 BC. A series of deportations ensued, and the temple was destroyed in 586 BC. The period of the exile followed, until 539 BC when King Cyrus of Persia allowed the exiles to return to Jerusalem. There are two exilic prophets, Ezekiel and Daniel, and three postexilic prophets, Haggai, Zechariah, and Malachi. Jeremiah prophesied in the transitional period before and after the fall of the southern kingdom. The dates of some of the prophets is quite precise, since they dated their oracles to the reigns of various kings. For others we are uncertain when they wrote.

The period of the prophets was a time of testing and decision for Israel and Judah. The great temptation the nation faced was whether they would stay faithful to the Lord and follow his covenant or whether they would follow the gods of the nations around them. The constant refrain of the prophets is a call to God's people to repent of their evil ways and return to the Lord. If they do so, he will bless them and give them peace and security in the land of Israel. If they reject him, they will face disaster and exile.

2. *What is the author's purpose in light of the prophecy's genre and historical and literary context?* Exegesis is essential for interpreting the prophets. The reader should first determine the general background to the prophetic book. What do we know about the prophet? What was happening in Israel at the time? Was this a period of security, peace, and prosperity? Or was there a threat of famine, war, or exile? Who was reigning in Israel and/or Judah and what was their reign like? Did they follow the Lord or worship idols? While these questions may seem daunting for the beginner, they are actually quite simple to answer. A good study Bible will provide a few pages of introduction to each prophet, identifying the time, place, and historical context of the book and its major themes. You can

also find this information in Bible dictionaries, encyclopedias, or handbooks.

Consider this passage in the *NIV Study Bible* from the introduction to the prophet Amos: "Amos prophesied during the reigns of Uzziah over Judah (792–740 BC) and Jeroboam II over Israel (793–753). . . . Both kingdoms were enjoying great prosperity and had reached new political and military heights (cf. 2 Kings 14:23–15:7; 2 Chronicles 26). It was also a time of idolatry, extravagant indulgence in luxurious living, immorality, corruption of judicial procedure and oppression of the poor. As a consequence, God would soon bring about the Assyrian captivity to the northern kingdom (722–721)."[14] In one short paragraph, you have a summary of the setting in which Amos wrote, including the social and economic situation in Israel, the nation's spiritual state, and its coming judgment. The introduction also provides a description of the author, more details concerning Israel's situation, the main themes of the book, and a detailed outline. This is quick access to everything you need to know to read the book intelligently in its historical and literary context.

With this general information in hand, you can move on to Amos's individual oracles. Interpreting these can also seem daunting. This is because the language is often metaphorical, and there may be allusions to things that were well known to the original readers but are obscure to you. For example, the book of Amos begins with a statement of the Lord's anger:

> The LORD roars from Zion
>   and thunders from Jerusalem;
> the pastures of the shepherds dry up,
>   and the top of Carmel withers. (Amos 1:2)

The Lord is angry because of Judah's sin and is metaphorically portrayed as a roaring lion and a thundering storm. Mount Zion was the location of the temple in Jerusalem and so became a poetic term for Jerusalem. Both Zion and Jerusalem here stand for the southern kingdom of Judah, which has fallen into sin. God will judge the nation by drying up her pastures and fields. Mount Carmel was a lush and beautiful area in Israel, so the point is that even the most fertile areas will be devastated.

What follows is a series of oracles against Israel's neighbors, beginning with Aram (Syria):

> For three sins of Damascus,
>   even for four, I will not relent.
> Because she threshed Gilead
>   with sledges having iron teeth,
> I will send fire on the house of Hazael
>   that will consume the fortresses of Ben-Hadad. (Amos
>   1:3–4)

Again we enter a world that may be unfamiliar to the reader because of its agricultural images, metaphorical language, and historical references. Damascus was the capital of Aram, or Syria, the nation to the north of Israel, and so represents that nation. The phrase "for three sins . . . even for four" is an idiomatic way of saying "for her many sins." A threshing sledge was a sledlike board or platform with sharp teeth used to thresh, or separate, the grain from cut stalks. Hazael was the king of Aram and "house of" refers to the dynasty (line of kings) that he established; Ben-Hadad was his son who would rule after him. Syria is thus described as crushing and oppressing God's people in Gilead, Israel's territory east of Galilee. God will judge Syria for this, coming like a fire to consume her. This fire is likely a metaphor for the invasion of the Assyrian army, which will devastate Syria.

This may seem like a lot of information, but having a basic understanding of these metaphorical and historical references is essential for interpreting the passage in its original context. But it is not so difficult as it might at first seem. All of the information above, for example, appears in brief notes below this passage in the *NIV Study Bible*, a one-stop tool for this kind of study. Many other study Bibles and tools like Bible handbooks provide similar information. If you need to go even deeper, the commentaries on Amos will take you there.[15]

3. *How does this passage inform our understanding of the nature of God and his purpose for the world?* Once you have identified Amos's purpose in writing, you can move on to the general question of what we learn about God and his purpose for the world and

for his people. Amos's prophecies confirm many things that are emphasized throughout the prophets and the Bible in general. God is the creator of all things, the righteous judge, and sovereign Lord of the universe (Amos 4:13; 9:5–6). He also cares for the smallest of creatures. Amos has a strong emphasis on social justice. God looks after the poor and outcast and wants his people to care for them as well. Israel of Amos's day was prospering economically, but this had not resulted in a heart of social concern. The nation had become rich and complacent, turning to idolatry and self-indulgence. The rich were ignoring God's law and exploiting the poor. Through Amos, God warns that judgment is coming because of the nation's immorality, corruption, idolatry, and complacency.

4. *What does this passage teach us about who we ought to be (attitudes and character) and what we ought to do (goals and actions) as those seeking to reflect the nature and purpose of God?* Once we have done our exegesis, we are ready to apply the message of the prophets to our present-day situation. Much of Amos's message translates directly into our context. God is the sovereign Lord of the universe, and he demands our loyalty. Idolatry of any kind—whether the idols of materialism, success, relationships, or lust—is a rejection of God's lordship over our lives. Loyalty to God means identifying with his values and then living out these values in our daily lives. Instead of selfishness and self-indulgence, the characteristics of God are love, justice, and compassion, and he expects the same from his people. Of course, recognizing these biblical values is not the same as doing them! The affluent West is not so different from Israel and Judah in Amos's day. When we have wealth, peace, and security, we tend to be self-centered, self-indulgent, and complacent in our relationship with God. Heeding the call of the prophets means reordering our lives in line with God's values and priorities.

Old Testament Poetry and the Psalms

When people think of poetry in the Bible, they commonly think of the Psalms. But as noted above, large sections of the Prophets are also poetry. In fact, over one-third of the Old Testament is written in poetic form, and there are poetic sections in almost every book in the Bible. Here we will first survey Hebrew poetry in general and then discuss the nature and application of the Psalms in particular.[16]

The Nature and Function of Hebrew Poetry

I have never been a very good reader of poetry. The reason, I suppose, is that I am more cognitive than emotive. I think things through and analyze them rather than experiencing and enjoying their artistic value. Though poetry can certainly be analyzed cognitively, it deals more with the aesthetic side of life. It is more concerned with feelings than with logic, with beauty than with argumentation. This makes poetry an ideal genre for expressing human emotions—joy, sorrow, love, anger, fear, relief, gratitude, and exhilaration.

Poetry can be difficult to identify and define. There is a continuum, rather than a clear demarcation, between poetry and prose. In general, poetry has an affective purpose and contains features like rhythm and meter, repetition and parallelism, pithiness and memorability, and emotive and figurative language.

In terms of its structure, Hebrew poetry seldom rhymes (though neither does much English poetry). Its most common structural feature is parallelism of lines. There are various types of parallelism, but the most common is *synonymous parallelism*. Psalm 89:1 reads,

> I will sing of the LORD's great love forever;
> > with my mouth I will make your faithfulness known
> > through all generations.

Notice how the first line expresses a thought similar to that of the second. Another type is *antithetical parallelism*, where the second line stands in contrast to the first. Consider Psalm 18:27:

> You save the humble
> > but bring low those whose eyes are haughty.

In *synthetic* (or *developmental*) *parallelism* the second line develops, elaborates on, or completes the thought of the first, as in Psalm 80:8:

> You transplanted a vine from Egypt;
> > you drove out the nations and planted it.

These three are very general categories of parallelism, and there are dozens of variants on each. The structure is also variable. There can be more than two lines of parallelism, with additional lines repeating, contrasting, or expanding upon the previous ones. Since poetry is emotive and evocative, there are few hard-and-fast rules.

Other structural features in the Psalms include refrains and acrostics. Refrains are repeated verses or lines, such as in Psalms 118 and 136, which repeat again and again the refrain, "His love endures forever." These were almost certainly liturgical psalms, where a song leader read the first line of each verse and the people responded with the refrain. In acrostic psalms, lines or stanzas begin with subsequent letters of the alphabet. Psalms 111 and 112, for example, both have twenty-two lines, one for each letter of the Hebrew alphabet. The most famous acrostic in the Bible is Psalm 119; there are twenty-two stanzas, and every line in an individual stanza begins with the same Hebrew letter. Unfortunately you can't see this in the English, since Hebrew and English letters and words are not the same, so most English Bibles print the Hebrew letter at the beginning of each stanza.

Figurative language is also common throughout Hebrew poetry. Especially frequent are metaphors and similes, metonymy and synecdoche, personification, hyperbole, and rhetorical questions. *Metaphors* and *similes* compare one thing to another. The only difference between the two is that similes use words such as "like" or "as" to make the comparison explicit, while a metaphor requires the reader to figure this out. "God is like a fortress" would be a simile. "God is a fortress" is a metaphor. The two have essentially the same meaning: there is something about God (his strength and ability to defend) that is like a fortress. The simile is an explicit comparison, while the metaphor may be more powerful rhetorically. Examples of each appear in the great poem to God's majesty in Isaiah 40. Isaiah 40:15 reads, "Surely the nations are like a drop in a bucket." This is a simile, meaning the nations are irrelevant before the power and majesty of God. A few verses earlier we read, "Surely the people are grass" (v. 7). This is a metaphor. The people are as fragile as a blade of grass that withers in the hot sun.

Consider these metaphors from Psalm 22:

I am a worm, not a man (v. 6)
Many bulls surround me (v. 12)

Roaring lions . . . open their mouths wide against me (v. 13)
Dogs surround me (v. 16)
All my bones are on display (v. 17)
Rescue me from the mouth of the lions (v. 21)
Save me from the horns of the wild oxen (v. 21)

Taking these images literally results in the absurd picture of the psalmist as a worm (with bones!) being threatened in a wild game park, rather than (correctly) interpreting them as a metaphorical description of his human enemies portrayed as wild beasts.

Metonymy and *synecdoche* also make metaphorical comparisons. Metonymy is when one thing stands for something else with which it is related. Psalm 22:20 says, "Deliver me from the sword." The sword stands for violent death. Psalm 34:13 reads, "keep your tongue from evil and your lips from telling lies." The tongue and lips stand for the things that we say. Synecdoche is similar, except in this case part of something is used for the whole, or the whole is used for a part. "I put no trust in my bow" (Ps. 44:6) means I don't trust in my weapons or military power. Paul says in Romans 1:16 that the gospel is the power of God for salvation, "to the Jew first and also to the Greek" (NASB). A part (Greeks) here stands for the whole (all Gentiles). Mark 16:15 says to preach the gospel to "all creation." The whole (creation) stands for the part (people within God's creation).

Personification is when inanimate objects are given personal attributes. Isaiah 55:12 uses personification to describe the restoration of creation: "the mountains and hills will burst into song before you, and all the trees of the field will clap their hands." This is also *hyperbole*, or intentional exaggeration, another common element in poetry. When Isaiah says, "All the stars in the sky will be dissolved and the heavens rolled up like a scroll" (Isa. 34:4), he is using hyperbole to describe the coming judgment against the nations.

While a real question is a request for information, a *rhetorical question* is used to make a point of some kind. There are many types of rhetorical questions. When God says in Isaiah 40:25, "To whom will you compare me? Or who is my equal?" he is not asking for names. The point is that no one can compare to God. When Samuel asks King Saul, "What . . . is this bleating of sheep in my

138

ears?" (1 Sam. 15:14), he means, "You have disobeyed the Lord by saving the plunder you took from the battle."

These are just a few of the many kinds of figurative language that Hebrew poetry uses for rhetorical effect and emotional impact. Consider, finally, the combination of figurative language in Psalm 22:14:

> I am poured out like water,
>> and all my bones are out of joint.
> My heart has turned to wax;
>> it has melted away within me.

All four lines are hyperbolic. In the first, "like water" is also a simile; in the third "heart . . . turned to wax" is a metaphor. "Heart" is synecdoche as well, the heart standing for the person's whole life. "Bones" is synecdoche for the body. Together the result is a forceful rhetorical expression of a person under enormous emotional and physical distress. Poetry is a powerful means to express our thoughts and emotions to God and to others.

The Nature and Function of the Psalms

There are 150 psalms in the Psalter.[17] In the book's present form, the psalms are arranged in five books, each ending with a doxology (Psalms 1–41; 42–72; 73–89; 90–106; 107–150). This number five is probably meant to recall the Old Testament Law, or Pentateuch, the first five books of the Old Testament. Just as there are five books of the Law, so there are five books of worship and praise.

Most of the psalms have titles, or superscriptions. These provide various kinds of information, such as author, type of psalm, the name of the collection, occasion of writing, and musical and liturgical notations. The Hebrew text sometimes differs from the Greek (Septuagint) on these titles, and so their historical accuracy is not certain. They should not be viewed as an inspired part of the psalm. Some of the psalms identify their author; others are anonymous. Seventy-three are associated with David in the Hebrew text, though whether he wrote all these or whether they were identified with him in some other way is not certain.[18] Other psalms are identified with Asaph (12 psalms), the sons of Korah (10), Solomon (2), Hemen (1),

Ethan (1), and Moses (1; Psalm 90). If these attributions are correct, most of the psalms were written during David's reign (1010–970 BC), but the collection ranges from the time of Moses (about 1500 BC) to the return from exile (about 500 BC; see Psalm 137).

The psalms were likely collated and arranged long after they were written, so that the book's overall structure and organization is secondary. More important for interpreting and applying the psalms is identifying the particular *type* of psalm and its original *purpose*. There are various types of psalms, each composed for a particular purpose or purposes in the life of Israel. One type is *praise psalms*, which celebrate God's greatness and his goodness. These are sometimes referred to as psalms of orientation, since they describe how God's people saw themselves in the context of God's creation and purpose for the world. Some examples of praise hymns include Psalms 8; 19; 66; 100; 145–47.

The most common psalms in the Psalter are *lament psalms*. These are cries to God for help in times of danger, pain, or sorrow. Lament psalms were sung when life was difficult and disappointing. These are sometimes called psalms of disorientation, as life gets out of kilter and the psalmist cries to God for help.[19] These psalms can be either individual laments (Psalms 3; 6; 22; 31; 54–57; 120; 139) or corporate laments (Psalms 12; 44; 79–80; 94; 137). Some lament psalms contain imprecations—angry cries to God to punish the wicked for the evil they have caused. The anger and even hatred expressed in these kinds of psalms may at times seem shocking. But we have to remember that these are the honest expressions of the psalmists' pain, sorrow, and frustration when the wicked seem to prosper and when justice seems far away. The psalmists are venting to God.

A third type of psalm is the *thanksgiving psalm*, a gracious response to God's goodness or help. These can be called psalms of reorientation, since they reflect the psalmist's grateful response that God has brought life back into order, rescuing the psalmist from danger, suffering, or sorrow. Thanksgiving psalms may be either individual (Psalms 18; 32; 40; 66; 118; 138) or corporate (Psalms 65; 67; 107; 136).

Though psalms of praise, lament, and thanksgiving are the most common types of psalms, there are many others as well. *Wisdom psalms*, which contain material similar to the book of Proverbs, are directed not to God but to other human beings, to instruct them in godly living (Psalms 1; 34; 36; 37; 49; 73; 112; 127; 128; 133). *Psalms of remembrance*, also called *salvation-historical psalms*, look back at God's great acts in history, like Israel's deliverance from slavery in Egypt during the exodus or Gideon's great victory over the Midianites (Psalms 78; 105; 106; 135; 136). By remembering, the psalmist gains confidence for the present and hope for the future. *Royal psalms*, composed for court occasions in the Davidic dynasty (the line of kings that followed David), celebrate the king that God has placed on the throne of Israel (Psalms 2; 18; 20; 21; 45; 72; 101; 110; 144). These may also be referred to as *messianic psalms*; though they were originally written with reference to the kings of Israel, they point forward prophetically and typologically to the coming of the Messiah, the great king who would arise from David's line.

Reading the Psalms Today

There are several points we should keep in mind as we read and apply the psalms.

1. *Join in the life experience of the psalmist.* Although these psalms were originally composed by and for the people of ancient Israel, they illustrate the common experiences of the people of God throughout the ages. Christians today go through the same kinds of trials, sorrows, suffering, joy, and delight in God's presence as did the people of God in the past. This helps to explain why the book of Psalms has been so popular throughout church history. We readily see ourselves in the experience of the psalmists, and their songs become ours. This also explains why copies of the Bible that only contain the New Testament often include the Psalms. The book is a helpful companion for our own corporate worship and for individual encouragement.

Of course, this does not take away the need for sound exegesis. We have to understand the experience of the psalmist in order to appropriately join in with a song of praise, lament, or thanksgiving.

2. *Apply the psalms to the purpose for which they were composed.* Throughout this book we have emphasized the need to apply the biblical text in line with the purpose of the original authors. The psalms are no exception. The different types of psalms discussed above provide the key to their application. Since different psalms

were composed for different occasions, we ought to apply them to analogous situations. For example, a psalm of corporate praise is an appropriate psalm for times of corporate worship, as we celebrate God's goodness to us. An individual psalm of lament is helpful to read when we are experiencing sorrow and difficulties. Psalms of wisdom provide us with the foundations for day-to-day living in line with God's purpose in the world. Understanding how these psalms originally functioned helps us to apply them appropriately.

3. *Read and apply each psalm as a whole, rather than taking individual verses out of context.* Related to the previous point, we should take into account not only the genre but also the literary context of each psalm. Although the organization of the book of Psalms is relatively random, so that reading through the book from beginning to end is not a priority, it is essential to recognize that individual psalms tell a story. Laments, for example, tend to follow a similar pattern. They begin with an appeal to God for help and an expression of the psalmist's confidence in the Lord. This is followed by a description of the trials or enemies the author is facing and cries to God for deliverance. The psalm ends with a statement of confidence, praising God for his salvation. It is important to follow the story through, as the psalmist resolves to trust God and affirms God's goodness and mercy.

Consider Psalm 10. It begins with a statement complaining that God seems far away and is hiding himself in times of trouble (v. 1). The wicked prosper even though they reject the Lord, oppress the weak, and exploit the poor (vv. 2–11). If we were to stop here, we would get a very distorted picture of God and his world. The psalm ends, however, with an affirmation that God will judge the wicked (vv. 14–15) and assurance that he is the sovereign king who will come to the aid of the weak:

> The LORD is King for ever and ever;
>> the nations will perish from his land.
> You, LORD, hear the desire of the afflicted;
>> you encourage them, and you listen to their cry,
> defending the fatherless and the oppressed,
>> so that mere earthly mortals will never again strike terror.
> (Ps. 10:16–18)

Only by reading to the end of the "story" will we understand the real message of the psalm.

4. *Recognize that the psalms can represent human words to God, rather than God's words to us.* Keep in mind when applying the psalms that not everything the psalmist says represents an appropriate response or a model for us to follow. The imprecatory lament psalms were mentioned above. Perhaps the most (in)famous of these is Psalm 137:

> Daughter Babylon, doomed to destruction,
>   happy is the one who repays you
>   according to what you have done to us.
> Happy is the one who seizes your infants
>   and dashes them against the rocks. (Ps. 137:8–9)

Smashing infants against rocks is clearly not a loving and merciful thing to do. Passages like this have to be balanced with those that remind us that vengeance is the Lord's (Deut. 32:35) and that we are to love even our enemies (Matt. 5:44). But the psalmist is venting to God his anger toward Babylon, the nation that has destroyed Jerusalem and the temple, slaughtered many in Israel, and taken others into captivity. The psalmist in his fury prays that God justly would do the same to them.

We have to recognize that a passage like this is not God's message to us about an action we should take. It is rather an angry and exasperated cry to God for his justice and vengeance. This does not make this passage any less divinely inspired or any less the Word of God. But the perspective of the psalmist must always be considered before appropriate application can be made. The imprecatory psalms represent an invitation to pour out our pain and sorrow to God. He wants us to be honest with him with our deepest feelings and strongest emotions, so that, through his Spirit, we can work through those feelings and find God's healing and restoration.

Answering the Four Questions for the Psalms

1. *Where is this passage in the larger story of Scripture?* While the Psalms are part of Israel's history and so arise from the context of the old covenant, their nature as prayers and worship provide more

direct relevance to us than other genres in the Old Testament. Old Testament people experienced the same kinds of trials, sorrows, temptations, anxiety, and stress, as well as the same joys, passions, and delight in the Lord, as people today.

2. *What is the author's purpose in light of the passage's genre and historical and literary context?* Two key exegetical questions related to the psalms were noted above. First, what is the type of psalm? Praises and thanksgiving psalms are models for our worship and gratitude toward God. Laments are examples of how we turn to God in times of testing and trials. In our application of the psalms, we should use them in ways that reflect their original purpose. Second, how does the figurative language contribute to the message of the psalm? Recognizing the function of figurative language—things like metaphors, similes, synecdoche, and hyperbole—enables us to determine the author's meaning.

3. *How does this passage inform our understanding of the nature of God and his purpose for the world?* The psalms are replete with teaching about the nature of God and his ways in the world. We learn from the psalms that God is a righteous and just God, who holds the wicked accountable for their actions and meets the needs of his people. We also see graphically illustrated God's purpose for his people: to love God, to worship him, and to live a life of trust and dependence on him through life's most challenging circumstances.

4. *What does this passage teach us about who we ought to be (attitudes and character) and what we ought to do (goals and actions) as those seeking to reflect the nature and purpose of God?* As the psalms celebrate who God is and what he has accomplished for his people in the past, so they illustrate who we ought to be and how we ought to live in relationship to him. In the psalms God's people are seen in worship and in prayer, celebrating his goodness and trusting in him for their daily needs. The application of the psalms arises naturally from their nature.

Old Testament Wisdom Literature

Three books in the Old Testament may be classified as wisdom literature: Proverbs, Job, and Ecclesiastes. A fourth, the Song of Songs (or Song of Solomon) is sometimes placed under this category, but is really a collection of love songs, celebrating the romance between a man and a woman. There is also wisdom teaching dispersed throughout the Bible. As we have seen, a number of psalms are classified as wisdom psalms (Psalms 1; 34; 36; 37; 49; 73; 112; 127; 128; 133) since they provide instruction similar to the book of Proverbs.

Wisdom literature arose in Israel especially during the period of the monarchy (tenth–sixth centuries BC) and continued through the Second Temple period (fifth century BC–first century AD). It has its roots in the royal courts of the ancient Near East, where advisors known as "the wise" (cf. Prov. 22:17) gave counsel and guidance to kings and governors.[20]

The Book of Proverbs

The sayings in the book of Proverbs are mostly attributed to King Solomon (1:1; 10:1; 25:1), but other authors are also named (22:17; 24:23; 30:1; 31:1). The proverbs were likely collated over time, edited, and eventually brought together in the present collection (see 25:1).

The nature and function of Proverbs. The primary purpose of biblical proverbs is to teach *wisdom*. Biblical wisdom, however, is not to be equated with intelligence or a high IQ. It is rather the ability to make good and godly choices, to live a life oriented toward God. The wise person is not someone who is smart or clever, but someone who has learned what it means to know God and serve him faithfully. Proverbs 1:7 sums this up: "The fear of the LORD is the beginning of knowledge, but fools despise wisdom and instruction." The opposite of the wise person is the fool. The fool is not someone who has low mental abilities, but rather someone who lives life in defiance of God and his law. The epitome of the fool is seen in Psalm 14:1: "The fool says in his heart, 'There is no God'" (see also Ps. 53:1). Fools live only for themselves and do not know God or care about his purpose for the world.

The book of Proverbs contains three main types of proverbs. The majority are what we could call *true proverbs*. These state a truth with an implied application. Proverbs 29:23 reads, "Pride brings a person low, but the lowly in spirit gain honor." A truth is stated about the result of pride and the benefit of humility. The implied application is to be humble, because pride results in a fall. *Instructional proverbs* teach more directly, using an imperative or command form. Proverbs 3:7 reads, "Do not be wise in your own eyes; fear the LORD and shun evil." Here the exhortation to humility is explicit. Much of the instructional wisdom in Proverbs is presented as a father giving wise guidance to his child (see, for instance, Prov. 3:21). A third type of proverbial material is the *example story*, which illustrates a truth with an example or mini-story. These can be very short and proverbial, as in Proverbs 29:20: "Do you see someone who speaks in haste? There is more hope for a fool than for them." Or the story can be much longer, like the extended account of a young man being lured into the home of a prostitute, a foolish act that will cost him his life (Prov. 7:6–27; cf. 6:12–15).

Reading Proverbs today. It should be clear from this discussion that as a literary genre, proverbs fit well our heart-of-God hermeneutic. Just as the goal of finding wisdom is to orient one's life toward God's will, so the method discussed in this book is to think God's thoughts after him, to live our story in line with God's story, and to pursue his purposes for the world. Here are some important cautions when applying proverbs to our lives.

1. *Proverbs are general rather than universal truths.* By their nature, proverbs are truths about how things generally happen, rather than expressions of what is always the case. Proverbs 10:4 says, "Lazy hands make for poverty, but diligent hands bring wealth." This is certainly true, but it is not universally true. You might know someone who has not done an honest day's work in their life but is very wealthy because of family money they have inherited. On the other hand, I know a gardener who works harder than anyone I have ever met, putting in long days in the hot sun and accomplishing in a day's work more than I could in a week. Yet he would still be classified as the "working poor." This does not make the proverb any less true, namely, that hard work results in material success. But it is not universally true. Similarly, Proverbs 10:25 says, "When the storm has swept by, the wicked are gone, but the righteous stand firm forever." I know for a fact that many wicked people have gone through storms in life unscathed, while righteous people have suffered catastrophically.

2. *Proverbs are not promises from God or legal guarantees.* Related to the fact that proverbs are general truths is the reality that they are

not promises or guarantees from God. Consider Proverbs 10:27: "The fear of the LORD adds length to life, but the years of the wicked are cut short." We could read this incorrectly as a guarantee from God for long life for those who serve him. But a few weeks prior to writing this chapter I attended the funeral of a courageous young boy of twelve. He loved the Lord and sought to serve him, touching the lives of everyone he came in contact with. But his body eventually succumbed to leukemia. This proverb is a general statement about the blessings that come to those who revere God. It is not a promise or guarantee of long life on earth.

3. *Proverbs do not necessarily represent the whole truth on a subject.* It follows from the two points above that proverbs do not represent the whole story on topics that they cover. A proverb about the righteous weathering life's storms does not take into account that God allows his people to go through difficulties, which build character and increase their trust in him. There are not always simple answers to the question of why bad things happen to God's people (see the discussion of Job below).

The nature of proverbs as incomplete truth is seen in the fact that Proverbs can apparently contradict one another. Consider two English proverbs. "Two's company, three's a crowd" means it is better to be with just one other person than with more. But another proverb, "The more, the merrier," means that it is better to have more people than fewer. Similarly, compare "Too many cooks spoil the broth" to "Many hands make light work." Is it better to have lots of help, or just a little? The answer is that it depends on the situation. In Proverbs 26, verses 4 and 5 stand right next to each other, yet they appear to contradict each other:

> Do not answer a fool according to his folly,
>   or you yourself will be just like him.
> Answer a fool according to his folly,
>   or he will be wise in his own eyes.

So should you answer a fool or not? The answer is, "It depends." In some situations, getting into an argument over something petty is a waste of time, and both parties look foolish. In other cases, however, someone may say something that is clearly wrong and could influence the attitudes and actions of others—a racial slur, or a bit of juicy gossip, or an inappropriate joke. These should not be ignored but must be answered with a word of rebuke or correction. There are times to answer a fool and times not to. Proverbs often address particular situations rather than universal ones.

4. *Proverbs must be interpreted and applied in light of the whole teaching of Scripture.* All of the points above remind us that the general truths taught in Proverbs must be viewed in light of the whole teaching of Scripture. Proverbs about righteous people gaining wealth and security have often been distorted to teach a "wealth and prosperity" gospel, which claims that God will bless materially those who have enough faith. This contradicts many other passages in Scripture where God's people, though faithful, often experience suffering, sorrow, persecution, and poverty (for example, Job 1:1–22; 2 Cor. 11:23–29; 12:10; Phil. 4:11–13; Heb. 11:36–39). Indeed, throughout Scripture wealth and prosperity are seen as potentially dangerous impediments to faith (Mark 10:17–25; Luke 12:16–21; 16:19–31). God's people are called to use whatever resources they have to help others and to accomplish God's kingdom purpose, rather than hoarding it for themselves (Luke 12:31–34; 2 Corinthians 8–9). Treasures stored in heaven will last forever, while those stored on earth will rust away and be eaten by moths (Matt. 6:19–21). Those who focus on material blessings instead of God's purposes in the world will face spiritual disaster. The teaching in Proverbs on material blessings and other subjects must therefore be read through the filter of the whole of biblical truth.

The Book of Job

The book of Job is a different kind of wisdom literature from Proverbs. After a short introductory narrative recounting how God allowed Satan to test Job with severe trials (Job 1–2), the book proceeds with a series of *wisdom dialogues*, or *disputations*, between Job and his friends, who have come to "encourage" him in his troubles. This dialogical style has sometimes been called *speculative wisdom*, since it raises and seeks to answer difficult questions about the nature of God and his ways in the world.

The message of Job. The question that is raised throughout the book of Job is, Why do the righteous suffer? Though apparently living an exemplary life, Job has suffered terribly, losing his wealth, his family, and his health. Three of Job's friends, Bildad, Zophar, and Eliphaz, try to convince him that all that happens to people is a result of their own good or evil actions. Job must therefore have sinned terribly to have brought such disaster upon himself. Job vehemently denies this again and again, claiming his own innocence. A fourth friend, Elihu, speaks up late in the book, rebuking the three friends for their inability to demonstrate Job's guilt and insisting that God must have a greater redemptive purpose for Job's suffering. In the end, God himself speaks (chaps. 38–41), proclaiming his own sovereignty and affirming that his ways are beyond human comprehension. He also rebukes the three and vindicates Job (42:7–9). The book concludes with a narrative describing the restoration of Job's life to an even greater state than before (42:10–17). After all this, the book does not actually answer the question, Why do people suffer? It rather affirms that God is sovereign over all things and that human beings are called to worship him and live in submission to his authority in the world.

Reading Job today. This is a timely message for believers. We will not always understand the reason for personal tragedy or debilitating disease or natural disaster. There is a tendency to seek some higher purpose in these events. I remember hearing someone claim that the devastating Indian Ocean tsunami of 2004, which killed over 200,000 people, was God's judgment against the people of those countries because of their pagan worship, idolatry, and immorality. But what about the Christians who were killed in the disaster? Or what about all those killed by wars or famine or earthquakes or disease around the world? While we can certainly say that all human suffering is a result of living in a fallen world, trying to figure out why some individuals suffer more than others is a precarious task. Instead we have to acknowledge that God's purposes are ultimately unfathomable to the human mind: "'For my thoughts are not your thoughts, neither are your ways my ways,' declares the LORD. 'As the heavens are higher than the earth, so are my ways higher than your ways and my thoughts than your thoughts'" (Isa. 55:8–9). This is ultimately the message of Job—that God is sovereign and we are not. That he is not asking us to figure it all out, but to trust him and live in dependence on him whatever the circumstances. All of our applications drawn from the book need to keep this central theme in mind.

Here are two key points to keep in mind when applying Job.

1. Individual statements must be interpreted in light of the central theme of the book: the sovereignty of God. The central theme is *not* the reason for suffering, and especially not that suffering is always the result of personal sin, as Job's three friends assert. Some of the counsel they give may be sound; some, not so sound. But ultimately the verdict pronounced on them is negative. In the end God himself rebukes them, and they escape judgment only by offering sacrifices to God and by having Job pray for them (42:7–9). Other statements throughout the book are enigmatic and difficult to judge. Is this positive counsel to be heeded, or negative counsel to be avoided? The character of Elihu, for example, is a mystery (chaps. 32–37). Is his counsel accurate, flawed, or some of both? Since Job does not answer Elihu's arguments (as he does the other three visitors), he may accept them as wise counsel. Nor does God rebuke specifically Elihu, only the other three. But Elihu still comes across as an arrogant windbag, not exactly the model of biblical wisdom.[21]

Despite these puzzles, the message of the book as a whole is clear. The climax comes in the closing chapters when God silences both Job and his companions with one of the most stirring declarations of God's sovereignty and omnipotence in the Bible (chaps. 38–41). God does not explain himself or try to justify why he allows the righteous to suffer. Instead, he proclaims his status as creator and sustainer of all things and the sovereign Lord of the universe. We apply Job in today's world by acknowledging this truth and living it out in our daily lives.

2. This primary emphasis on God and his sovereignty raises the secondary question of whether we should find application from Job's own example. Though Job is rebuked for complaining and for not understanding God's sovereign control over all things (38:1), he is still presented as a model to follow. The book begins with a statement of his righteousness (1:1), going so far as to describe him as the most righteous man in the world (1:8). Even when Job loses everything, he refuses to "curse God and die," as his wife counsels (2:9). Instead, he praises God and accepts that God has every right to both give and take away: "The LORD gave and the LORD has taken

away; may the name of the L ORD be praised" (1:21). The repeated refrain is that despite his suffering, Job "did not sin" against God (1:22; 2:10). The end of the book vindicates Job (42:7), and God blesses him with more land, property, and children than he had before (42:10–17). Three things about Job are worth emulating. First, he is a righteous person whose desire is to love and serve God (1:1, 8). Second, Job affirms that the chief aim of humanity is to worship and praise God whatever the circumstances (1:21–22; 2:10). Third, when God rebukes Job, he acknowledges the truth of God's word and repents "in dust and ashes" (42:6). A rock-solid faith and the readiness to repent of sin are keys to faithfully serving God.

The Book of Ecclesiastes

If Job is an example of speculative wisdom in a dialogue format, Ecclesiastes is speculative wisdom presented as a *monologue*. The basic theme of the book is the meaninglessness and futility of life apart from God. A key word that appears throughout the book is the Hebrew word *hebel* ("breath," "mist," "vapor") which is variously translated as "vanity" (KJV), "meaningless" (NIV; NLT), "futility" (NJB; HCSB), "pointless" (GW), "useless" (GNT), or even "enigmatic."[22] The speaker, who identifies himself as Qoheleth, or the "Teacher," describes all human strivings "under the sun" as *hebel*. Apart from God, there is no meaning in life.

The message of Ecclesiastes. Ecclesiastes is one of the most challenging books in the Bible because of its odd mix of themes and seemingly conflicting messages. On the one hand, the book seems to affirm that, in light of the shortness of life and reality of death, the best thing you can do is enjoy life to its fullest under God's heaven. On the other hand, the book points to the futility of all pursuits in life since everything is meaningless. These apparently contradictory messages have resulted in two distinct approaches to the book. The optimistic view is that the book teaches the *right way to live* in light of the inevitability of death. Since all human strivings are meaningless in themselves, the best you can do is follow wisdom's way and enjoy life as a gift from God (2:24; 3:13). The pessimistic interpretation is that the whole book in fact represents *the wrong way to live* and is meant to be a foil for the rest of the Bible. In the pessimistic view, the last part of the book provides an answer and correction to the rest. At the end the Teacher says, "Remember your Creator in the days of your youth" (12:1), and "Now all has been heard; here is the conclusion of the matter: Fear God and keep his commandments, for this is the duty of all mankind" (12:13).

Reading Ecclesiastes today. Here are three principles to keep in mind when interpreting and applying Ecclesiastes.

1. First, whether you take the optimistic or pessimistic approach, the central theme of the book is *the meaninglessness of life apart from God*. All else that the book teaches, whether good or bad, needs to be interpreted in light of this point.

2. Second, like Job, but unlike Proverbs, the book needs to be interpreted and applied *as a whole* rather than by pulling individual sayings out of context. This is not just a collection of wisdom sayings but a monologue about the meaning of life and how to live in response to this.

3. Third, as with Proverbs, individual statements should not be viewed as the "last word" on a particular topic but may be qualified elsewhere in the book or in the rest of the Bible. For example, the repeated refrain in the book, "everything is meaningless," must be qualified whether you take the optimistic or pessimistic view. In the optimistic view, the refrain is qualified within the book itself by the counsel to enjoy life and acknowledge God's sovereignty. In the pessimistic view, the refrain is qualified by the teaching of the Bible as a whole that there is indeed ultimate meaning in life because of the reality of God as a just and impartial judge.

Answering the Four Questions for Wisdom Literature

Wisdom literature is particularly appropriate for the heart-of-God hermeneutic, because the purpose of wisdom is to shape our lives in line with God's nature and purpose for the world. The whole Bible, therefore, could be viewed as a message of wisdom. The Bible's many genres—stories, songs, laws, letters, prophecies, and parables—all guide us in living as God's people in the world.

Here we will apply our four key questions to the wisdom genres.

1. *Where is wisdom literature in the larger story of Scripture?* As noted above, wisdom literature has its roots in the period of the

monarchy in Israel (tenth–sixth centuries BC). Yet the nature of wisdom literature as general truth for godly living renders this first question less important than it is for other genres. For example, while the Old Testament law must be interpreted and applied in the context of Israel's covenant at Mount Sinai and in light of the law's fulfillment in the new covenant, wisdom literature is more generally relevant for all people everywhere. This does not mean, however, that exegesis is unimportant for wisdom literature, as our second question reminds us.

2. *What is the author's purpose in light of the passage's genre and historical and literary context?* In wisdom literature the exegetical questions of meaning and purpose are tied more closely to *genre* than to historical and literary context. In other words, we do not need to know precisely when Job was written or the historical context and situation of the author in order to determine the book's meaning and purpose. On the other hand, understanding how the genre of a proverb, disputation, or wisdom monologue works is crucial for correct application. As we have seen, a proverb should not be understood as a universal truth or a promise of what must happen or a legal guarantee from God. Similarly, a disputation like that in Job includes both good and bad counsel. Just because the words of Job's friends appear in the Bible does not make them godly counsel. The same is true of Ecclesiastes. The declaration of the meaninglessness of everything under the sun is the resigned view of the Teacher, not a God's-eye view. Understanding the nature and function of these genres is crucial for accurately interpreting and applying them.

While genre is the most critical element in exegeting wisdom literature, understanding the *historical context* can also be important for accurate interpretation and appropriate application. For example, Proverbs 21:9, "Better to live on a corner of the roof than share a house with a quarrelsome wife," seems very strange unless we recognize that Middle Eastern roofs were flat and used as living space. In a culture of tiled or shingled inclined roofs, the equivalent might be something like, "Better to live in an attic . . . ," or, as Eugene Peterson's *Message* reads, "Better to live alone in a tumbledown shack than share a mansion with a nagging spouse."[23]

3. How does this passage inform our understanding of the nature of God and his purpose for the world? Proverbs tend to focus on human actions and attitudes rather than on God's nature and purpose. We might say that for the book of Proverbs, questions 3 and 4 should be reversed. We ask first what the proverb teaches us about who we ought to be and how we ought to live, and then ask what this teaches us about the nature and purpose of God. Some proverbs, however, do describe something about the nature of God, and our application follows from this. For example, Proverbs 11:1 reads, "The LORD detests dishonest scales, but accurate weights find favor with him." Here we learn that God is a God of justice and righteousness and that he is pleased with those who practice honest and fair business dealings.

In contrast to the Proverbs, the speculative wisdom of Job tells us a great deal about God's nature. God's speech in Job 38–41 is one of the great sections in the Bible on the sovereignty and majesty of the creator God. God's sovereign control over all things is also a major theme in Ecclesiastes, though sometimes with the cynical response, "If God controls everything, why bother doing anything?"

4. What does this passage teach us about who we ought to be (attitudes and character) and what we ought to do (goals and actions) as those seeking to reflect the nature and purpose of God? This fourth question flows naturally, and usually easily, from the wisdom literature. Proverbs teaches that we ought to be upright, honest, loving, giving, and self-sacrificial. We need to avoid greed, selfishness, dishonesty, injustice, cruelty, and oppression. We do all this because God is a loving, righteous, giving, and self-sacrificial God.

Conclusion

This chapter has applied the heart-of-God hermeneutic to the five main Old Testament genres: narrative, law, prophecy, poetry, and wisdom literature. Whatever the nature and function of the literature, in each case we learn much about God's nature and purpose for the world. This in turn allows us to make good and godly decisions in life and to live as the people of God. In the following chapter, we will turn to the main New Testament genres.

Discussion and Reflection Questions

1. What are the two main purposes of Old Testament narratives? At what three levels do Old Testament narratives function?

2. What does it mean to take a paradigmatic approach to applying the Old Testament law?

3. With reference to the Prophets, what is the difference between foretelling and forthtelling? What are some qualifications the "fulfillment" of Old Testament prophecies?

4. What are the main types of the psalms, and how were they used in Israel's religious life? How should they be used in ours?

5. What is the purpose of biblical proverbs? Are proverbs universal truths, guarantees, or promises from God? If not, what are they?

6. What is the central message of Job? What do we learn about God and the reason for human suffering in the book?

7. Why is wisdom literature particularly appropriate for a heart-of-God hermeneutic?

7

Finding the Heart of God in the Diverse Genres of the New Testament

ABIZARRE STORY APPEARED IN THE NEWS AFTER THE DEATH of billionaire tycoon Howard Hughes in April 1976. A hand-written will had been discovered, signed by the eccentric recluse and expressing his desire to leave one-sixteenth of his estate—156 million dollars!—to the Mormon Church and another 156 million to a man named "Melvin DuMar." Dummar (the actual spelling of his last name) turned out to be a service station attendant who claimed he had discovered Hughes wandering in the Nevada desert in 1967 and saved his life, dropping him off at a Las Vegas hotel. The remarkable story electrified the nation. But after a series of court battles, in 1978 a Las Vegas jury declared the will to be a forgery. The controversy continues, however, with some still claiming that the will was authentic.[1]

Here is an example of the importance of genre identification. Was the will a clever ruse to bilk the Hughes estate out of millions of dollars? Or was it an authentic expression of the desires of the eccentric billionaire? Identifying the purpose of the document and the intention of the author (whether Hughes or a forger) makes all the difference in the world. All of us do "genre identification" every day. Someone watching an Oliver Stone movie, like *JFK* (1991) or *Nixon* (1995), for example, must decide what they are watching. Is this an attempt to accurately portray historical events based on hard evidence? Or is it fanciful embellishment arising from the creative imagination of the writer and director? Making this genre decision will determine how you watch the film and what sort of truth you discern in it.

The last chapter discussed various Old Testament genres and guidelines for reading, interpreting, and applying the Old Testament text. Genre identification is equally essential in the New Testament. This chapter will survey the four main New Testament genres: the four Gospels, the book of Acts, the Epistles, and the book of Revelation. As with Old Testament genres, each of these has unique features and unique principles that guide their interpretation and application.

The Four Gospels

The New Testament Gospels—Matthew, Mark, Luke, and John—provide four unique perspectives on the life and ministry of Jesus Christ. Together they give us a fuller, more multifaceted portrait of who Jesus is and what he has accomplished.[2]

The Nature and Function of the Gospels

The word "gospel" comes from the Anglo-Saxon word *godspel*, which means "good news." It is a translation of the Greek word *euangelion*, which is used in the New Testament to refer to the "good news" of the salvation provided through the life, death, and resurrection of Jesus Christ. While *euangelion* originally referred to the oral message about Jesus preached by the apostles (1 Thess. 1:5), it came to be applied to the four written accounts of that message. This tells us something about the nature of the Gospels. These are not merely historical reports or biographies of a great person. They are, rather, written versions of the public preaching that God's long-awaited salvation has arrived through the life, death, and resurrection

158

of Jesus Christ. The Gospel writers are sometimes called Evangelists because their purpose is to announce the good news—the *euangelion*—of God's salvation.

The Synoptic Gospels and the Gospel of John. The first three Gospels—Matthew, Mark, and Luke—are known as the Synoptic Gospels. The word "synoptic" means "viewed together" and applies to these three because they follow a similar outline of Jesus's life and tell many of the same stories, sometimes with nearly exact verbal agreement. Scholars debate the relationship between these three Gospels and whether they borrowed material from one another. The most widely held view is that Mark wrote his Gospel first, and that Matthew and Luke used Mark and various other sources to compose their works. All of the Gospel writers drew from the large body of oral and written material being passed down by the followers of Jesus.

John, the Fourth Gospel, offers a unique perspective in terms of its content, themes, and structure. Only a few of the stories from the Synoptics appear in John. While 90 percent of the content of Mark's Gospel appears in similar form in Matthew or Luke, less than 10 percent of this material appears in John. The nature of John's content is also different. The Synoptics tend to contain short, semi-independent vignettes, or mini-stories (in the singular, known as a *pericope* [pronounced "períkopē"]) and Jesus teaches mostly in parables and short sayings (aphorisms). John tends to contain longer conversations, dialogues, and debates, especially between Jesus and the religious leaders. John's themes are also different. The Synoptics stress Jesus's preaching about the kingdom of God and the need to repent and believe the good news. In John, Jesus speaks more about knowing God and attaining eternal life, identifying himself as the unique Son of God who reveals the Father. The reason for these differences is related to both time and circumstances. John probably wrote late in the first century, when the church faced new challenges and new opponents. The primary stress in the Synoptics is that Jesus is the Jewish Messiah, who has been vindicated by God through his resurrection. In John the church is facing challenges from false teachers who deny the real humanity and true deity of Jesus Christ. John stresses that Jesus is both fully human and fully divine (John 1:1, 14, 18), the one true way to the Father (14:6).

Why four Gospels? Diverse communities, diverse purposes. This brings up an important point about the Gospels and the answer to the question, Why four Gospels instead of one? The answer is that each of the four was written to a different community within the early church and was meant to address the unique needs, concerns, and challenges facing that community. This does not mean that the Gospel writers did not also envision larger audiences, expecting their works to be copied and passed on to other communities.[3] But, as with all books of the Bible, each Gospel was written within a particular historical and cultural situation to address certain issues and meet certain needs.

Matthew, for example, was likely written to a predominantly Jewish-Christian community or communities and was meant to assure these believers that Jesus was indeed the Messiah who had fulfilled the promises made to Israel in the Old Testament. Mark's Gospel was written to a persecuted church (or churches), perhaps in Rome, and was intended to encourage them to persevere and stay faithful to Jesus in the face of severe suffering and even death. Mark's readers are called to follow the suffering path of the Servant-Messiah, who called on his disciples to "take up their cross" and follow him (Mark 8:34). Luke was likely written to a mixed or predominantly Gentile community. It was intended to confirm that the message of salvation was for all people everywhere, whatever their race, gender, economic status, or social and cultural background. In this regard Luke's Gospel is the most inclusive of the four, confirming that the message of salvation that began in Israel is now going out to all people. Somewhat later in the first century, John's Gospel was written to believers who were experiencing increasing alienation from their Jewish roots and increasing hostility from society at large. John assures them that they have found the truth in the One who is the way, the truth, and the life.

The gospel genre: History, narrative, and theology. In terms of their genre, the Gospels may be characterized as *historical narrative motivated by theological concerns*.[4] They are historical in that they are meant to pass on reliable information about Jesus Christ. Consider the prologue to Luke's Gospel:

> Many have undertaken to draw up an account of the things that have been fulfilled among us, just as they were handed down to us by those

160

who from the first were eyewitnesses and servants of the word. With this in mind, since I myself have carefully investigated everything from the beginning, I too decided to write an orderly account for you, most excellent Theophilus, so that you may know the certainty of the things you have been taught. (Luke 1:1–4)

Notice the piling up of historical terms: "eyewitnesses," "carefully investigated," "orderly account," "know the certainty." There is no doubt that Luke was striving to pass on accurate historical information about the events of Jesus's ministry. This does not mean that the Gospel narratives necessarily follow a strict chronological order or produce verbatim accounts of Jesus's words. Much of the material is ordered topically, and the Gospel writers sometimes summarize, paraphrase, and interpret the significance of Jesus's words. Yet their goal is to produce a trustworthy account of Jesus's words and actions.

Though historical, the Gospels are not simply lists of historical facts, but are historical *narrative*, history told as story. As described in chapter 3, all stories have certain features, including characters, settings, and plot. Properly interpreting the Gospels means acknowledging each of these features. It means carefully following the *plot* of the story from beginning to end, through introduction, conflict, crisis, and resolution. It means seeking to understand the nature and function of the *characters* in the story, characters like Jesus himself, the disciples, the religious leaders, the crowds, and even Satan and his demons. It means determining the importance of various settings in the Gospels. These settings can include regions, such as Galilee, Samaria, or Judea. They can be towns and cities, like Capernaum, Jesus's base of operations while in Galilee, or Jerusalem, his ultimate destination. They can be geographical features, like mountains, as when Jesus gives his famous inaugural Sermon on the Mount (Matthew 5–7) or when his appearance is changed on the Mount of Transfiguration (Matt. 17:1–8).

Such settings are not just backdrops for the events of the story; they also carry theological and symbolic significance. Samaria, for example, is a place where one would expect conflict and hatred, since the Jews and the Samaritans hated one another. Instead, in John 4 Jesus finds a welcoming audience in Samaria and a positive response to the gospel. We find here hints that the gospel will break down barriers of ethnic and racial hatred between peoples (see also Acts 8). Mountaintops are places of divine revelation in the Old Testament, as God reveals himself to Moses and gives his law to the Israelites on Mount Sinai. It is significant, therefore, that Jesus reveals a radical new take on the law at the Mount of Beatitudes (Matt. 5:17, 21, 27, 31, 33, 38, 43) and reveals his true identity on the Mount of Transfiguration (Matt. 17:2). Reading the Gospels as story keeps us attentive to these kinds of narrative and theological features.

Not only are the Gospels history and narrative, they are also *theology*. This means they are not simply unbiased or "neutral" accounts about Jesus; they were rather written for a purpose: to proclaim the message of the salvation accomplished through the life, death, and resurrection of Jesus the Messiah. This purpose is clear in the prologue to Luke's Gospel. Luke writes to Theophilus "so that you may know the certainty of the things you have been taught" (Luke 1:4). Similarly, John writes his Gospel "that you may believe that Jesus is the Messiah, the Son of God, and that by believing you may have life in his name" (John 20:31). The goal of all four Gospel writers was to confirm the truth of what Jesus said and did, to strengthen the faith of his followers, and to call others to faith in him.

Some people have claimed that acknowledging this theological nature of the Gospels necessarily compromises their historical accuracy. The Gospel writers are surely biased and so cannot be writing accurate history. But this is flawed reasoning. Nobody writes history free of bias. Everyone has a worldview and a perspective concerning the existence of God and the nature of reality. The question therefore becomes not whether the Gospel writers have a viewpoint (everyone does), but whether their historical reports are accurate and reliable. A discussion of the reliability of the Gospels is beyond the scope of this book, and we would simply point to significant works like Craig Blomberg's *Historical Reliability of the Gospels*,[5] and the recent Institute for Biblical Research historical Jesus project, *Key Events in the Life of the Historical Jesus*.[6] Here we simply assert that there is no necessary contradiction in the claim that a document is both theologically motivated and historically accurate. Indeed, one of the great passions of the Gospel writers is to affirm the *truth* of the events they are describing. One would think that those most passionate about truth would be careful to get it right.

Reading the Gospels Today

In light of the nature and function of the Gospels, here are important guidelines for reading and applying them today.

1. *Read the Gospels "vertically" (downward through each story), rather than harmonistically (merging them into a single story).* There has been a common tendency in the past, especially among conservative Christians, to try to produce a chronologically accurate account of Jesus's ministry by reordering and combining the four Gospels into a single "life of Christ" or "harmony of the Gospels." There are three problems with this cut-and-paste approach. First, such reconstructions are hypothetical and are unlikely to produce reliable results. The Gospel writers often structure their material topically rather than chronologically. Second, and more important, the four Gospels are literary masterpieces. Each Gospel tells its own story in a particular way to bring out certain aspects of Jesus's life and ministry. Cutting up the Gospels and reordering them risks losing each author's unique style, themes, and theological contributions. Third, and even more important, the Holy Spirit gave the church four distinct Gospels. He could have given just one. Reordering and rearranging the Gospels is taking God's inspired and authoritative Word and turning it into something else. To hear the Holy Spirit speak we ought to listen to each story as it was given rather than rearranging them together into a new story. This idea of reading each of the Gospels from beginning to end has sometimes been called reading vertically, which means reading downward through the text from introduction, to crisis, to climax, and finally to resolution.

Reading the Gospels vertically also encourages the student to read each passage in its appropriate literary context. The Gospel writers ordered their narratives in a particular way to bring out their unique themes and theology. For example, after a brief introduction, Mark's Gospel presents a series of episodes that demonstrate Jesus's authority—authority in calling disciples, in teaching, in healing, and in exorcisms (1:14–2:12). This is followed by a series of controversy stories, where the religious leaders challenge Jesus's authority

(2:1–3:6). The episode of the healing of a paralyzed man (2:1–12) comes in the middle and forms a transition between these two sections, functioning as both a healing (2:9) and a controversy story (2:6–7). The account also provides the framework for understanding Jesus's miracles, since it connects his authority to heal with his authority to forgive sins (2:10). Mark is teaching his readers that the salvation Jesus is bringing provides forgiveness of sins and, through this, the restoration of a fallen world. Reading vertically means interpreting each Gospel episode in the flow of the narrative to discern its purpose in the larger story.

2. *Compare the Gospels "horizontally" to determine their unique perspectives.* While a harmonistic approach to the Gospels should generally be avoided, it is helpful to compare the four Gospels with one another by reading them horizontally (across the page). A synopsis of the Gospels is a book that places the four Gospels in parallel columns.[7] The goal of a synopsis is not to produce a single story (a harmony), but rather to compare their accounts to determine each Gospel's unique perspectives and theological themes. Since Matthew, Mark, and Luke have so many common stories, examining them side by side can teach us about each author's unique purpose in writing.

Consider, for example, the account of the temptation of Jesus in Matthew and in Luke. In Matthew 4:1–11, Satan tempts Jesus in this order: (a) temptation to turn stones into bread; (b) temptation on the pinnacle of the temple to test God's ability to save him; and (c) temptation on a high mountain, where Satan offers Jesus the kingdoms of the world in exchange for his worship. Luke 4:1–13 has the same basic account, but the order of the last two temptations is reversed, with the final temptation taking place at the temple in Jerusalem. The climax in Matthew is significant for his Gospel, where mountains are places of divine revelation (Matt. 5:1; 17:1; 28:16). The climax in Luke is equally significant for his Gospel, since Jerusalem and the temple play a pivotal role in both Luke and Acts (e.g., Luke 1:9; 9:31, 51; 13:34–35; 24:53; Acts 1:4–8). By comparing the two accounts side by side (reading them horizontally), we can see each author's unique theological contributions.

3. *Recognize the Gospels' two levels of historical context.* All narratives have two levels of context, the context of the events of the story and the context of the authors and original readers. For

example, J. R. R. Tolkien's classic fantasy series, *The Lord of the Rings*, take place in the mythical world of Middle Earth. Understanding the story means learning about hobbits, elves, dwarfs, Orcs, and a variety of other mythical creatures and places. It also helps, however, to understand Tolkien's background as a professor of Anglo-Saxon at Oxford University, his Roman Catholic background, and his longtime friendship with people like C. S. Lewis and the members of literary society known as the Inklings. These influences provide insight into the nature and significance of Tolkien's work.

The Gospels, though historical rather than mythical, also reflect two contexts, the context of the events of the story and the context of the author and the original readers. The events described in the Gospels took place around AD 30 in Palestine under Roman rule. Interpreting them accurately means learning about the world of first-century Judaism, including things like geographical locations (Galilee, Judea, Samaria, Jerusalem, etc.); religious groups and institutions (Pharisees, scribes, temple, synagogue, Sanhedrin, etc.); governmental rulers (Tiberius Caesar, Herod Antipas, Pontius Pilate, etc.); and political, social, and cultural settings (patron/client relationships, honor/shame society, patriarchal households, etc.). This kind of background material is readily available in a variety of sources: books on New Testament background, commentaries on the Gospels, and Bible encyclopedias, and more briefly in study Bibles, Bible handbooks, and Bible dictionaries.

While they describe the events of Jesus's day, the Gospels were written twenty-five to sixty years later to Christian churches scattered throughout the Roman Empire.[8] Interpreting and applying them in a modern context means taking into account the original context as well. For example, to understand Mark's Gospel it is necessary to understand the world in which Jesus lived, and specifically the historical places and persons mentioned above. Yet we must also recognize that Mark is writing decades later to a church that is likely suffering under severe persecution. When Jesus tells his disciples that they must deny themselves, take up their cross, and follow him (Mark 8:34), Mark uses this exhortation to encourage his readers to persevere and press ahead despite the prospect of suffering and even death. As noted above, the Gospels are not just "the bare facts" about the life and times of Jesus; they are announcements of the good news and exhortations to God's people to respond in faith to what God is doing in the world.

Answering the Four Questions for the Gospels

With these points in mind, we can turn to our four questions for drawing appropriate application from the Gospels.

1. *Where are the Gospels in the larger story of Scripture?* In the grand drama of Scripture, the coming of Jesus represents the middle point of salvation history.[9] The Old Testament repeatedly points forward to the promise that God will one day send a Savior, who will bring restoration and renewal to a fallen creation (Isa. 9:1–7; 11:1–16). The Gospels tell the story of the coming of the Messiah, the initial fulfillment of that promise, and point forward to its final fulfillment at the second coming of Christ.

The place of the Gospels in the biblical story is closely related to the central theme of Jesus's preaching: *the kingdom of God.* When Jesus begins his public ministry, he announces, "The time has come. . . . The kingdom of God has come near. Repent and believe the good news!" (Mark 1:15; cf. Matt. 4:17; Luke 4:43; John 3:3, 5). The "time" that has come is the center point of human history, the fulfillment of God's promise of salvation (Gal. 4:4).

Much debate has focused on the nature of the phrase "the kingdom of God." Does it refer to God's universal and eternal reign, or a temporal kingdom in space and time? Is it a physical realm or a spiritual reign? Is it present or future? The answer to all of these questions is yes. God's kingdom is both a reign and a realm, both present and future. The kingdom refers first of all to God's authority as the king of the universe. He is the sovereign Lord over all: "Your kingdom is an everlasting kingdom, and your dominion endures through all generations" (Ps. 145:13). Yet since the fall of Adam and Eve, human beings have been in revolt against God's authority, resulting in their slavery to sin, suffering, and death. Throughout the Old Testament God promises to one day reestablish his sovereign reign and restore all things to himself: "The Lord will be king over the whole earth. On that day there will be one Lord, and his name the only name" (Zech. 14:9).

While the Jews expected the kingdom to come with the restoration of creation at the end of time, Jesus announced that through his own words and actions, God's kingdom was already breaking into human history. From the perspective of the New Testament writers, the life, death, and resurrection of Jesus Christ represent the *inauguration* of the kingdom of God. His second coming represents its *consummation*. The kingdom is both already and not yet. It is already present in the accomplishment of salvation through Christ's death and resurrection. It is still future in the consummation of that salvation with the coming of a new heaven and a new earth (Isa. 65:17; Revelation 21–22).

Appropriately interpreting and applying the Gospels means recognizing this already/not yet nature of the kingdom. It also means acknowledging the transitional nature of the period of Jesus's ministry. As we have seen, Jesus at one point tells his disciples to preach the gospel only to the people of Israel, not to Gentiles or Samaritans (Matt. 10:5). He also tells a Gentile woman that he was sent "only to the lost sheep of Israel" and (at first) refuses to heal her daughter (Matt. 15:24). If we were to apply these commands directly now, we would have to share the gospel only with Jews. Yet when we view this from the perspective of the New Testament as a whole, we recognize that Jesus is here gathering a remnant from within Israel, which he will then send out to preach to all nations (Matt. 28:18–20).

There are other examples of the transitional nature of this period. Jesus describes his followers as offering sacrifices at the temple (Matt. 5:23) and commands a man healed of leprosy to follow the purification rituals and offer the sacrifices stipulated by the Old Testament law (Matt. 8:4; Mark 1:44; Luke 5:14). Since Christ's death ended the sacrificial system, these commands are clearly not for the present-day church. Passages like these remind us that Jesus's ministry was a transitional period, when salvation was being announced but had not yet been accomplished.

2. What is the author's purpose in light of the gospel genre and the historical and literary context of the passage? As with all the Bible's genres, application of the Gospels begins with sound exegesis. For the Gospels this means understanding the general historical context, the life and times of Jesus of Nazareth. Recognizing that the Jews had been under the authority of the Roman Empire for ninety years at the time of Jesus's ministry helps us to understand the people's intense hope and expectation that John the Baptist might possibly be the Messiah who would free them from foreign oppression (Luke 3:15). Understanding the loathing that the people had for their Gentile overlords elucidates the rage of the Nazareth townspeople when Jesus declares God's love and concern even for Gentiles (Luke 4:25–29). Knowing the history of enmity between Samaritans and Jews shows how shocking a parable like the "good" Samaritan would have sounded to Jesus's contemporaries. Before we can appropriately apply a text from the Gospels we have to discern how it would have been heard by Jesus's hearers and what the Gospel writers were trying to communicate through it.

Social and cultural background is also important for sound exegesis. For example, at one point Jesus tells his disciples to stop preventing the children from coming to him because "the kingdom of God belongs to such as these." He then adds, "Truly I tell you, anyone who will not receive the kingdom of God like a little child will never enter it" (Luke 18:15–17). Today we might think that children are worthy of the kingdom because they are pure or innocent, not having learned the evil ways of the world. But in the first century children were not viewed as pure or innocent. They were viewed as insignificant, irrelevant, and totally dependent on adults. Jesus's point is that the only way to enter the kingdom of God is by acknowledging our insufficiency and total dependence on God. Without understanding the social and cultural world of the first century, we could misapply this passage. Exegesis is essential for sound application.

3. *How does this passage inform our understanding of the nature of God and his purpose for the world?* Like the rest of the Bible, the Gospels constantly point to God's nature and his purpose for the world. This is true of all of the passages discussed above. Jesus's teaching about the kingdom of God reminds us that God has not forgotten his wayward people but has a plan to bring them back into a right relationship with him. The parable of the Good Samaritan teaches that God loves all people, whatever their race or ethnicity, and expects his people to practice this same self-sacrificial love for enemies and outsiders. Jesus's teaching about children reminds us that there is nothing we can do to save ourselves, and that we live in absolute dependence on God our Father. The Great Commission to make disciples of all nations (Matt. 28:18–20) confirms that

God's purpose in the world is to bring humanity back into a right relationship with him.

4. *What does this passage teach us about who we ought to be (attitudes and character) and what we ought to do (goals and actions) as those seeking to reflect the nature and purpose of God?* Not everything Jesus says in the Gospels necessarily applies directly to the church today. When Jesus sent his disciples out to preach the gospel and told them not to take a bag for their journey, or an extra shirt, or sandals, or a staff (Matt. 10:9–10), he was not establishing missionary guidelines for all time. Those commands were given to his disciples for their particular journey. So while not everything Jesus says in the Gospels is a command to us, everything we learn about God and his purpose has application for us. God's love for his enemies reminds us that we too must love our enemies, whether that means the person who just cut us off on the freeway, the hostile boss who constantly berates us, or the Muslim family that has just moved in across the street. When Jesus teaches his disciples that they must become like children to enter the kingdom of God, we recognize that God is our heavenly Father who wants us to live in dependence on him for our every need. Jesus's Great Commission, although given to his twelve disciples, applies to us as well since Jesus is not just giving his disciples particular instructions for this journey (as in Matt. 10:9–10), but is outlining God's purpose and plan to bring people of every nation back into a right relationship with him. As heirs of this apostolic tradition and the people of God in the present age, our commission is the same as their commission.

We can illustrate the application process for the Gospels with a text that is puzzling for many people, the account of the rich ruler in Luke 18:18–30 (cf. Matt. 19:16–29; Mark 10:17–30). When a man approaches Jesus and asks what he must do to inherit eternal life, Jesus first gives the traditional Jewish answer: keep the commandments. The man responds that he has done this since he was a boy. Jesus then says that he lacks one thing. He must sell everything he has, give the money to the poor, and come follow Jesus. This is a shocking passage. Is Jesus saying that salvation comes from selling our things and giving the money to the poor? Is this something all believers are commanded to do?

As with all commands in the Bible, this one has a specific context. It was given to this man in his particular situation. It was not given to us. This does not get us off the hook, so that we can breathe a sigh of relief and say, "Thank goodness I don't have to sell all my stuff!" Though this command was not given to us, it is *for us*. The question is how to apply it. It cannot be that God is commanding all believers to sell their possessions and give the money to the poor. This is taught nowhere else in Scripture. God did not tell Abraham to sell his possessions, nor does the Old Testament law command such action of the Israelites. Similarly, in the New Testament we see believers retaining their possessions and still serving God faithfully. Barnabas, for example, voluntarily sells some property and gives the proceeds to the poor (Acts 4:36–37), but he does not sell everything he owns.

Instead of either directly obeying this command or simply disregarding it (as most do), we have to ask our key questions: What does this passage teach us about the nature and purpose of God? How should we live in response to this? In this context, the rich man's wealth has become his god, the thing that is keeping him from complete surrender to God. Throughout Scripture we learn that God is our sovereign Lord, who demands not just part of our life but our whole life. Salvation comes by putting our faith in him instead of in ourselves. This does not mean just being *willing* to give up everything but actually giving up all to follow him. For most believers, this probably won't mean selling everything and giving it to the poor. But it does mean living in such a way that *all* of our resources—whether time, treasures, or talents—are used for his purposes.

Anything that takes the place of God in our lives is an impediment to eternal life. Jesus says as much in the last part of this passage. When he points out that it is easier for a camel to go through the eye of a needle than for a rich man to enter the kingdom of God, the people express shock and dismay, asking, "Who then can be saved?" Jesus responds, "What is impossible with man is possible with God" (Luke 18:24–27). Salvation comes when we cease striving in our own power and with our own resources and put our trust in God. This application will take different forms for different people. For some whose wealth has become their god, it could mean selling everything and giving it to the poor. For others, it may mean giving up their pride and submitting to God's authority in their lives. For still others, it may mean getting out of a destructive relationship that is keeping them from obeying God. Though Jesus's command here may have been given to this particular man, it has relevance for all Christians everywhere, since it teaches us about the nature of God and his purpose for his people.

If, after reading this section, you breathed a sigh of relief that you don't have to sell everything you own, then you have missed the point of the passage. You need to go back and practice a bit of *lectio divina* (see chap. 5) by listening more intently to God speak. Properly applying this text means entering into the story, feeling the same rapid heartbeat and shock and dismay that this man felt at Jesus's words, examining your life to see what parts you haven't given to God for his service, and then taking steps to do just that. Applying Scripture doesn't mean just affirming the principles it teaches; it means being transformed and renewed by living out the story in our daily lives.

The Book of Acts

The book of Acts, like the Gospels, is historical narrative, so the same basic rules for interpreting and applying narratives apply to Acts. The book has unique features and a unique role in Scripture, however, so it is treated separately here.

The Nature and Purpose of Acts

Acts continues the story that began in the Gospels, relating how Jesus's followers spread the good news of salvation from Jerusalem to Rome and beyond. The book covers a period of about thirty years, from around AD 30 to AD 60, beginning with Jesus's postresurrection appearances to his disciples (1:1–8) and concluding with Paul's imprisonment in Rome (28:11–31).

The unity of Luke and Acts (Luke–Acts). Acts was written by the same author as the Gospel of Luke and therefore shares a similar style of writing and many of the same themes. Church tradition tells us that the author was Luke, a physician and missionary partner of the apostle Paul (Col. 4:7–17; Philem. 23, 24). At several places in the narrative of Acts, the author stops speaking about Paul and his companions in the third person ("he"; "they") and uses the first-person plural ("we"), confirming that he was traveling with Paul at this time (16:10–17; 20:5–21; 21:1–18; 27:1–28:16).

Church tradition claims that Luke was a converted Gentile. This is also suggested by Paul, who lists Luke as one of his non-Jewish associates (Col. 4:11, 14). Luke's detailed acquaintance with the Old Testament and Judaism may suggest that prior to becoming a follower of Christ he was a God-fearer, that is, a Gentile who worshiped the God of Israel but who had not undergone full conversion to Judaism. This helps to explain Luke's strong interest throughout Acts in confirming that the message of salvation that began in Israel is now going forth to all nations everywhere.

Scholars view Luke and Acts not simply as two books by the same author but as two volumes of a single work, commonly referred to as Luke–Acts. At the beginning of Acts, the author refers back to his "former book," which relates "all that Jesus began to do and to teach" (1:1). While the Gospel of Luke records what Jesus *began to do* through his life, death, and resurrection, Acts records what he *continues to do* as the risen Lord of the church through the Holy Spirit he sends to guide and empower his followers (2:33).

Both the Gospel of Luke and Acts are addressed to a certain individual named Theophilus (Luke 1:3; Acts 1:1). This name means "one who loves God," and some have suggested that Luke was writing to all those who are seeking God, or perhaps to all Christians everywhere. More likely, Theophilus was an individual, perhaps the patron who sponsored the writing of the two books. Since Luke addresses him as "most excellent" (Greek: *kratiste*) Theophilus (Luke 1:3), he was likely a Gentile of high social status.

Central purpose and theme. If Luke and Acts are a single, two-volume work, then they share the same overall purpose. Luke sets out this purpose in the prologue of the Gospel (Luke 1:1–4). Having researched the events thoroughly, he is writing an "orderly" and "accurate" account, "so that you may know the certainty of the things you have been taught" (v. 3). Theophilus evidently had a basic knowledge of the gospel, but needed further instruction and confirmation. The overall purpose of Luke–Acts is therefore *the confirmation of the gospel.* Luke writes to confirm for his readers that God's great plan of salvation, promised in the Old Testament, has come to fulfillment in the events of Jesus's life, death, resurrection, and ascension and continues to unfold in the growth and expansion of the early church.

If the overall purpose of Luke–Acts is to confirm the gospel message and the gospel messengers, the narrative of Acts shows how the explosive growth of the church represents the work of God and the fulfillment of his purpose for the world. Acts 1:8 provides the central theme and an overall outline of the book. Following his resurrection and before his ascension, Jesus commands his disciples to remain in Jerusalem until they receive the Holy Spirit. The Spirit will empower them to accomplish the task Jesus has set out for them: "But you will receive power when the Holy Spirit comes on you; and you will be my witnesses in Jerusalem, and in all Judea and Samaria, and to the ends of the earth" (Acts 1:8).

The rest of Acts is an account of how the church, in the power of the Spirit, accomplishes this commission by being Christ's witnesses outward in concentric circles: from Jerusalem, to Judea, to Samaria, and to the ends of the earth. Throughout the book, despite opposition and hardship, the gospel moves forward, confirming that this Christian movement is indeed the work of God. A key defining moment comes in Acts 5, when the apostles are arrested and brought before the Jewish high council, the Sanhedrin. The religious leaders are furious at the apostles for continuing to preach the message about Jesus despite being warned to stop. As the Sanhedrin is debating how best to punish the apostles, one of the Jewish leaders, a man named Gamaliel, stands up to speak. He describes several individuals who arose in opposition to the government but whose movements were quickly suppressed or abandoned. He then gives this advice: "Therefore, in the present case I advise you: Leave these men alone! Let them go! For if their purpose or activity is of human origin, it will fail. But if it is from God, you will not be able to stop these men; you will only find yourselves fighting against God" (Acts 5:38–39).

Gamaliel says that if this movement is from God, no one will be able to stop it. Though Gamaliel himself does not believe the Christian movement is from God, his words prove to be prophetic. Throughout the book of Acts, nothing can stop the progress of the gospel. The Christian missionaries are harassed, arrested, beaten, put on trial, thrown in prison—even bitten by snakes (28:3). But nothing can stop the advance of the gospel. The book ends with Paul in prison in Rome. Surely chains in prison will stop this energetic apostle from proclaiming the gospel message. But the last thing Luke tells us in the book is, "For two whole years Paul stayed there in his own rented house and welcomed all who came to see him. He proclaimed the kingdom of God and taught about the Lord Jesus Christ—with all boldness and without hindrance!" (Acts 28:30–31). Paul is under house arrest and chained to a Roman guard. But he is still preaching the gospel "with all boldness and without hindrance." While the opponents of the church can chain the gospel messenger, they cannot chain the gospel message.

The Acts of the Holy Spirit. Although the traditional title of the book is The Acts of the Apostles, Acts is not really an account of the "acts" of Jesus's twelve apostles. The eleven disciples (minus Judas Iscariot; 1:18–19) are listed by name at the beginning of the book (1:13), and the apostles are prominent in the early chapters of Acts, as they teach, heal, and provide leadership for the Jerusalem church (2:42–43; 4:2, 33–37; 5:12, 18–41). But they appear only sporadically after that (8:1, 14; 15:2) and disappear completely after chapter 16. They play no role in the advancement of the gospel beyond Jerusalem.

Nor is Acts the history of the first-century church. After an introductory section related to the beginning of the church in Jerusalem (chaps. 1–8), the book focuses almost exclusively on the missionary activities of the apostle Paul westward into Asia Minor and Greece (chaps. 9, 13–28). We learn nothing about the church's work in regions where Paul did not go. The book tells us nothing, for example, about how the church was established in Rome and Italy to the west, Egypt or North Africa to the south, or eastward into Mesopotamia, Armenia, or Parthia. The author's purpose is clearly not to give us a biography of the apostles or a comprehensive history of the church. It is rather to narrate the miraculous work of God in the progress of the gospel from its Jewish origins in Jerusalem outward to the Gentile world.

The most important character in the book of Acts is not the apostles but God himself, who is at work through his Spirit. The Holy Spirit is referred to more than sixty times in the book. The outpouring of the Spirit in Acts 2 marks the beginning of the church and signals the dawn of the new age of salvation (Joel 2:28–32). Throughout the book the Holy Spirit fills and empowers believers, and guides and

174

directs the progress of the gospel (Acts 2:4; 4:8, 31; 6:3, 5; 7:55; 9:17; 11:24; 13:2; 16:6–7). Luke's purpose is to show that this movement is initiated and driven not by human beings but by God himself.

The most prominent human characters in the book—Peter, Stephen, Philip, Barnabas, Paul, and so on—are important not because they are apostles (of these, only Peter was one of the Twelve) but because they play key roles in *breaking down barriers* to the advancement of the gospel. Peter, for example, takes the gospel both to the Jews of Jerusalem (chap. 2) and to Cornelius, the first Gentile convert (chaps. 10–11). Stephen's martyrdom results in the scattering of the church and so provokes the spread of the gospel outside Jerusalem (8:1–2). Philip takes the gospel to the Samaritans and to an Ethiopian court official (8:4–40). Barnabas plays a key role in establishing the Gentile church in Antioch (11:19–30) and then, together with Paul, leads the first missionary outreach to the Gentiles (13:2). Paul becomes the apostle to the Gentiles, whose missionary activities comprise the rest of the book (chaps. 13–28). These characters are not important because of their *status* as apostles but because of their *function* as bridge-builders and groundbreakers for the advancement of the gospel.

Reading Acts Today

Understanding the theme and purpose of Acts as *the unstoppable progress of the gospel* is essential for applying the book of Acts appropriately today. Acts was not intended to be a biography of the apostles or a comprehensive history of the early church. Nor is it a detailed manual on how to "do church." One of the most common errors in applying Acts is assuming that everything that happened in the book is the standard or norm for the present-day church. There is an understandable desire to return to the purity and power of the earliest church. People sometimes say, "We want to be just like the church in Acts!" The problem is that while the church in Acts is certainly a model for us to follow in terms of its overall mission and purpose, the book was not written to provide details of church polity and procedure.

For example, while Acts mentions the "breaking of bread" (2:42), probably a reference to the Lord's Supper, it does not give us guidelines on how often the church should take the Lord's Supper, who can administer it, or what words should be spoken during the ceremony. Although we see people being baptized in Acts, the book does not tell us whether baptism is to be done by sprinkling, effusion (pouring), or full immersion (dunking). Nor are we told explicitly whether baptism is to be administered only to adults or whether infants should also be baptized. It is not that these are unimportant issues or that Christians should not seek to answer them. But we need to be cautious in appealing to Acts for those answers since the book was not written for this purpose.

The same ambiguity applies to church governance in Acts. Although the churches established in the book certainly had leaders, Acts does not set out the nature, function, or selection process for church offices like pastors, elders, deacons, or overseers. Nor is a standard for church government established, whether elder rule, bishop rule, or congregational rule. All of these are areas of debate within the modern church, and those trying to prove their view often appeal to the patterns in Acts.

One of the more contentious issues in the church is when and how believers receive the Holy Spirit. Does this occur immediately after professing faith in Jesus or at a later "second baptism"? In Acts 10, Cornelius and the members of his household are filled with the Holy Spirit immediately when they believe. Yet in Acts 8, the Spirit delays coming upon the Samaritan believers until Peter and John come from Jerusalem and lay hands on them. Which is the norm? Related to this is the question of whether the coming of the Holy Spirit is accompanied by speaking in tongues. Sometimes in Acts believers speak in tongues when they receive the Holy Spirit (10:46; 19:6); sometimes they don't (8:17; cf. 1 Cor. 12:30). These and other pressing questions are not answered in Acts because the book was never intended to be a handbook for church order and function.

If Acts is not a handbook on how to do church, how do we apply the book today? Here are three principles to keep in mind.

1. *Apply individual passages in the context of the overall purpose of Acts.* Luke's purpose in Acts is to show that the unstoppable progress of the gospel from its Jewish roots to the Gentile world is the fulfillment of God's promise of salvation. Individual passages should be interpreted and applied within this larger purpose. Consider,

for example, the question of the delayed appearance of the Holy Spirit in Samaria (Acts 8:4–25). In terms of the purpose of Acts, Philip's ministry in Samaria represents the fulfillment of Acts 1:8 ("you will be my witnesses . . . in Samaria"), the breaking down of ethnic barriers to the gospel (since Jews hated Samaritans), and the continued expansion of the gospel message (from Jews to Samaritans ["half-Jews"] to Gentiles). The delayed coming of the Holy Spirit (8:14–17) is understandable in this context. If the Samaritans had received the Holy Spirit immediately when they believed, they may have viewed themselves as independent of the Jerusalem church, and a rival Samaritan church may have sprung up. The Spirit's delay until Peter and John came from Jerusalem confirmed *for the apostles* that the Samaritans were truly saved (something most Jews would have had trouble believing), and confirmed *for the Samaritans* that they were necessarily linked to the Jerusalem church. The unity of the church—a major theme in Acts (4:32)—was preserved. This passage is not meant to establish a permanent theology for how the Spirit comes upon believers; rather, it illustrates the unstoppable progress of the gospel.

2. *Look for repeated and consistent patterns.* How, then, do we know when something that happens in Acts is a standard for today? One key is consistency and repetition. For example, some have wondered whether the apostles' method of choosing a new apostle by casting lots (Acts 1:23–26) is still an appropriate method of decision making. If every time the church made a decision in Acts they cast lots, we would probably have to say yes. But, in fact, this is the only time in Acts where this method is used. As Duvall and Hays point out, the early church in Acts was guided in a variety of ways, including by the Spirit (8:29; 10:19), angels (8:26; 12:7), visions (9:10–12; 16:9–10), the Scriptures (1:20; 8:30–35), and circumstances (8:1).[10] Nowhere else are lots used. The casting of lots also occurs *before* the disciples have received the Holy Spirit, their ultimate guide (2:1–4). This suggests that using lots was an interim method for discerning God's will rather than a model for us now. Without a repeated and consistent pattern, we should not assume that something that happens occasionally in Acts is the standard for the church for all time.

3. *Treat as normative what the book treats as normative.* Closely related to the previous point is the principle that we should treat as

normative (an obligatory rule or standard) what Acts itself treats as normative. Though the experience of the Spirit by new believers varies depending on the circumstances, the one constant is that all true believers receive the Holy Spirit. This is the consistent testimony throughout Acts (2:38; 8:17; 10:44; 11:15–16; 15:8; 19:6) as well as the rest of the New Testament (Rom. 8:9; 1 Cor. 2:12; 12:13). Similarly, although the book tells us little about the mode of baptism, it clearly and consistently identifies baptism as a mandatory initiatory rite for believers (Acts 2:38, 41; 8:12, 36–38; 9:18; 10:47–48; 16:15, 33; 18:8; 19:5). Jesus commanded baptism (Matt. 28:18–19), and there is no suggestion in Acts or throughout the New Testament that the practice was merely optional for believers. Though Acts gives few details about leadership roles in the church—including titles, specific functions, or methods of appointment—the one constant is that leaders in the church must be filled and empowered by the Spirit of God (Acts 4:8, 31; 6:3, 5; 7:55; 9:17; 11:24).

Answering the Four Questions for Acts

1. *Where is Acts in the larger story of Scripture?* Acts is an essential part of the story of redemption, representing the transition from the time of Jesus to the church age. As noted above, the transitional nature of this period calls for caution in application. Apostles who have not yet received the Holy Spirit (1:4), casting lots to discern God's will (1:26), followers of Jesus worshiping in the temple (3:1), church members struck dead for practicing deceit (5:1–10), disciples holding to Jewish dietary laws (10:14)—these are not necessarily patterns for the church for all time. They are part of the transition from the age of promise to the age of fulfillment.

So while Acts does not necessarily provide the details of how to do church, it teaches the nature, mission, power, and potential of the church. Returning to our theme verse in Acts 1:8, we see the *nature* of the church is to be Christ's "witnesses," his representatives to a lost world. The *mission* of his church is to take his message of salvation outward from Jerusalem to Judea, Samaria, and "the ends of the earth." The *power* Christ provides to accomplish this task is his very presence, the Spirit of God who fills, empowers, and guides the followers of Jesus. The *potential* of the church is the transformation of the world through the good news of Jesus Christ. As the spiritual heirs to the commission Jesus gave to his disciples, we apply the message of Acts by learning what it means to live out this fundamental mission through the power of the Holy Spirit in our own place and time.

2. *What is the original author's purpose in light of the passage's genre and historical and literary context?* As we have seen, the question of purpose is particularly crucial for reading and applying the book of Acts. Every individual passage fits into the larger story of Acts. Finding this place provides us with the key to applying the text. For example, in Acts 6:1–7 the church faces a crisis when the Greek-speaking Jewish widows are being neglected in the daily distribution of food. The church solves the problem by appointing seven men to oversee this service to those in need.

It would be inappropriate to conclude from this passage that every church should have a council of seven deacons to oversee the distribution to the poor. Luke does not call these men "deacons" (they are an ad hoc committee), and nowhere else in Acts is a seven-man committee formed for this purpose. There *is* evidence that the term "deacon" (Greek: *diakonos*; literally, "servant") became a title for a church office in some first-century churches (Rom. 16:1; Phil. 1:1; 1 Tim. 3:8–13), but Luke's purpose here is not to describe the establishment of this office. Rather, he is making several points. First, he is certainly showing that the church cared for its own, a point he has already stressed in Acts (2:42–47; 4:32–37). He is also confirming the crucial role of the apostles in passing on the message that Jesus passed on to them: "the ministry [or "service"; *diakonia*] of the word of God" (6:2). Most important, perhaps, he is introducing Stephen and Philip, two of the seven, who will play a key role in propelling the gospel beyond the walls of Jerusalem. Stephen will do this through his martyrdom, which forces the church to scatter (8:1). Philip will do it when he takes the gospel to Samaria and to an Ethiopian court official (8:4–40). For Luke, it is all about the nature, mission, power, and potential of the church.

3. *How does this passage inform our understanding of the nature of God and his purpose for the world?* The answer to this third question flows naturally from our understanding of the overall message of

179

Acts. By the power of the Spirit, the church is taking God's message of salvation to the ends of the earth. And each individual passage contributes to this theme. The choice of the seven in Acts 6 reminds us that God is a loving God who cares for the needs of the lowliest of his people. The widow and the fatherless are models throughout the Old Testament of the most vulnerable and needy members of society. God cares especially for them and expects his people to do the same. Just as important, this passage teaches that God uses human instruments to accomplish his purpose. The apostles are given the task of proclaiming the message of Jesus. The seven are given the responsibility of caring for the people of God. Both Stephen and Philip also turn out to be powerful evangelists. The theme of Acts—the unstoppable progress of the gospel—plays out in the martyrdom of Stephen. Though the church suffers a terrible setback in the death of one of its most eloquent spokesmen, this does not stop the gospel, which spreads far and wide through the persecution that follows. We learn here that God even takes the deeds of evil men and through them accomplishes his good purposes (cf. 2:23–24; 3:17–18; 4:24–30).

4. *What does this passage teach us about who we ought to be (attitudes and character) and what we ought to do (goals and actions) as those seeking to reflect the nature and purpose of God?* Although Acts 6:1–7 does not establish the office of deacon, it does remind us of the responsibility of all Christians to care for those among us with needs. It also teaches the importance of the ministry of God's Word and its faithful transmission to succeeding generations. The role of the apostles in transmitting the Jesus tradition is carried forward today through the church's teachers and preachers. The early church may not give all the specific details about how to do church, but it certainly teaches us who we ought to be and what we ought to do as the people of God in the present age. We are to be the Spirit-filled, Spirit-guided, and Spirit-empowered people of God, who care for those in need and whose passion is to take the message of salvation from our own hometown to the ends of the earth. The application of Acts, as with the rest of Scripture, means learning to walk with God along life's journey and pursuing his purpose and passion for the redemption of a lost world. This is not just *their* story. It is also ours.

The New Testament Letters

In addition to the four Gospels and the book of Acts, there are twenty-one epistles, or letters, in the New Testament. These letters were written by early church leaders to various Christian churches and individuals throughout the Roman Empire. Thirteen of the letters were written by the apostle Paul (though some of these are disputed[11]). Of these thirteen, nine were written to churches (Romans, 1 & 2 Corinthians, Galatians, Ephesians, Philippians, Colossians, 1 & 2 Thessalonians) and four to individuals (1 & 2 Timothy, Titus, Philemon).

The rest of the letters in the New Testament are known as the General Epistles, since they were written to more general audiences. These are named for the author (James; 1 & 2 Peter; 1, 2, 3 John; Jude). The letter to the Hebrews is unique. It is anonymous in the sense that the author is not explicitly named, although the original readers clearly knew the author (Heb. 13:18–19, 22–24). Historically, some have attributed Hebrews to Paul. This is unlikely, however, since the letter is very different from Paul's other letters in terms of format, literary style, and theological content. Other authors have been suggested, including Apollos, Luke, Barnabas, Priscilla, or Silas, but all of these are little more than guesses. The authorship of the letter remains a mystery.

The Nature and Function of the Letters

The format of New Testament letters. The New Testament letters are similar in many respects to other letters found in the ancient Mediterranean world.[12] Such letters followed a common format:

- Name of author
- Identification of recipients
- Greeting
- Sometimes a thanksgiving or prayer for the recipients
- Body of the letter
- Concluding remarks

Unlike modern letters, which usually begin with an address to the reader ("Dear . . ."), first-century letters usually started with the name of the *author*, followed by their titles or credentials. This would be followed by the name of the *recipients* and a *greeting*. Second Corinthians, for example, begins: "Paul, an apostle of Christ Jesus by the will of God, and Timothy our brother, to the church of God in Corinth, together with all his holy people throughout Achaia: Grace and peace to you from God our Father and the Lord Jesus Christ" (2 Cor. 1:1–2). While the most common greeting in secular Greek was *chairein* ("greetings" or "hello"), Paul "Christianizes" this with the term *charis* ("grace"), followed by a typical Jewish greeting, "peace" (Greek: *eirēnē*; Hebrew: *shalom*). Outside of the Pauline letters, this "grace and peace" formula also appears at the beginning of 1 and 2 Peter and Revelation (1:4). The source of grace and peace is not the human author but God himself; as Paul writes in 2 Corinthians: "grace and peace to you from God our Father and the Lord Jesus Christ."

The greeting in ancient letters was often followed by *a thanks-giving or a prayer* for the person's health. For example, one ancient letter reads: "Herm[(es) (to Sarapion)], greetings, and that you may always remain in good health in your whole person for long years to come, . . . I pray for your safekeeping during your entire life and for the health of your children and all your household."[13] Paul, too, generally follows his greeting with a prayer and/or thanksgiving for the recipients. In Philippians, after greeting the church, Paul writes, "I thank my God every time I remember you. In all my prayers for all of you, I always pray with joy because of your partnership in the gospel from the first day until now" (Phil. 1:3–5). For Paul, this thanksgiving was not just a courtesy but also a way to introduce themes that would appear later in the letter. For example, the joy Paul experiences from his "participation in the gospel" with the Philippians is a major theme throughout the letter. When Paul skips this thanksgiving section, it is also significant, as in his letter to the Galatians. Paul is hopping mad and deeply disturbed that some of the Galatians are abandoning faith in Jesus Christ for a "different gospel" and so finds little to be thankful for.

This thanksgiving or prayer would be followed by *the body of the letter*, which dealt with whatever issue the author was writing about. The New Testament letters were written for a variety of purposes: (1) to praise and encourage actions or attitudes, (2) to address doctrinal or behavioral problems in the churches, (3) to refute false teaching, and (4) to pass on news about the author's circumstance. First Corinthians, for example, is written primarily to address problems in the church at Corinth and to answer questions from the church. Galatians is written to refute false teaching in the churches of Galatia. First Peter is written to encourage the churches of Asia Minor to persevere through suffering and persecution. Letters can also have multiple purposes. Philippians is a more general letter, written to pass on news about Paul's situation in prison, to thank the church at Philippi for a gift they sent, to call the church to greater unity, and to refute certain false teaching.

After the body of the letter, authors would end with *concluding remarks*. These might include final instructions or exhortations, personal news, greetings to mutual friends, a benediction, and a personal signature. Some New Testament letters have no concluding remarks (1 John, James); in others, the remarks are very brief (Ephesians), while in yet others, they are extensive (Romans). In Romans, Paul takes almost two chapters to bring the letter to a close, including two benedictions, news of his plans, and an extensive list of greetings to Christian friends (Rom. 15:13–16:27).

While the New Testament letters are similar in most respects to other ancient letters, their length sets them apart. The average length of a private letter from the ancient world was a few hundred words. A more general letter meant for the public might be anywhere from a few hundred to a few thousand words. Paul's letters are generally much longer and *average* about twenty-five hundred words. They range from Philemon, the shortest and most personal of his letters (about three hundred words), to Romans, which is over seven thousand words. Paul clearly viewed his letters as more than quick reports or updates. They were theological instruction meant to replace his personal apostolic presence and to guide and teach the church in right doctrine and practice.

The composition of New Testament letters. Ancient writers often dictated their letters to a copyist or *amanuensis*, who wrote down the author's words. At the end of Romans, for example, the amanuensis suddenly appears and identifies himself: "I, Tertius, who wrote down this letter, greet you in the Lord" (Rom. 16:22). Although the letter is from Paul (who speaks in the first person throughout), Tertius wrote it down. The same is likely the case in 1 Peter, where Peter notes at the end, "With the help of Silas, whom I regard as a faithful brother, I have written to you briefly" (1 Pet. 5:12). The degree to which an amanuensis was responsible for the content varied from case to case. For some letters an author might tell the scribe generally what he wanted to say and the scribe would compose the letter. Other times the letter might be dictated verbatim. Some differences in style in the New Testament (such as between 1 and 2 Peter) may perhaps be due to the degree of involvement by an amanuensis.

At the end of a letter, an author would often sign it in their own hand to confirm its authenticity. At the end of 1 Corinthians, Paul writes, "I, Paul, write this greeting in my own hand" (1 Cor. 16:21; cf. Gal. 6:11; Col. 4:18; 2 Thess. 3:17). In 2 Thessalonians the authenticity of the letter is a pressing concern, since Paul refers to the possibility of forged letters written in his name (2 Thess. 2:2).

In some letters Paul names others in his greeting, such as Timothy (2 Cor. 1:1; Phil. 1:1; Col. 1:1), Silas (1 Thess. 1:1; 2 Thess. 1:1), and Sosthenes (1 Cor. 1:1; perhaps the amanuensis). These are more co-workers than co-authors, however, since Paul most commonly refers to himself in the first person singular ("I" or "me").[14] What the inclusion of co-workers in the greetings tells us is that Paul viewed his apostolic ministry as a team effort, with others serving as partners in the gospel.

The audiences of the New Testament letters. The New Testament letters were intended to be read publicly rather than privately. Most people in the ancient world were not literate, and communication in general was more oral than written. The New Testament letters would have been delivered to the church by courier and then read aloud when the church gathered as a community. Letters would often be copied and passed on to other churches (see Col. 4:16). Even letters to individuals, like 1 and 2 Timothy, Titus, and Philemon, were likely read publicly to the church when it gathered for worship and fellowship. Philemon, though a personal letter, is addressed not only to Philemon but also to Apphia and Archippus (likely Philemon's wife and son, respectively), ". . . and to the church that meets in your home" (Philem. 2).

Letters in the ancient world ranged from very general literary works meant for the public at large to personal letters written for a single individual. Compare, for example, a letter to the editor published in a newspaper with a personal note written to a friend. The letter to the editor is more like an essay and is written to persuade anyone willing to listen to a particular point of view. The note is personal and private, meant only for the eyes of the addressee. Most letters lie on a spectrum between these two extremes of exclusively public or private. A fund-raising letter from an aid organization would be targeted to a specific group (say, past donors) but would be a very general appeal. A missionary prayer letter full of news could be targeted to a group of churches or to individuals who have known and supported these missionaries.

The New Testament letters exhibit a similar range from very general to very specific audiences. On one extreme is a letter like James, written broadly to "the twelve tribes scattered among the nations" (1:1), probably a general reference to Jewish believers scattered throughout the Mediterranean world. Moving across the spectrum, we see 1 Peter written to the churches of the large area of five provinces of Asia Minor (1 Pet. 1:1), Galatians to several churches in the single province of Galatia, Philippians to a single church in the Macedonian city of Philippi, and Philemon to a single individual in the church at Colossae.

Noting such differences, scholars have sometimes distinguished between "real letters" and "epistles."[15] Real letters are private, personal, and nonliterary, intended to pass on information to a single individual or group. Epistles are more like essays, impersonal and conventional literary works written for the public at large (like the letter to the editor mentioned above). While this distinction can be helpful, none of the New Testament letters fit neatly into either category. This is because all of them are both personal and public, both real letters and literary compositions. Consider Hebrews, for example. In many respects Hebrews looks more like an essay than a letter. It begins like a sermon or a theological treatise, without naming the author or the recipients, and is a carefully crafted literary and theological masterpiece. The author systematically demonstrates the superiority of Christ and the new covenant to the old covenant system of priests and sacrifices. Yet while the book is highly literary and rhetorically powerful, it is also a very personal letter, written by a church leader to a group of believers who are in danger of drifting away from the faith and returning to their old life in Judaism.

The occasional nature of the New Testament letters. This brings up the important point that all the letters in the New Testament are *occasional* documents. They were written to a specific group of people to address specific needs and concerns. Some of these occasions are more specific than others. Galatians, for example, was written to address the false teaching of a works-oriented salvation that was taking root in the churches of Galatia. A letter like Ephesians, on the other hand, has a more general purpose of instructing the churches of Asia Minor on Christian identity and practice. Even the most theological of the letters, however, is occasional. Romans, Paul's greatest theological work, was written to prepare the house churches in Rome for his missionary campaign into Spain and to call Jewish and Gentile believers in Rome to unity around the core message of the gospel of grace through faith in Jesus Christ. This occasional nature of the letters has important implications for how we read them today.

Reading the Letters Today

In some ways, the New Testament Epistles are the trickiest of the biblical documents to apply. This is because—at first sight—they seem to be so directly applicable to us. After all, they were written to churches, and we are the church. The believers they address stood in the same period of salvation history as we do now, the new age of salvation inaugurated by Jesus Christ. Yet we must also recognize that these letters were occasional documents written to address specific issues and needs in first-century churches.

Consider, for example, 1 Corinthians 15:58, where Paul writes, "Therefore, my dear brothers and sisters, stand firm. Let nothing move you. Always give yourselves fully to the work of the Lord, because you know that your labor in the Lord is not in vain." We can see here direct applicability to our lives. As believers we are called to devote ourselves to the work of the Lord. Yet a few sentences later we read, "On the first day of every week, each one of you should set aside a sum of money in keeping with your income, saving it up, so that when I come no collections will have to be made" (1 Cor. 16:2). Here Paul is giving a command to the Corinthians that does not (directly) apply to us. He is telling them to collect ahead of time the money they are planning to send to the poor believers in Jerusalem, which he and others will take to Jerusalem. Since none of us are expecting a visit from the apostle Paul in the near future, this command would be a hard one for us to obey. Similarly, a few paragraphs later Paul adds, "When Timothy comes, see to it that he has nothing to fear while he is with you, for he is carrying on the work of the Lord, just as I am" (1 Cor. 16:10). This is personal information meant for this church at this time.

While the applicability or inapplicability of these particular passages may be relatively easy to determine, a few paragraphs later Paul says, "Greet one another with a holy kiss" (1 Cor. 16:20). Does this fall into the first category above (applicable today) or the second (only for the Corinthians)? More controversially, shortly before this Paul says, "Women should remain silent in the churches. They are not allowed to speak, but must be in submission, as the law says" (1 Cor. 14:34). Is this passage meant as a command for all believers at all times and places? Or was it meant only for the churches of the first century, or even more specifically for the church at Corinth? The Epistles seem so directly relevant to our lives that we are often lulled into forgetting that we are reading someone else's mail, letters written to specific churches to address specific social and theological concerns. In the next chapter, we will examine in more detail criteria for distinguishing universal truths from culturally conditioned commands. Here we introduce some basic principles for interpreting and applying the Epistles.

1. *Get to know the general historical context of the first-century church.* Learning about the Jewish and Greco-Roman worlds of the first century and the historical circumstances of the first-century churches is important for both understanding and applying these letters in the present. For example, Paul's warning to the church at Corinth concerning their participation in the Lord's Supper (1 Cor. 11:17–34) has to be understood in the context of first-century Greco-Roman meals, social status, and social values. Banquets or dinner parties in the first century were rituals of social status, a place where your position in society was established and confirmed. The host at such a party would invite guests of similar social status and would provide them with a seat and food equal to their status in the community. The guests of honor would be seated close to the host and

would receive the best food. People with lesser status would receive gradually lower-quality food and a "cheap seat" farther from the host.[16] The host's expectation was that the wealthy people would reciprocate by inviting him to their parties and so raise his status in the community. While today we might be horrified by such social prejudice, this was the norm of the day.

The church, by contrast, was to be a great equalizer. Christianity affirms that all people are equal in Christ. All have sinned and fallen short of God's glory and all are equally saved by God's free gift of grace (Rom. 3:23–24). In a world of social hierarchy this was a radical and revolutionary concept; Paul's words in Galatians 3:28 would have sounded far more radical to first-century ears than they do to us now: "There is neither Jew nor Gentile, neither slave nor free, nor is there male and female, for you are all one in Christ Jesus."

Throughout 1 Corinthians, Paul has been calling this struggling church away from its divisions caused by pride and elite attitudes and toward the unity they share as believers in Jesus Christ. Paul has heard that some in the church were practicing the same kind of social exclusion common in the secular world. This occurred during their "love feast" (*agapē*), a banquet the church held in conjunction with the Lord's Supper. Some of the wealthy people were evidently arriving early and gorging themselves on food and drink, while the poor would arrive later and be hungry (1 Cor. 11:20–22). Paul is furious at this humiliation of the poor and warns the church of the grave danger of shattering the church's unity: "those who eat and drink without discerning the body of Christ eat and drink judgment on themselves" (1 Cor. 11:29). Practicing this kind of social exclusion and prejudice is absolutely contrary to the equality and value of all believers in the body of Christ.

When Paul warns "whoever eats the bread or drinks the cup of the Lord in an unworthy manner" (1 Cor. 11:27), there is a tendency today to think of "unworthy" as referring to personal or private sins. At the Lord's Supper, believers are often told to quietly prepare their hearts before God for taking the bread and the cup. Yet in context Paul is talking about the corporate sins that are causing disunity, such as greed, pride, prejudice, and hypocrisy. The Lord's Supper, focusing as it does on the reconciliation we have with God through Jesus Christ, should be a time of unity and reconciliation for the church, the body of Christ. Understanding the social and cultural world of the first century helps us to appropriately apply a passage like this in the current day and age.

2. *Identify the specific occasion of the letter.* In addition to understanding the general social and cultural world of the first century, we must identify the specific purpose and occasion for which each letter was written in order to interpret the Epistles well. First Thessalonians, for example, was written by Paul from Corinth to the recently established church at Thessalonica. Paul had started the church on his second missionary journey while traveling through Macedonia (northern Greece). Shortly afterward, severe persecution forced Paul to leave and flee southward to Berea, Athens, and then Corinth. He was very concerned about the young church in Thessalonica and wondered how they were holding up under the pressure of persecution. Finally, he sent Timothy to check on the church. Timothy visited the church and then returned to Paul in Corinth with the positive report that the church was thriving despite persecution. In response, Paul wrote a letter full of praise and encouragement for this young group of believers. Understanding this general occasion and Paul's purpose in writing is critically important for interpreting the individual passages in the letter.

How do we learn all this information? The letter itself is the best source. If you read through the first three chapters you will see that Paul refers back to both the circumstances surrounding the establishment of the church and the circumstances of his writing (see especially 1 Thess. 2:17–3:9). The material from the letter can be supplemented from the book of Acts, which describes the establishment of the church (Acts 17:1–9). There are also the reference books referred to earlier, including study Bibles, Bible handbooks and dictionaries, and commentaries. All of these will discuss the occasion and purpose of the letter and can be used to check what you learn from the letter itself.

3. *Follow the progress of the argument (the literary context).* Context refers not only to the historical context, or life setting, of the letter, but also to the *literary context*, the flow of the author's argument. In the Epistles it is particularly important to read through the letter in its entirety from beginning to end. There are many benefits to doing this. First, you will be able to follow the author's argument

and pick up keys to the letter's occasion and purpose. For example, although at the beginning of Romans Paul expresses his hope and desire to visit the church at Rome, it is only near the end of the letter that he mentions his plans to launch a missionary outreach into Spain and solicits the church's support for this mission. This is an important part of Paul's purpose in writing that might be missed if the letter is not read in its entirety.

Second, reading the letter from beginning to end helps to avoid taking passages out of context, that is, misinterpreting them because you don't have the whole picture. Paul's command, mentioned above, for women to remain silent in the churches (1 Cor. 14:34) can hardly be taken at face value since Paul earlier assumes that it is appropriate for women to pray and prophesy in the worship services of the church (1 Cor. 11:5). By reading the letter all the way through, we recognize that there must be more to 1 Corinthians 14:34 than a command to absolute silence. A passage like this also reminds us that we are only hearing part of the conversation and that there is much we don't know about the historical, cultural, and social situation at Corinth. It would be unwise to assume that this passage is a universally binding command for the church of all time until we can better understand what it actually means. As I have said, clear passages with theological themes that are pervasive throughout Scripture should be central to our application, while obscure and ambiguous passages should be kept on the periphery.

Third, reading the letter through in its entirety helps the reader to pick up key themes and motifs developed by the author. For example, in 1 Corinthians 3:10 Paul says, "By the grace God has given me, I laid a foundation as a wise builder." The Greek word for "wise" here is *sophos*. Some Bible versions, recognizing that "wise" is an unusual word to describe a builder, translate this word as "skilled" or "expert" (ESV, NLT, HCSB, etc.). But by reading through the letter from beginning to end, we recognize that earlier Paul has been contrasting the false wisdom of the world with God's true wisdom. God's wisdom is the message of the cross of Christ, a stumbling block to Jews and foolishness to Gentiles. But to believers who have been transformed by its message, it is the power of God and wisdom of God (1 Cor. 1:20–24). By following the progress of Paul's argument, we see that a "wise" (*sophos*) builder (NIV, NASB) is one who builds not on fleeting human wisdom but on the sure foundation of the cross of Christ.[17]

4. *Apply the letters in truly analogous historical, social, and cultural situations.* This point will be taken up in greater detail in the next chapter, which will provide various criteria to determine whether a particular command or statement in Scripture is directly or indirectly applicable for us. Here the point is that determining the applicability of a command depends to a great extent on whether our social and cultural situation is analogous to the situation the original author is addressing.

In 1 Corinthians 7:27, for example, Paul encourages the Corinthians to stay in their current marital state: "Are you pledged to a woman? Do not seek to be released. Are you free from such a commitment? Do not look for a wife." Young people today may wonder about this last statement, "Do not look for a wife." Is it wrong to pursue marriage? There is obviously more going on at this time in the church at Corinth than meets the eye. Just before this statement, Paul writes, "Because of the present crisis, I think that it is good for a man to remain as he is" (1 Cor. 7:26). What is this present crisis? Commentators can guess, but we simply don't know. This should give us pause before assuming that 1 Corinthians 7:27 is a command for all believers for all time. Nowhere else in Scripture are believers commanded to avoid marriage, and even in 1 Corinthians 7, Paul assumes that marriage is the norm for most believers (7:1–2). The point here is that before we assume that a command *to them* is necessarily also a command *for us*, we must determine whether the historical, social, and cultural situation is truly analogous to our own. More on this in the next chapter.

Answering the Four Questions for the Letters

1. *Where are the letters in the larger story of Scripture?* One of the reasons the New Testament letters are still so applicable is that they were written to churches and believers who lived in the same place in salvation history as we do. They, like us, are new covenant believers living after the death and resurrection of Jesus Christ, but before his second coming. We therefore approach the commands of Paul, Peter, James, John, and Jude on a different level than we do

191

the commands of the Old Testament law, which were clearly given to the nation Israel living under the old covenant.

At the same time, we have to acknowledge that even new covenant commands are embedded in culture and were given to address specific cultural and social situations. We cannot merely assume that all New Testament commands—such as those related to greetings, clothing, hairstyles, propriety in worship, slaves, male and female roles, and so forth—are necessarily commands for all time. In other words, the Epistles, like the rest of the Bible, must be *contextualized* to determine how they apply to us.

2. *What is the author's purpose in light of the passage's genre and historical and literary context?* The question of purpose is crucial for interpreting and applying a New Testament letter. Consider, for example, Paul's command in Colossians 2:16: "Therefore do not let anyone judge you by what you eat or drink, or with regard to a religious festival, a New Moon celebration or a Sabbath day." Does this mean that it is inappropriate for Christians to judge one another in terms of food or drink? If I am abusing food or alcohol, should another Christian confront me about this?

A closer look at this passage reveals that Paul's purpose here is not about holding others accountable for their actions. Rather, false teachers at Colossae were claiming that faith in Jesus Christ was not enough for salvation but that Christians needed to follow other (probably Jewish-based) rules, such as dietary laws, Sabbath observance, and other religious rituals. Paul rejects this and throughout the letter points to the absolute supremacy of Christ and his death on the cross as the sole means of our salvation. In 2:16 Paul tells the Colossian believers not to let false teachers judge them by their own human legalistic standards. He is not talking at all about Christians keeping one another accountable. Understanding the *purpose* behind the command is essential for finding relevant application for today.

3. *How does this passage inform our understanding of the nature of God and his purpose for the world?* The most important thing we learn in the Epistles, as in any part of Scripture, is who God is, who we are in relationship to him, and what his purpose for the world is. The Epistles represent "task theology"—God's truth brought to bear on specific life situations. Paul writes Colossians,

for example, to combat a growing heresy in Colossae, false teaching that is challenging the supremacy of Christ and replacing it with a works-oriented message. Paul's purpose in writing is to call the believers in Colossae to remain faithful to the gospel that was originally preached to them.

Paul accomplishes this purpose by affirming who Jesus Christ is and what God has accomplished through him. "The Son," Paul says, is "the image of the invisible God," the creator and sustainer of all things (Col. 1:15–17). God is not only the creator but also the redeemer: "For God was pleased to have all his fullness dwell in him, and through him to reconcile to himself all things, whether things on earth or things in heaven, by making peace through his blood, shed on the cross" (Col. 1:19–20). Because Christ alone is the savior and redeemer of all of creation, seeking to be saved through our own works or merit is useless.

4. *What does this passage teach us about who we ought to be (attitudes and character) and what we ought to do (goals and actions) as those seeking to reflect the nature and purpose of God?* This fourth question is probably easier to answer with reference to the Epistles than with any other biblical genre, since these letters are brimming with the practical application of God's truth (where the rubber meets the road). As practical exhortations to real-life churches, the New Testament letters constantly move from who God is and what he has accomplished to how we ought to live in response. In Ephesians, for example, the first three chapters concern God's sovereign purpose in choosing, calling, and redeeming his people. Chapters 4–6 then turn to how we ought to live in response. In 4:1 Paul writes, "As a prisoner for the Lord, then, I urge you to live a life worthy of the calling you have received." Similarly, in Romans 1–11 Paul describes the sinful fallen state of all people and God's great purpose in saving and sanctifying them. Beginning in Romans 12:1, he turns to the practical application of these truths: "Therefore, I urge you, brothers and sisters, in view of God's mercy, to offer your bodies as a living sacrifice." Following a description of Christ's supremacy and his saving work on our behalf, Colossians 3:1 reads, "Since, then, you have been raised with Christ, set your hearts on things above, where Christ is, seated at the right hand of God." The truths about who God is and what he has accomplished for us are meant to be lived

out through a life of submission and service to him and his purpose for the world.

The Book of Revelation

The name of the book of Revelation comes from its first line: "The revelation of Jesus Christ, which God gave him to show his servants what must soon take place" (1:1). The Greek word for revelation is *apocalypsis*, so the book is often called "the Apocalypse." Scholars debate the meaning of the phrase "the revelation of Jesus Christ." Is this a revelation *about* Jesus Christ, or is it a revelation *from* Jesus Christ? In fact, both are true in the book. The revelation is given by Jesus ("which God gave him to show his servants"), and it is Jesus, the "Lamb who was slain," whose sacrificial death on the cross and victory over death allow the visions of the book to unfold (5:5–6). Yet it is also a revelation *about* Jesus. Revelation 1 contains a vision of the glorified Christ at the right hand of God (1:12–20), and Jesus's nature and saving work are revealed throughout the book. It is possible that the author here intends a double meaning: the revelation is both from and about Jesus Christ.[18]

The Message of Revelation

For most modern readers, Revelation is the most difficult book in the Bible, filled as it is with strange images (angelic creatures, dragons, beasts, demonic locusts), cryptic symbols (lamp stands, scrolls, bowls, trumpets, seals), mysterious numbers (666; 144,000; many sevens), and descriptions of cataclysmic judgment upon the earth. The main problem for modern readers is that there is nothing in contemporary literature quite like this book. While most other biblical genres—narrative, poetry, law, letter—have modern parallels, readers struggle for a frame of reference to comprehend Revelation.

Central theme. Despite the many challenges of interpreting and applying the book, the central theme is crystal clear: God is the sovereign Lord of history, the Alpha and the Omega, the Beginning and the End. No matter how bad things get in the world, no matter how much evil may seem to triumph, in the end God will judge the wicked, vindicate the righteous, and establish an eternal kingdom of justice and righteousness. This victory has been accomplished already through the death and resurrection of Jesus Christ and will be consummated when he returns in glory. At that time there will be no more evil, suffering, or death. God will create a new heaven and a new earth; the new Jerusalem will descend from heaven, and God will dwell with his people forever (Revelation 21–22). The Bible that begins, "In the beginning," with the creation of the present heaven and earth (Gen. 1:1) ends with a new beginning, the creation of a new heaven and a new earth (Rev. 21:1; cf. Isa. 65:17).

Summary of contents. Following an introduction identifying the author and the occasion of the book, Revelation presents a vision of the glorified Christ, who commands John to write down what he is about to see (chap. 1). This is followed by letters to seven churches in Asia, calling them to perseverance and faithfulness (chaps. 2–3). John is next shown a vision of heaven, where God sits on his glorious throne. In his right hand is a scroll, which is sealed with seven seals and contains the future about to unfold. John weeps since no one is found worthy to open the scroll. No one, that is, except Jesus Christ, the Lamb who was slain to redeem people from every tribe, language, and nation (chaps. 4–5). The Lamb opens the seals, initiating three sets of cataclysmic judgments against the earth: seven seals, seven trumpets, and seven bowls (chaps. 6–16). These are periodically interrupted by mysterious interludes: the sealing of 144,000 with the mark of God, two witnesses martyred for Christ, the allegory of the woman and the dragon, and the appearance of the two beasts.

The three sets of sevenfold judgments are followed by a description of the rise and fall of Babylon, a symbol of Rome and the evil world system. Babylon is portrayed as a great prostitute who rules the earth and persecutes the people of God (chaps. 17–18). As the revelation climaxes, the prostitute Babylon is destroyed and Christ returns, riding a white horse and accompanied by the armies of heaven (chap. 19). The great dragon (Satan) is seized and locked in the abyss, and Christ establishes a thousand-year reign (the millennium). Following this thousand years, Satan is released and leads a final rebellion against God. He is defeated and thrown forever into the lake of fire (chap. 20). God creates a new heaven and a new earth, and a glorious new Jerusalem, the eternal home of God's people, descends to earth (chaps. 21–22). The book ends with an encouragement to persevere, for Jesus is coming soon (22:18–21).

The Genres of Revelation

Identifying the genre of the Revelation is crucial for understanding its message. The book is a combination of three distinct genres: *letter, prophecy,* and *apocalypse.*

1. *Letter.* After an introductory prologue (1:1–3), Revelation begins with an introduction typical of other ancient letters, including author, recipients, and a greeting. The author identifies himself as "John." This has traditionally been considered to be John the apostle, son of Zebedee and brother of James. Some scholars, however, note differences in style between Revelation and the other Johannine writings and suggest this may be another John, identified by the early church historian Eusebius as John the Elder.

The book is addressed to seven historical churches in the Roman province of Asia (1:4) and contains seven individual letters addressed to these churches: Ephesus, Smyrna, Pergamum, Thyatira, Sardis, Philadelphia, and Laodicea (chaps. 2–3). References in these letters indicate that at least some were experiencing persecution (2:10, 13). Their greatest present danger, however, is not persecution but complacency and compromise with the evil world system. They are called to wake up and put their spiritual house in order, since Jesus is coming soon to save and to judge.

Since these are letters, it is important to determine their occasion and purpose. The occasion of Revelation is described in 1:9–19. Because of his teaching and testimony concerning Jesus, John has been exiled to Patmos, a small island in the Aegean Sea, southwest of Ephesus. John is "in the spirit" on the Lord's day (Sunday), when a vision is given to him. He is commanded to write in a book "what you have seen, what is now and what will take place later." John is first given the seven letters to the seven churches, then an extended vision concerning "what will take place later"—coming judgments against the world and the consummation of all things. The purpose of the book, then, is to provide a glimpse into God's sovereign plan for the future to encourage these churches to persevere in their present circumstances.

2. *Prophecy*. The author identifies Revelation not only as a letter but also as a prophecy (Rev. 1:3; 22:7, 10, 18, 19), and the book contains many elements common to prophetic literature. These include messages from God to his people, warnings against unbelief, and oracles of coming judgment and deliverance. As we have seen, the most important function of prophecy is not *foretelling* (predicting the future) but *forthtelling*, announcing God's message to his people. The prophetic message of Revelation is to remain faithful through trials and persecution. Though God's people will experience suffering and even death, God will protect the faithful from the judgment and wrath that is coming upon the world. Those who remain faithful will become heirs of God's eternal kingdom and glory.

3. *Apocalypse*. The third genre of Revelation is the most difficult for modern readers. It is apocalypse, a type of literature that flourished in Israel from the second century BC to the second century AD. Apocalyptic literature has its roots in the Old Testament, especially the prophetic books of Daniel, Ezekiel, Zechariah, and parts of Isaiah.

Apocalyptic literature has a number of key characteristics. (a) Apocalyptic writings tend to be *crisis literature*, written during periods of political instability and foreign oppression, when God's people were severely tested. The message is that things are going to get much worse before they get better, but that God is in charge and will faithfully deliver his people. (b) Apocalyptic literature is *eschatological* (from the Greek word *eschatos*, "last" or "end," used in reference to the end times), meaning that the present crisis is the beginning of the transition from the present evil age to the "age to come"—the kingdom of God. The images of judgment tend to be cosmic in scope. Creation itself is about to be shaken as the present world gives way to the world to come. (c) The term "revelation" is appropriate for this literature since the authors usually receive *divine mysteries* concerning spiritual realities and/or the events leading up to the end of history and the final judgment. These mysteries are often delivered through angels. (d) Apocalyptic literature is highly *symbolic*, using both common objects (bowls, trumpets, scrolls) and bizarre imagery (dragons, beasts, human-faced locusts) to portray spiritual realities. Numbers often have symbolic significance. The number seven, for example, appears throughout the book of

Revelation and probably indicates completeness. There are seven churches, lamp stands, seals, trumpets, bowls, last things, and spirits; the lamb has seven eyes and seven horns (5:6). Other symbolic numbers are 666 (the mark of the beast; 13:18) and 144,000 "servants of God," 12,000 from each tribe of Israel (7:4–8). (e) Most Jewish apocalyptic writings are *pseudonymous* (written under an assumed name), attributed to a great Old Testament figure, like Adam, Enoch, Abraham, Elijah, or Ezra.

The book of Revelation has all of these features, with one exception: it is not pseudonymous. Whether written by John the apostle or another John, such as John the Elder, the author clearly knows his readers and they know him.

Reading Revelation Today

Overall interpretive strategy. The strange and symbolic world of Revelation has resulted in a variety of approaches to the book throughout history. There are at least four main interpretive lenses through which the book has been read.

1. The *historicist* interpretation views Revelation as a summary of church history from the first century AD to the second coming of Christ. In this view the symbols in the book refer to specific persons and events throughout history. Though this interpretation has been popular in the past, especially during the Protestant Reformation (sixteenth century), it currently has few supporters. This is due to its extreme subjectivity and the fact that each generation has a tendency to interpret the events through its own lens and to view itself as the final generation.

2. The *idealist* interpretation sees the book as a wholly symbolic description of spiritual conflict throughout the ages, eventually climaxing in the victory of God at the end of history. Unlike the historicist view, which sees the symbols of Revelation as representing actual persons and events, the idealist view treats them as abstract symbols for good and evil and the eventual triumph of Christianity over paganism. In this interpretation, the book is equally applicable to any period of church history. For idealists, the thousand-year reign of Christ described at the end of the book (the "millennium"; 20:1–7) is not a literal reign of Christ on earth but a spiritual reign

that began with the resurrection and will conclude with the second coming and the establishment of a new heaven and a new earth.

3. The *preterist* interpretation places the events of the book entirely in the first century. In this view, Revelation symbolically represents the struggle between the church and its opponents, especially the Roman Empire. The book predicts the church's victory and deliverance at the imminent return of Christ. More liberal interpreters claim the author was mistaken and the end of the world did not occur as he expected. More conservative preterists see the judgments described in the book as fulfilled in the destruction of Jerusalem in AD 70 and in the eventual collapse of the Roman Empire. The cosmic nature of these judgments (stars falling from the sky, etc.) is meant to be taken symbolically rather than literally and is characteristic of apocalyptic hyperbole.

4. The *futurist* interpretation claims that the great majority of events in the book, with the exception of the opening visions and the letters to the seven churches, are still future and yet to be fulfilled. The book mostly concerns the events leading up to and including the second coming of Christ and the end of the age. The judgments described in the book will occur during the period known as the great tribulation, which will be followed by the return of Christ, the final judgment, and the creation of a new heaven and earth. There are two main futurist approaches, *historical premillennialism* and *dispensationalism*. Both consider the thousand-year reign of Christ to be an actual reign on earth that will precede the establishment of a new heaven and new earth. The primary difference is that dispensationalists stress the importance of the restoration of the nation Israel and its crucial political and spiritual role in the events of the end times.

The best approach to Revelation is one that combines a preterist and futurist perspective. The first-century conflict between Christianity and its opponents is certainly the backdrop to the book and must be taken into account when interpreting the symbols and imagery. But the book also envisions a still-future climax to these events, including a period of intense persecution and tribulation for the people of God, the victorious return of Christ with the armies of heaven, and the establishment of a new heaven and a new earth where God's people will live with him forever.

Principles of interpretation. Without a doubt, Revelation has been the most misunderstood and misinterpreted book in the Bible. People tend to go to one of two extremes. Some are so put off and confused by the bizarre imagery and outrageous interpretations of the past that they completely avoid the book. Others become obsessed with it and are convinced they have discovered the key to every image, usually finding its fulfillment in contemporary world events. Neither approach does justice to this important biblical book. Here are some important principles for a more sane and balanced approach.

1. *Recognize that the first century is the historical context of the book.* While Revelation certainly describes the consummation of all things at the end of time, it was written to seven historical churches and must be understood within the world in which these Christians lived. Whatever future events the book concerns must have been understandable—at least in a general sense—to its first-century readers. The book should be interpreted first and foremost from the perspective of the church's first-century struggle with paganism and with an increasingly hostile Roman Empire.

Too often Revelation is read through a modern lens instead of a first-century one. For example, when Iraq invaded Kuwait in the first Gulf War of 1991, popular books immediately began to identify Iraq as the Babylon of Revelation 17–19 and the invasion of Kuwait as the fulfillment of biblical prophecy. While it is true that Iraq is located in the general region of ancient Babylon, a first-century reader would have likely recognized "Babylon" as a code name for Rome (see 1 Pet. 5:13) and, symbolically, for the evil world system under Satan's power.[19] Too often readers try to interpret Revelation by reading today's news instead of by considering its own historical context.

2. *Recognize the symbolic nature of apocalyptic imagery.* The apocalyptic genre of the Revelation uses symbolic imagery to communicate both historical realities and spiritual truths. Trying to identify the images of Revelation literally generally runs counter to the nature of apocalyptic literature. Locusts from the pit, for example, symbolize destructive evil and should not be interpreted as literal descriptions of modern warfare (such as attack helicopters, as some have claimed). The original readers would never have recognized such an identification. Similarly, it is unlikely that the reference to a

third of the earth being burned up in Revelation 8:7 is a prediction of nuclear holocaust, as some have suggested. This is rather apocalyptic hyperbole, a symbolic way to describe the severity and cataclysmic nature of God's judgment.

3. *Understand that the Old Testament is the "code book" and "answer key" for the symbols of Revelation.* The book of Revelation has more allusions to the Old Testament than any other New Testament book, and it is this background that provides the best clues to the meaning of its symbols. The four horsemen of the apocalypse (6:2–8), for example, find their counterpart in the horsemen and chariots of Zechariah 1:8–17; 6:1–8. The beast that comes out of the sea in 13:1 is an echo of Daniel's vision of four beasts from the sea in Daniel 7:2–7 (symbolizing a succession of world empires). The invasion of Gog and Magog in 20:7–8 has its background in Ezekiel 38–39. Though the symbols used in Revelation are certainly fluid and may not carry the same meaning as their Old Testament counterparts, this Old Testament background is a much more reliable guide to their meaning than contemporary world events. The popular dispensationalist identification of Gog and Magog with the Soviet Union during the Cold War, for example, never had credibility either from the perspective of the Old Testament or from historical geography.

4. *Focus on general rather than specific meanings.* Throughout history the identification of images in Revelation with specific persons or events has always proved to be mistaken. From the first century onward, people have identified the antichrist with a bewildering array of individuals and ideas, including the Roman emperor Nero, the Roman Empire in general, the Pope (identified by Martin Luther), Martin Luther (identified by the Pope), Peter the Great of Russia, Rasputin, Hitler, Stalin, Anwar Sadat, Ronald Reagan, Mikhail Gorbachev, and Barack Obama. Such misguided interpretations discredit both Christians and the authority of the Bible in the eyes of the world. The book of Revelation was not written as a mystery to be solved but as a prophetic message to be heard and obeyed. Its essential message is clear: God's people are called to perseverance and faithfulness in light of the certainty that God is the sovereign Lord of the universe who will eventually triumph over Satan, sin, suffering, and death. The victory has already been won through Jesus,

the victorious Lamb who was slain, and will be consummated soon at his return in glory.

Answering the Four Questions for Revelation

1. *Where is Revelation in the larger story of Scripture?* From a canonical and theological perspective, the book of Revelation represents the "end of the story" (and the beginning of a new one). If the narrative of Scripture as a whole is the drama of redemption, then the book of Revelation is the final act. The account that began in Genesis 1–3 with the creation of the world and fall of humanity now ends with the reversal of the results of the fall and the restoration and renewal of all things.

This consummative function of the book is significant for application. The images of the people of God here represent the church in its perfected state. In Revelation 7, for example, an innumerable multitude from every nation, tribe, people, and language stands before the throne in white robes praising God and worshiping the Lamb (7:9). The glorified assembly of God's people reflects ethnic and cultural diversity. Their white robes represent purity, achieved not by personal merit but because they have "washed their robes . . . in the blood of the Lamb" (7:14). Their role is to stand before the throne of God and to "serve him day and night" (7:15). God himself will be their provision and their protection. He will "shelter them with his presence" and be their shepherd, feeding them, protecting them from the scorching sun, providing living water, and wiping away every tear (7:15–17). Here we see humanity in its glorified and perfect state. Our goal for the church should be to become a body of diversity and purity, whose purpose and passion is to praise and glorify God in all that we do.

2. *What is the author's purpose in light of the passage's genre and historical and literary context?* The central theme and principles of interpretation set out above enable us to interpret individual passages in Revelation. Even if the specific identification of the image eludes us, we can determine its general function in the book with a high degree of certainty.

Consider, for example, in Revelation 13 the image of a beast that emerges from the sea. As noted above, there has been a great deal of discussion and debate concerning the identity of this figure. Some consider him to be an individual antichrist who will emerge during the last days. The word "antichrist" actually does not appear in Revelation but is applied here based on its use by the author of 1 and 2 John, who refers to a coming "antichrist" who "denies the Father and the Son" (1 John 2:18, 22; 4:3; cf. 2 John 7). Paul similarly speaks of the "man of lawlessness" (2 Thess. 2:3), who "sets himself up in God's temple, proclaiming himself to be God" (2:4). Others view the beast as a symbol for the first-century Roman Empire, which was persecuting the church as the beast of Revelation does. Evidence for this, it is said, is the fact that the beasts that emerge from the sea in Daniel 7 are a succession of world empires. Still others consider the beast to represent the evil world system more generally, which throughout history has opposed God's purpose and his people.

All of these interpretations can be well defended with solid evidence from the text and from the historical context of Revelation, and there are able scholars on various sides of this debate. One's conclusion will likely depend as much on their overall interpretation of the book—whether futurist, preterist, or idealist—as on any individual piece of evidence. What is beyond dispute, however, is that the beast—whether individually or corporately—represents the Satanic forces in opposition to God, seeking to destroy his people and to thwart his purpose for the world. Together with the dragon (Satan; see 12:9; 20:2) and the beast from the earth (13:11), this beast forms an unholy "trinity" allied against the true Trinity and the people of God. This struggle between God and Satan, good and evil, right and wrong, has been going on since the beginning of human history and will be consummated on the final day of judgment.

This is not to say that a more precise identification of the beast is unimportant, or that we should not engage in detailed exegesis to try to solve the puzzle. Yet we should not allow the ambiguity and mystery that is so much a part of apocalyptic literature to distract us from the more important central message of the text.

3. *How does this passage inform our understanding of the nature of God and his purpose for the world?* No book in the Bible informs us better about the nature and purpose of God for the world than the book of Revelation. From the picture of the glorified Christ (chap. 1), to the throne room of God (chap. 4), to the innumerable

multitude standing before the throne and the Lamb (chap. 7), to the description of the new Jerusalem (chaps. 21–22), God's holiness, perfection, and sovereign lordship are on center stage. Throughout Revelation we learn that God alone is worthy of worship, that humankind's inclination is to turn away from him and worship idols, but that those who remain faithful to him throughout trials and persecution will triumph in the end.

Every passage in Revelation can be seen from this vantage point. In the episode about the beast from the sea (chap. 13), the beast is allied with Satan and his forces of evil in opposition to God. He utters blasphemies against God and makes war against God's people. All the people of the world will worship the beast—all, that is, except true believers, whose names have been written in the Lamb's book of life (13:8; cf. 21:27). They will remain faithful despite persecution, suffering, and even death. In the end, they will be vindicated, rising from the dead, reigning with Christ for a thousand years, and then becoming heirs of the new heaven and new earth (chaps. 20–22). While it is debated among interpreters how these events will actually play out on the stage of history, the central message comes through loud and clear.

4. *What does this passage teach us about who we ought to be (attitudes and character) and what we ought to do (goals and actions) as those seeking to reflect the nature and purpose of God?* Just as the nature of God and his purpose for the world are clear in the book of Revelation, so is the appropriate response of believers in Jesus Christ. True believers are characterized by faithfulness to God and his Son Jesus Christ, by trust in him through difficult circumstances, and by steadfast endurance in the face of persecution. The hero of the story of Revelation and the one who conquers in the end is the "Lamb who was slain," the one who was willing to sacrifice everything in order to be faithful to God. All those who wish to serve God must similarly take up their cross and follow him.

Conclusion

This chapter has discussed the interpretation and application of the major New Testament genres: the Gospels, Acts, the Epistles, and the book of Revelation. Though diverse in terms of their nature and function, all these are part of the grand narrative of the Bible and fit into the story of redemption.

Throughout these last two chapters we have seen that the diverse biblical genres were given in the context of human history and were shaped by the cultures and contexts in which they arose. One implication is that what a biblical author says to the people of a particular culture may not necessarily be God's message for every culture and context. In the following chapter, we will look more closely at how we can determine the will of God for today within the culturally embedded texts of the past.

Discussion and Reflection Questions

1. What does it mean that the Gospels are historical narrative motivated by theological concerns? In what ways are the Gospels history, story, and theology?

2. Why is it important to read the Gospels as individual narratives, rather than to merge them together into a single story?

3. What is the "kingdom of God"? Is it present or future? A reign or a realm?

4. What was Luke's purpose in writing Acts? How does this purpose play out throughout the book of Acts?

5. Is Acts meant to be a history of the early church? Is it a handbook on church order and function (church governance, baptism, the Lord's Supper)? If not, what is it?

6. What does it mean that the New Testament Epistles are "occasional" documents? Why is it important to determine the occasion and purpose of each of these letters?

7. What is the central theme of the book of Revelation?

8. What are some key principles for interpreting the book of Revelation?

8

When Cultures Collide

Discerning the Heart of God in Cultural Context

WAS RAISED IN A VERY CONSERVATIVE CHRISTIAN CHURCH. Every Sunday morning, and then again on Sunday evening, the Bible would be read and preached. The Bible was also taught at Wednesday youth group and small group Bible studies throughout the week. We memorized Scripture (King James Version, of course), and had "sword drills," where the prize went to the person who could find the verse in their Bible first. We were Bible-believing Christians who stood firm on the Word of God as our highest authority. I grew up hearing statements such as, "The Bible is God's inerrant, infallible, inspired, and authoritative Word. Every word of the Bible is true!" In Sunday school, we would sing heartily, "I stand alone on the Word of God, the B-I-B-L-E!"

What separated us from the "liberals" was that we took the Bible seriously and they did not. We believed what it literally said. They softened it to a mushy message of self-help and social platitudes—the words of humans, not the Word of God.

Looking back, I realize we did not always take the Bible quite as literally as I thought we did. We certainly took the Bible literally when it came to certain matters of leadership in the church. A woman could not be a pastor or an elder in our church because Paul explicitly taught that he didn't allow a woman to teach or exercise authority over a man (1 Tim. 2:11–15). We weren't quite so literal about Paul's command—in the same passage—that women must not wear braided hair, gold, pearls, or expensive clothes (2:9–10). When I was growing up, I saw a lot of gold jewelry, pearls, and expensive clothes in church.

Nor did we require the men of the church to "lift up holy hands" during worship, despite Paul's explicit command to do so (again, in the same passage; 1 Tim. 2:8). In fact, nobody in our church ever lifted up their hands—whether holy or otherwise. This was because the charismatics lifted their hands in worship, and everyone knew the charismatics were whacked-out emotionalists, who allowed their emotions to take precedent over their obedience to God's Word. *They* certainly didn't take the Bible seriously, with all their speaking in tongues and dancing in the aisles. The apostle Paul said that "God is not a God of disorder but of peace," and "everything should be done in a fitting and orderly way" (1 Cor. 14:33, 40). That ruled out the babbling and disorder of speaking in tongues and prophetic utterance.

Yet while we took the command for order in worship in 1 Corinthians 14:40 quite literally, we weren't so literal when it came to the previous verse, 1 Corinthians 14:39. Paul says, "be eager to prophesy, and do not forbid speaking in tongues." Nobody in our church was eager to prophesy, since we believed prophecy had ceased two thousand years earlier, and we *did* forbid the speaking in tongues, since we believed it too had long since ceased. Tongue speaking was considered pure emotionalism and even demonic. We were cessationists when it came to the charismatic gifts, believing that the so-called sign gifts—tongues, prophecy, interpretation of tongues, healing, and so on—had ceased at the close of the canon of Scripture in the first century AD. Despite the claim of taking the Bible literally, we did a fair bit of picking and choosing about *which* passages to take literally and which to dismiss as "not relevant."

The same could be said of my church's approach to Bible prophecy. Like the rest of Scripture, we interpreted the book of Revelation "literally" (as good dispensationalists). We believed in the imminent return of Christ and that the church would be raptured at the beginning of a seven-year period of persecution known as the tribulation. During this period, the antichrist would arise as a world leader and make a covenant with the Jews. He would subsequently break that covenant and begin persecuting them, or at least those 144,000 Jews who had come to faith in Jesus Christ. Those who followed the antichrist would receive the mark of the beast, 666, on their hands or foreheads. Those who refused would be martyred. At the climax of this persecution, the battle of Armageddon would take place. Russia and China would invade Israel, but Christ would return with the armies of heaven and wipe them out. He would then establish his kingdom on earth—the millennium—and we would reign with him for a thousand years.

This future could be mapped out so clearly because, we believed, we took Revelation literally. Others, like those amillennialists and covenant theologians, did not. They allegorized everything and did not believe in the rapture, the great tribulation, the antichrist, or the millennium. They didn't take the Bible seriously enough.

Looking back, however, I realize my church did not take Revelation quite as literally as I thought. After all, Russia and China do not appear in Revelation by name, and the supposed references to them are dubious at best. The word "antichrist" never appears in Revelation, and the "person" identified as the antichrist is not a person at all. It is a hideous beast with ten horns and seven heads that crawls out of the sea (Revelation 13). If you *really* took Revelation literally, you would have to conclude that the antichrist is going to look more like Godzilla than like the handsome Nicolae Carpathia (the character of the antichrist in the *Left Behind* novels). In reality, nobody takes the book of Revelation literally. Everyone takes it symbolically. What differs is how they interpret those symbols and the relationship of those events to world history.

Please don't get me wrong. I am still a dispensationalist, and I certainly still believe the Bible is God's inspired and authoritative Word. In fact, I am more convinced now than ever before. But I also recognize that all of us come to the text with a worldview, a theological framework, a family history, and our own agendas. Learning to read and apply the Bible well means learning to acknowledge those agendas and hear God speak to us—sometimes in very countercultural ways.

This brings up one of the most difficult aspects of application, touched on at various points throughout this book: How do we determine which commands, exhortations, and examples in Scripture are culturally relative, and so may not apply to us today, and which represent absolute standards of right and wrong that apply to every culture and context? This chapter will address this question.

The goal here, however, is not to identify which commands in the Bible are cultural and which are not. As we have seen throughout this book, all biblical revelation is contextualized theology. All the Bible's commands, promises, exhortations, narratives, laws, prophecies, and so on are given within the context and limitations of human language and culture. A particular truth may be *transcultural* (equally true for all human cultures), but nothing is *supracultural* (outside of human culture). Nor is the intent here to distinguish between commands intended for an original audience (say, the churches in Asia Minor, or an individual like Timothy) and those intended for all believers. Virtually all commands in Scripture were intended for a specific audience, whether a nation (Israel), a particular church or churches, or an individual. The goal, rather, is to seek the "heart of God"—the divine ethic, standard, or purpose that is expressed through the text. If we can determine this, we can discern God's will for us in new and changing contexts and circumstances.

We will first examine three *models* that have been proposed for envisioning the process of contextualization. I believe all three provide helpful insight for the cultural analysis of biblical texts. Like all models, these three also have certain deficiencies. Next, we will turn to various *criteria* that have been proposed to discern this heart of God or divine ethic within the culturally and historically embedded statements of Scripture.

Models for Cultural Analysis

Models are helpful in that they give us a concrete picture as we seek to conceptualize abstract truths and methodological schemes. The three models discussed below are (1) a *hermeneutical bridge* spanning the chasm between two cultural and historical contexts; (2) a *pyramid or ladder of abstraction* moving from the top down, from general truths to specific, culturally unique applications; and (3) a *trajectory of the Spirit,* whereby biblical commands are seen to lie somewhere along the path between God's condescension to human culture and the absolute ethic to which he is leading them.

These models are not necessarily mutually exclusive. They can be complementary, as are the models of *story, drama,* and a *journey* proposed in chapter 4 with reference to scriptural engagement. Each model provides a unique angle or vantage point to envision the task of applying culturally embedded texts.

Crossing the Hermeneutical Bridge and Back

The first model or analogy for cultural analysis is used frequently in hermeneutical circles: a bridge stretching across a gorge, chasm, or river. The gorge represents the time, space, culture, and language that separate us from the original authors and settings of Scripture. Our first hermeneutical task is *exegesis:* crossing the bridge from our world to theirs to determine the author's *meaning* in its original context. Our second task is then *contextualization:* bringing that message back across the bridge and determining its *significance* for today.

In their well-written and accessible volume on biblical interpretation, *Grasping God's Word,* Scott Duvall and Danny Hays adopt this model and consistently apply it to the Bible's various genres.[1] The hermeneutical task is envisioned as a trip from one town to another, requiring the traveler to cross a historical and cultural bridge between the two. Duvall and Hays propose four essential steps for us as interpreters to bring the meaning home to our own time and place: (1) grasp the text in the other town (What did the text mean to the original audience?); (2) measure the width of the river to cross (What are the differences between the biblical audience and us?); (3) cross the principlizing bridge (What is the theological principle in this text?), and (4) grasp the text in our town (How should individual Christians apply the theological principle in their lives?).

One strength of this analogy is its simplicity, describing the hermeneutical process as two basic steps: exegesis and contextualization.

Another strength is that it drills into readers the reality of the historical and cultural distance between the world of the Bible and our own, and hence the need for careful and critical exegesis. There is always a danger we will misread the Bible because of our own cultural blinders. This strength, however, can also be a weakness, because of the model's emphasis of discontinuity over continuity. The world of the text is not in fact a different *world*, but another place in the same redemptive story as our own. Those on the other side of the bridge are not strangers or foreigners but our spiritual ancestors. We are not outside observers evaluating the redemptive story as passive observers but rather active participants in that story. This is *our story* as well.

Joel Green argues that it is false to draw a strict dichotomy between meaning and significance. The church needs to read the Bible *as Scripture*, rather than as an historical artifact. He writes:

> Critical exegesis today tends toward a hermeneutical theory that presumes that we must make pilgrimage into the world of the biblical text in order to ascertain its truths, then return to our world in order to transform those truths into contemporary thought and language forms. The exegetical vision I am sketching presumes that the idea of "pilgrimage" is thus wrongly applied. "Pilgrimage" is more appropriately a description of the character of our lives in this world, with our status as strangers in the world attributed to our making our home in the world of Scripture. In this hermeneutical scenario, *it is not the message of the Bible that requires transformation; it is we who require transformation.*[2]

The greatest problem we face in reading the Bible, Green says, is not our lack of information about the world of the text (the exegetical questions). The problem is theological—learning to hear the text *as addressed to us*. "We may happily reconstruct our portrait of the [disenfranchised] recipients of the Letter of James in historical terms. We may be less happy to read it as though it were addressed to us. . . . We do not desire the status of societal misfits, deviants in the world around us." Until we do, he argues, we cannot hear the letter of James *as Christian Scripture*.[3]

Green's caution is well taken. The Bible was written to the people of God, and we are the people of God. It is easy to read a text of

212

Scripture and say, "That was for them. In our cultural context it means such and such." The result can be a watered-down message that fits comfortably into a modern Western lifestyle, while it neglects the radical demand that the authentic gospel makes on our lives. While Green's caution does not negate the need for sound exegesis and a recognition of the original context of Scripture, it does remind us that we are not passive observers who "glean principles" from the lives of biblical characters. We are rather fellow travelers on the same salvation-historical journey that they are on. Green's description of reading the Bible as Scripture sounds a great deal like our heart-of-God hermeneutic: "It aims for its readers to embark on a journey of theological formation bounded only by the character and purpose of God."[4]

Another possible shortcoming of the bridge analogy is that, while it emphasizes the need to establish theological principles and to cross the cultural bridge, it doesn't actually provide insight into how this is done. Saying, "cross the bridge with a principle," is one thing. Knowing how to decide which principle to carry across is another. In defense of Duvall and Hays, they do provide helpful guidelines on how to discover these principles. But the model itself does not provide the guidelines. Our second model focuses more specifically on the means by which to discern principles from the text.

The Pyramid or Ladder of Abstraction: In Search of Principles

Jack Kuhatschek, in his clear and practical volume *Taking the Guesswork out of Applying the Bible*, develops a method for discerning cultural factors in Scripture using the model of a pyramid and "levels of application."[5] At the very top of the pyramid are the two greatest commands: love God and love others. Principles closer to the top of the pyramid are more general and abstract (e.g., "love one another"). They do not, however, tell us specifically how this ought to be practiced. As we move downward on the pyramid, commands become more specific culturally and situationally. For example, Paul's specific statement about eating food sacrificed to idols (1 Cor. 8:13) is based on a more general principle: do not cause a brother or sister to fall into sin (1 Cor. 8:9). This principle, in turn, is based on an even more general principle: do only what builds others up (1 Cor. 8:1). The key for applying the more specific cultural commands is to identify their place on the pyramid, move up to the general principle, then move down again to specific application in a new cultural context. From the specific command related to idol meat, for example, we move up to the general command to never tear down others by our behavior, and then down again to find a specific application in our own cultural context (e.g., not to drink alcohol in front of a recovering alcoholic).

Walter Kaiser has similarly proposed a "ladder of abstraction," which functions essentially the same as Kuhatschek's pyramid of application.[6] Kaiser illustrates this two-sided ladder with the command in Deuteronomy 25:4 not to muzzle oxen that tread grain:

> Here is how the Ladder of Abstraction works: from the *ancient specific situation* (oxen that tread out grain) we move up the ladder to *the institutional or personal norm* (animals are God's gifts to humanity and should be treated kindly), to the top of the ladder, which gives to us *the general principle* (giving engenders gentleness and graciousness in those mortals who care for and can minister back to those who serve them as well, whether they are animals or people). As we descend the ladder on the other side, we meet *the theological and moral principle* behind our general principle ("love your neighbor" . . .), to the contemporary or New Testament *specific situation* (pay those pastors ministering to you, including Paul, 1 Cor. 9:9–12).[7]

In this model, identifying the level of specificity becomes the key to applying culturally embedded texts. It is the top of the pyramid that represents the heart of God, or the essential divine ethic. This heart of God can be expressed in a variety of ways, depending on the cultural context.

If the bridge analogy for cultural analysis is helpful for its clarity, the pyramid of abstraction model is helpful for its practicality. Most commands in Scripture fit quite well along a line from the very general to the very specific. Paul's warning to the Gentile Christians in Galatia not to be circumcised (Gal. 5:2–3) is a very specific command, pointing to the more general truth that no one can be justified by keeping the Old Testament law (Gal. 5:4). This, in turn, points to the even more general truth that no human effort can achieve salvation (Gal. 3:3).[8] While the first two truths do not have much direct application for (Gentile) Christians today, the third certainly does.

Another strength of the pyramid approach is its simplicity, with the clearly delineated goal of establishing principles to live by. The task of application gets boiled down to the simple formula of finding in each scriptural passage a general proposition or statement about truth. These general principles are then used to address ethical issues and contemporary situations not directly addressed in Scripture.

While the pyramid or ladder of abstraction is a very helpful tool, it does have some shortcomings. One weakness is that, although it is relatively clear and straightforward with reference to propositional statements in Scripture, it is not so clear how it functions with a variety of other literary forms in Scripture. Principles may be quite easily derived from direct commands, warnings, instructions, and proverbs but less clear-cut in narrative, prophecy, psalms, parables, and apocalyptic literature. The method needs further explication with reference to these literary forms.

In this way principlizing can inappropriately privilege certain literary forms over others. Yet the diverse literary forms of Scripture are an asset rather than a liability, and other literary forms can communicate truth as well and even better than propositional statements. I sometimes ask my students what is the greatest text in the Bible on grace. They often point to Ephesians 2:8–9 (or some other propositional statement): "For it is by grace you have been saved, through faith—and this is not from yourselves, it is the gift of God—not by works, so that no one can boast." This is a great answer, but what about the parable of the prodigal son? Although the parable does not include the word "grace" or make any propositional statements about grace, the story powerfully illustrates the meaning of grace. Why should we privilege principles over story? Daniel Doriani makes a similar point with reference to Jesus's rhetorical questions in Mark 8:17–21.[9] After the disciples fail to comprehend Jesus's warning about the "leaven" of the Pharisees, Jesus responds with a series of questions.

> "Why are you talking about having no bread? Do you still not see or understand? Are your hearts hardened? Do you have eyes but fail to see, and ears but fail to hear? And don't you remember? When I broke the five loaves for the five thousand, how many basketfuls of pieces did you pick up?"

"Twelve," they replied.

"And when I broke the seven loaves for the four thousand, how many basketfuls of pieces did you pick up?"

They answered, "Seven."

He said to them, "Do you still not understand?"

Jesus's eight rhetorical questions clearly represent a more effective means of communicating truth than if Jesus had simply stated a general principle: "I can provide all that you need." Flattening everything into propositional statements can reduce the powerful effect of God's Word.

Taking this a step further we might ask whether establishing "principles" is the ultimate goal of interpretation. The Christian life is not just about knowing the right answer; it is also about living in light of God's nature and will. For example, which is more important when reading the parable of the prodigal son: identifying the principle of unqualified forgiveness, or living out the story as the loving father did by offering God's forgiveness to others? This critique could be leveled at any method of application, including the heart-of-God approach advocated in this book. Application is about more than simply knowing the answers—it is about walking with God in his story and realigning our attitudes and actions in light of his purpose and will. It is about being and doing, not just knowing.

Another possible weakness of the pyramid or ladder of abstraction model is that principlizing may downplay the significance of the interpreter's own context by assuming that a propositional truth or principle is somehow above culture. David Clark, for example, suggests that "principlizing obscures the fact that any articulation of the allegedly transcultural principles still reflects the culture of the translators."[10] While this may well be true, this critique again could be applied to almost any method of application. All interpreters have a tendency to apply texts in line with their own cultural biases and worldview. Paul's command for women to cover their heads in worship in 1 Corinthians 11 will likely be interpreted by a complementarian as a call for female subordination but by an egalitarian with reference to propriety in worship. The goal for all of us should be to try to look beyond our personal biases to discern the heart of God reflected in the passage.

These cautions, though important, do not negate the value of the pyramid or ladder of abstraction to establish principles. Indeed, almost all methods of contextualizing, even those that eschew "principles," eventually resort to some form of principlizing. We are people of order and logic, and we appreciate statements that say it like it is.

One final concern with principlizing is that it tends to gloss over the necessity for serious engagement with the cultural problems in the text. To say that the command for a man to marry a woman he has raped (Deut. 22:28–29) teaches the principle of personal responsibility may be true, but it glosses over the larger ethical question of why God would allow (what appears at first sight to be) such abusive exploitation of women. Another model for cultural engagement, the "trajectory of the Spirit," seeks to engage these more serious cultural challenges found in Scripture.

Tracing the Trajectory of the Spirit: A Redemptive-Movement Hermeneutic

A third, and more controversial, model for cultural analysis is William Webb's "Trajectory of the Spirit," or Redemptive-Movement Hermeneutic (RMH).[11] Webb's basic thesis is that many of the commands of Scripture represent a less-than-ultimate ethic because of the limitations of history and culture. Though the Bible does not necessarily give us the final word on a particular topic, it reveals a clear redemptive movement, or trajectory of the Spirit, which enables the reader to move beyond the specifics of inculturated texts toward an ultimate ethic. This ultimate ethic represents God's will for us today.

Webb finds the strongest support for his model in the Bible's teaching on slavery. The commands related to slavery for Israel in the Old Testament reveal a vast improvement over the treatment of slaves found in surrounding ancient Near Eastern cultures. Slaves in Israel were treated as people, not just property, and penalties were imposed for abuse of slaves. Yet these Old Testament laws still seem a far cry from mandates for an ideal society. Slaves were still treated as property to be bought and sold, and masters, though warned against excessive cruelty, were at liberty to beat their slaves with impunity (Exod. 21:20–21). The New Testament shows a clear "redemptive movement" beyond the Old Testament, with affirmations that both slave and free have the same Master and that all believers are equal in Christ (Eph. 6:9; Gal. 3:28). At the same time, New Testament writers never condemn slavery outright, and they encourage their readers to live righteously within the system rather than to work to abolish it. From a modern perspective, it looks as though the New Testament does not establish an ultimate ethic on slavery, but rather a trajectory or arrow pointing in the direction the Spirit wants God's people to go, namely, toward full emancipation.

Webb finds the same kind of redemptive movement in the Bible's teaching on corporal punishment.[12] Pro-spanking advocates often use Old Testament texts about corporal punishment to defend their view of discipline (e.g., Prov. 13:24: "Whoever spares the rod hates their children"). Webb argues, however, that they are not reading their Bibles very closely, since the Old Testament view of corporal punishment is far more severe than pro-spanking advocates would allow. For example, most of these advocates teach that spanking should be done primarily in the preschool years, diminishing up to ages ten to twelve, and should not be used at all in the teen years. It should be as infrequent as possible, entailing only one or two smacks on the bottom, and never leaving welts or bruises. It should never be done in anger. Webb points out that, by contrast, when the Old Testament speaks about corporal punishment, it sets no age limit, encourages the use of frequent beatings, allows for up to forty lashes on the back (not the bottom), accepts bruises and welts as appropriate, and assumes that anger is the disposition of the one who disciplines (Exod. 21:20–21; Deut. 25:1–5; Prov. 10:13; 18:6; 19:29; 20:30; 22:15; 26:3; Isa. 50:6; cf. Sir. 23:10; 28:17; 30:12).[13] Webb's point is not that these modern pro-spanking advocates are wrong. In fact, he agrees with their moderate approach. But then he shrewdly suggests that they are unconsciously adopting the same redemptive-movement hermeneutic that he is advocating. Because of cultural and historical factors, the Bible's teaching does not represent the ultimate ethic in terms of disciplining children, but rather points forward to where the Spirit wants the church to go.

Webb's main thesis is that if this hermeneutic is true for slavery and corporal punishment, it is likely true for other ethical issues where the canonical text may not represent an ultimate ethic. He especially brings this argument to bear on the role of women in the church and the home, affirming an egalitarian perspective with respect to leadership roles of women. Commands in the New Testament such as those in 1 Timothy 2:11–15, which apparently forbid women from teaching or leading men, should be seen as adaptations to particular cultural contexts rather than as an ultimate ethic related to the roles of women and men.

What is most controversial about Webb's theory is the claim that this ultimate ethic is not found within the limits of the canon of Scripture. In some cases the ultimate ethic must be determined by a trajectory that begins in the Bible but reaches its fullest expression beyond the first-century world in which the New Testament arose. So what is to prevent an anything-goes hermeneutic, where contemporary culture, rather than the Bible, dictates our theology and ethics? Webb's answer is that if the Bible reveals no redemptive movement or upward trajectory, then there is no justification for going beyond the biblical text. The consistent condemnation of homosexual practice throughout Scripture confirms the transcultural nature of these commands. There is no danger of ethical relativism, since it is the Bible—not culture—that establishes the trajectory.

In response to strong opposition to his views, Webb has answered a number of misconceptions. He denies, for example, that an RMH seeks a "better ethic" than that of the New Testament. It rather seeks to identify the ethics of the Old and New Testaments *rightly understood and applied*.[14] Against critics, he affirms that an RMH views the New Testament as the final and definitive revelation. But being the final *revelation* "does not automatically mean that the New Testament contains the final *realization* of social ethics in all its concrete particulars."[15] Webb clarifies his position: "The idea of a RM hermeneutic is not that God himself has somehow 'moved' in his thinking or that Scripture is in any way less than God's word. Rather, it means that God in a pastoral sense accommodates himself to meeting people and society where they are in their existing social ethic and (from there) he gently moves them with incremental steps towards something better."[16]

There are important strengths in a redemptive-movement hermeneutic. Webb recognizes that all Scripture comes to us in inculturated form. As God accommodated to frail human flesh in the Incarnation, so he accommodates to less-than-ideal human cultures in order to incrementally move his people toward his greater purpose for the world. Since we are at a different place culturally from the people of God in the Old and New Testaments, the message to them is not necessarily the application for us. Old Testament texts have traditionally been easier to recontextualize *covenantly*, that is, on the basis of their old covenant context. A redemptive-movement hermeneutic allows similar flexibility *culturally* with reference to New Testament texts.

Another strength of a redemptive-movement hermeneutic is that it enables Webb to face head-on the most troublesome and perplexing biblical texts. If *all* Scripture is inspired by God and is profitable for teaching, rebuking, correcting, and training in righteousness (2 Tim. 3:16), then why do we tend to avoid the slave-beating and daughter-selling texts of the Old Testament? Webb's method allows the preacher to say, "Wow! Look at how far the Old Testament message has advanced beyond the pagan cultures around it, and look at where the Holy Spirit is taking us. God really is redeeming his world!"

Yet Webb's approach is also fraught with hazards.[17] Identifying trajectories can be a daunting task. As children of our own culture, we will tend to view those things that our culture finds acceptable as a "better ethic." In critiquing Webb, Daniel Doriani raises the intriguing question of whether Westerners too quickly dismiss the benefits of corporal punishment of adults. In his own informal survey, "every man chose painful blows over lost years [in prison]."[18] We must be cautious about assuming too quickly what is or is not a better ethic.

I also wonder whether a trajectory model is sufficient to explain the diversity of ethical instruction and cultural contexts found in Scripture. A trajectory model implies that if you have two points along the line, you can project outward to the ultimate goal. But can such a consistent trajectory be discovered in the biblical text? Even the issue of women and men that is central to Webb's thesis in *Slaves, Women & Homosexuals* yields mixed results. Paul's most egalitarian statement appears in what is likely his earliest letter (Gal. 3:28) and his most restrictive statement in one of his latest (1 Tim. 2:11–15). Is Paul moving in the wrong direction?

Instead of a trajectory approach, it is preferable to speak of commands given to fit particular cultural situations and contexts. Old Testament commands related to slavery were given in the historical context where indentured servitude was an accepted fact, considering the social and economic system in which Israel existed. So God allowed it, but with stipulations protecting slaves from exploitation and cruelty. Slavery was also endemic to Greco-Roman society, so Paul provided instructions on how to live a God-honoring life within this cultural situation, rather than commanding Christian masters to free their slaves. Is this the establishment of a trajectory, or is it different commands appropriately addressing different social and cultural contexts?

This raises the intriguing and potentially disturbing question of whether there might be cultural situations today where Christians should not call for the abolition of certain controversial practices—such as polygamy, slavery, or the inequality of women—but would instead provide ethical guidelines related to their practice. Imagine, for example, the gospel penetrating a particular tribal context, where society was structured around polygamous relationships and unmarried women were subject to danger, exploitation, or deprivation. Should the missionary insist upon divorce and the abolition of polygamy in society? Or would it be more ethical to teach that love, kindness, and fairness should be shown to each wife? Or suppose that a limited form of slavery or indentured servitude provided the social welfare system for another tribe. Should missionaries insist upon emancipation or, like Paul, should they teach that believers show kindness and love to one another and that they—whether slave or free—are one in Christ and servants of the same ultimate Master?[19]

In cases like these, even if we decided that the missionaries should condescend to a less-than-ultimate ethic, we would expect them to gradually encourage the people toward a higher standard of ethical behavior, that is, to move toward God's "ultimate ethic" or "ethical ideal." This brings us to the primary topic of this chapter: how to determine standards of theology and ethics that represent God's ultimate will and purpose for human behavior and belief. The following section will propose a series of criteria to help us discern the heart of God in cultural context.

Criteria for Discerning the Heart of God in Cultural Context

There are three basic steps for contextualization that are generally agreed upon among biblical scholars: (1) establish the meaning of the text in its original historical and literary context (exegesis); (2) identify the divine ethic, ethical ideal, or principle behind the specific teaching or command of Scripture; and (3) determine ways in which this ethical ideal can be lived out in contemporary contexts. The first step is sometimes divided into two, with the second evaluating the distance or differences between the culture of the text and our own contemporary culture.[20] These three (or four) steps are not necessarily linear, and each informs the others. It is impossible to exegete a text, for example, apart from a broader perspective on Christian theology and ethics.

Informing such steps are rules, guidelines, or criteria that aid in cultural analysis. These criteria guide us in determining how cultural factors are affecting the text and so help us to discern God's purpose and will (the process of moving from step one to step two). Almost all hermeneutical theorists, whatever their model for hermeneutical engagement, utilize such criteria to evaluate the ethical and theological issues of Scripture. Grant Osborne discusses eight criteria or "principles for determining supracultural content."[21] Charles Cosgrove provides five hermeneutical rules for appealing to Scripture in moral debate.[22] Walter Kaiser identifies five guidelines for cultural interpretation.[23] William Webb develops eighteen (!) criteria for cultural analysis.[24] Similar lists are provided by Fee and Stuart;[25] Klein, Blomberg, and Hubbard;[26] and others.

In the following discussion, we will survey eight key criteria for delimiting God's ultimate ethic from within the culturally and historically embedded commands of Scripture.[27] Of these eight, the first three may be seen as *primary* or *controlling principles*. The remaining five come into play especially when the first three produce mixed, conflicting, or uncertain results.

1. Criterion of Purpose

This criterion is of fundamental importance, since determining the original purpose of the command, instruction, law, or rule allows us to apply its message to analogous situations today. Cosgrove states the criterion of purpose this way: "The purpose (or justification) behind a biblical moral rule carries greater weight than the rule itself."[28] Suppose, for example, I give my son ten dollars and ask him to go down the street and take the car through the automatic car wash. He comes back an hour later, hands me my ten dollars, and says, "I washed and waxed it myself, and vacuumed the inside." Has he obeyed me? While he did not obey my direct command (go to the car wash), he recognized the purpose of the command (a clean car) and fulfilled that purpose. In fact, he exceeded my command by cleaning the interior and returning my money.

The same principle applies to biblical commands. The rationale behind the commands by Peter and Paul for believers to greet one another with a kiss (1 Pet. 5:14) is not to make sure lots of kissing takes place in the church. It is to emphasize that believers are family and should show familial affection toward one another (Rom. 16:16; 1 Cor. 16:20; 2 Cor. 13:12; 1 Thess. 5:26). This purpose was fulfilled one way in its first-century context but may be fulfilled in a variety of ways in other cultural contexts. Indeed, in some cultural contexts kissing could run contrary to the purpose of the command. For this reason, the rationale behind the rule is more important than the rule itself.

It should be evident how this principle of purpose relates to the pyramid or ladder of abstraction discussed above. Abstract commands tend to be related more directly to their purpose, while more specific and concrete commands tend to reflect cultural applications. Paul's purpose for commanding believers not to eat food sacrificed to idols was not because the food itself was evil or because other gods actually existed. Paul points out that "an idol is nothing at all in the world" and "there is no God but one" (1 Cor. 8:4). Furthermore, all food is clean since "the earth is the Lord's, and all it contains" (1 Cor. 10:26 NASB, citing Ps. 24:1), and so the person who eats such food is no better or worse spiritually than the person who doesn't eat (1 Cor. 8:8). Rather, the purpose for Paul's instruction is to avoid causing other believers to fall into sin (1 Cor. 8:9). Suppose, for example, Paul's readers avoided idol meat but caused their fellow believers to sin in some other way. Though keeping the letter of the law, they would be violating its purpose and spirit. Jesus's teaching in the Gospels also often looks beyond the letter of the law to its spirit. For instance, he states that the purpose of the Sabbath commandment is not slavish observance of a ritual but rest and renewal for human beings (Mark 2:23–3:6). Likewise, the ultimate purpose of the commands against murder and adultery goes beyond external behaviors to reconciliation and healthy relationships (Matt. 5:21–30).

By determining the purpose of a command, we can apply it appropriately in our own cultural context. For the holy kiss, this might mean a hug or handshake, or some other appropriate means of family affection. For commands related to idol meat it would mean avoiding situations that could cause someone else to sin. Here is an illustration. At one point I was counseling a married couple, and the husband, who was a rock musician, asked me if I would come hear his band play. I said, "Sure." That weekend I visited the club he was playing at, bringing along a friend. After a few minutes my friend became very agitated. I could tell something was wrong, and so we left. As we talked about it afterward, I learned that before he became a Christian he had been involved in the club scene, an area of sin and continuing temptation in his life. What was not a temptation or cause of sin for me was a real danger for him. Though Paul could not have envisioned a modern nightclub in his letter to the Corinthians, identifying his purpose enables us to apply his commands in appropriate contemporary contexts.

The criterion of purpose confirms the need for careful exegesis. Only by understanding the genre of the text and its historical and literary context can we determine the author's purpose in writing. It follows that the more difficult the interpretation, the more cautious we need to be in our application.

Consider Paul's command in 1 Corinthians 11:5–6 for women to cover their heads in worship. The text is notoriously difficult to exegete, and major problems confront the interpreter. Consulting a good commentary on the passage, you will see a bewildering array of difficult questions: Is the passage as a whole about wearing head coverings or about long hair and short hair (see the note in the NIV on v. 7)? What is the historical background to head coverings (Jewish or Gentile? Secular or religious?)? Does the figurative use of "head" in verse 3 mean "authority" (cf. Eph. 1:22) or "source" (cf. Eph. 4:15)? Is this text about men and women, or about husbands and wives? (In Greek, the same word can mean either "man" or "husband"; likewise, the word for "woman" can also mean "wife.") Does the phrase literally translated "having down the head" (11:4) mean a physical head covering, long hair, or loose, flowing hair? Similarly, does "uncovered" (11:5) mean "having no covering" or "having short hair"? Is uncovered hair the mark of a prostitute, or something else, such as a pagan religious tradition? Whose "head" is dishonored in verse 5 (the woman's head or the man, as her head)? Why the command to shave the head (11:6)? What does it mean that the woman is the "glory" of man (11:7)? Is the "authority" upon the woman's head a sign of her own authority, or the man's authority (11:10)? What does "because of the angels" mean in 11:10? Some of these questions are easier to answer than others, but together they present a formidable obstacle for us to be certain of the interpretation. In cases like this, the degree of exegetical uncertainty should cause us to have an equal degree of humility and caution in application.

2. Criterion of Cultural Correspondence (Coherence or Analogy)

This criterion asserts that the closer the cultural or historical context to our own, the more likely we can apply the command directly. Fee and Stuart speak of "comparable particulars": "Whenever we share comparable particulars (i.e., similar specific life situations) with the first-century hearers, God's Word to us is the same as his Word to them."[29] Osborne similarly writes that "we must determine the degree to which the commands are tied to cultural practices current in the first century but not present today."[30] Cosgrove calls this the criterion of *analogy*, quoting a definition by James M. Gustafson: "Those actions of persons or groups are to be judged morally wrong which are similar to actions that are judged to be wrong or against God's will under similar circumstances in scripture."[31] This principle is sometimes called the criterion of *coherence*, since commands that cohere with contemporary practice are more likely to apply directly today.

Paul's command not to get drunk with wine (Eph. 5:18) provides a good example of this criterion. Drunkenness in the ancient Near East and the Greco-Roman world resulted in the same kinds of social and societal damage as alcoholism does now: loss of control, poor judgment, a tendency toward physical or verbal abuse. The application for us is therefore the same as it was for them: avoid drunkenness, which results in dissipation.

Contrast this with the issue of a head covering in worship, which clearly does not have the same cultural connotations in most Western cultures now that it did in the first century. In the great majority of churches in America, a veil or head covering is not a sign of piety or reverence, and the lack of a head covering does not bring shame to a woman or to the church. One can see how this criterion is used in concert with the criterion of purpose. The purpose of a head covering today differs from its purpose in the first century, and so culturally the command does not have the same relevance.

Consider also haircuts on men, an issue addressed in this same passage in 1 Corinthians 11. We are again at a loss exegetically when Paul writes, "Does not the very nature of things teach you that if a man has long hair, it is a disgrace to him, but that if a woman has long hair, it is her glory?" (1 Cor. 11:14–15a). What is strange about this statement is that while in the Old Testament men are prohibited from dressing like women (Deut. 22:5), nothing is said about men wearing their hair long. On the contrary, the Old Testament Nazirite vow *requires* that those taking the vow avoid a haircut for a period of time (Numbers 6). In the book of Acts, Paul himself is described as keeping such a vow, ending it with a haircut in Cenchreae (a harbor city near Corinth) shortly after leaving Corinth on his second missionary journey (Acts 18:18). Ironically, this means that Paul had long hair while establishing the church at Corinth, only to write a few years later to that same church that it is a "shame" for a man to have long hair!

So what does this text mean? Paul probably does not mean that long hair is "unnatural," since the natural process would be to grow hair long. The Greek word *physis*, translated "nature" (NASB) or "the nature of things" (NIV), in this context probably means "custom," referring to the Greco-Roman custom of short hair on men. Since the standards of hair length on men have varied over different times and cultures (and since it is not altogether clear what Paul intended), we should be reluctant to view this statement as binding for all Christians for all time.

This criterion of cultural correspondence can be brought to bear on various commands throughout Scripture. We have discussed earlier the question of tattoos, which are expressly forbidden in the Old Testament (Lev. 19:28). This command was likely related to pagan religious markings and so has little in common with modern tattoos. If the situation is not analogous, the command does not apply today. The likely purpose of the command, however, was to avoid anything that would indicate loyalty to a "god" other than the one true God. This could, of course, relate to some modern tattoos, depending on their purpose, or to any number of other things: the clothing we wear, the music we listen to, the movies we watch, the "toys" we buy for our homes and garages.

Consider also Paul's New Testament command to Timothy: "Stop drinking only water, and use a little wine because of your stomach and your frequent illnesses" (1 Tim. 5:23). If we took all commands in the New Testament as binding today, we would have to insist that all Christians drink wine whenever they have stomach problems. But the criterion of cultural correspondence reminds us that these situations are simply not analogous. This command has as its context a culture where water was often contaminated and wine functioned both as a purifying agent and for medicinal purposes. The situation is very different in cultures where clean water is readily available and where a range of medicines can be used to treat stomach ailments. This does not prohibit the use of wine in moderation, but it does mean that none of us are commanded to drink it.

These first two criteria—purpose and cultural correspondence—work in conjunction with each another.[32] By identifying the purpose of the command or instruction in its own historical context and then carefully comparing this to cultural practices today, we can evaluate the relevance of most biblical commands for a variety of cultural contexts.

3. Criterion of Canonical Consistency

This third criterion asserts that ethical imperatives that remain consistent and unchanged throughout the Bible—in diverse cultural, social, and historical situations—are more likely to reflect God's universal purpose and will than those that change depending on the time and place.[33] This criterion comes into play especially with distinctly moral commands, since God's fundamental standards of right and wrong do not change over time or culture. Commands against murder, stealing, lying, cheating, coveting, adultery, exploitation of the poor, and idol worship remain consistent throughout the Old Testament and the New and so are binding for all time.

This criterion also relates to the radical transition from the Old Testament to the New, when Israel's covenant given through Moses at Mount Sinai gave way to the new covenant age inaugurated through the life, death, and resurrection of Jesus Christ. The change of ages brought the fulfillment of the law, a transition we see working itself out in the New Testament through the abrogation of many Old Testament laws. Israel's sacrificial system, for example, was fulfilled through the once-for-all sacrifice of Christ, and so new covenant believers are no longer bound to offer animal sacrifices (Heb. 10:11–14). Similarly, while Israel was commanded to avoid a whole range of foods that God deemed "unclean," in the New Testament all foods are declared clean (Mark 7:19; Acts 10:15; Rom. 14:14; 1 Cor. 8:8).

The Old Testament law also commanded that all Israelites tithe, giving to the Lord a tenth of all they produce (Lev. 27:30). The tithe, however, is never explicitly commanded in the New Testament, and believers are instead encouraged to give generously from their hearts (2 Cor. 9:6–7). This is in line with the New Testament testimony that believers have the law written in their heart and so live by the power of the Holy Spirit. This does not get Christians off the hook with reference to giving, however. Indeed, when Jesus speaks of the fulfillment of the law in the Sermon on the Mount, he *raises* the standard of righteousness. It is no longer enough to avoid murder; you must also stop hating, since hate is equivalent to murdering someone in your heart. It is not enough to avoid adultery; you must no longer lust, since lust is committing adultery in your heart (Matt. 5:20–30). Though believers are no longer commanded to tithe, this heart-righteousness frees them up to give even more!

This principle of canonical consistency applies not only to the transition from the Old Testament to the New but also within the New Testament itself. We know that Jesus's specific instructions related to the missionary outreach of his disciples do not represent universal norms for all missionaries, since they change from one set of instructions to the next (Luke 10:4; 22:36). Similarly, the rich young ruler is called to sell everything he has and give to the poor

(Matt. 19:21; Mark 10:21; Luke 18:22), but other believers are told to use their resources to accomplish God's purpose. The universal principle here is that everything we have belongs to the Lord and should be used in his service.

As noted above, these first three criteria—purpose, cultural correspondence, and canonical consistency—serve as foundational and controlling principles for cultural evaluation. For the great majority of ethical imperatives, these should be sufficient to render a decision. However, with a number of issues we face greater difficulty, either because of ambiguity in Scripture or because of more complex social and cultural situations. The following five criteria can help us find a way through this uncertainty. However, not all of the five will be equally relevant for every passage or issue.

4. Criterion of Countercultural Witness

This criterion claims that when "teaching transcends the cultural biases of the author and readers, it is more likely to be normative."[34] Jesus's command to love one's enemies, for example, runs contrary to the conventional wisdom of his day (Matt. 5:44). In comparison, the Wisdom of Jesus ben Sirach, a book of classical Jewish wisdom from the second century BC, instructs love for friends and hatred for enemies: "If you do good, know to whom you do it. . . . Give to the devout, but do not help the sinner. Do good to the humble, but do not give to the ungodly. . . . For the Most High also hates sinners and will inflict punishment on the ungodly. Give to the one who is good, but do not help the sinner" (Sir. 12:1–7 NRSV).[35] In a context where hate for enemies was assumed, Jesus's instruction to turn the other cheek, to love enemies, and to pray for those who persecute you was strikingly countercultural and without doubt represents the heart of God (Matt. 5:39–46; cf. Rom. 12:14–21).

Similarly, Paul's instruction to husbands to model Christ's self-sacrificial love toward their wives (Eph. 5:25) was given in a culture where wives were generally viewed as the property of their husbands. First Corinthians 7 presents what would have been viewed as a radical sexual ethic for the first century. Paul says not only does the wife owe her husband conjugal rights (a given in that culture), but the husband owes the same to his wife: "The wife does not have authority over her own body but yields it to her husband. In the same way, the husband does not have authority over his own body but yields it to his wife" (1 Cor. 7:4). While the former was expected, the latter would be surprisingly countercultural in the patriarchal world of the first century.

The higher status women were accorded in the early church was no doubt a result of Jesus's own attitude. Jesus had women followers, which was countercultural and potentially scandalous in a day when Jewish rabbis would not consider women worthy of discipleship. The Mishnah, a body of Jewish traditions codified around AD 200, reads, "Every man who teaches his daughter Torah is as if he taught her promiscuity" (Mishnah, *Sotah* 3:4). The Jerusalem Talmud, compiled somewhat later, says, "Let the words of Torah be burned up, but let them not be delivered to women" (Jerusalem Talmud, *Sotah* 19a). While such anti-women sentiments were probably not the view of all Jewish teachers of Jesus's day, they appear to be predominant. Jesus challenged this traditional wisdom by accepting women as his disciples (Luke 8:1–3; 23:49). When he visited the home of Mary and Martha of Bethany, for example, Mary sat at Jesus's feet—the position of a disciple—learning from him. After Martha complained that Mary was not helping to prepare the meal (the traditional role of a woman), Jesus said, "Mary has chosen what is better, and it will not be taken away from her" (Luke 10:42). These are countercultural words indeed.

Paul is similarly revolutionary when he says, "There is neither Jew nor Gentile, neither slave nor free, nor is there male and female, for you are all one in Christ Jesus" (Gal. 3:28). There is a significant debate among modern interpreters whether Paul is referring here to full equality of gender roles or to equal access to salvation (see the case study below). In either situation, however, he is certainly being countercultural, since the ethnic (Jew/Gentile), social (slave/free), and gender (male/female) distinctions he mentions were considered inviolable and part of the very fabric of society. The gospel, Paul says, is the great leveler, giving all people equal status before God.

When commands and teaching like these run counter to contemporary cultural standards, they can be viewed as transcultural divine correctives to the failures of human culture.

5. Criterion of Cultural Limitations

The flip side of the fourth criterion is that we must exercise caution in instances where an author was operating within strong cultural or societal constraints.[36] An example of this is in Acts 16:1–3, where Paul circumcises Timothy before taking him on the second missionary campaign. Paul did this "because of the Jews who lived in that area, for they all knew that [Timothy's] father was a Greek" (16:3). Does this mean that in our own day all Christians with mixed Jewish and Gentile ancestry ought to be circumcised? The answer is no. Whereas Paul would likely have preferred to leave Timothy uncircumcised, since in Christ "neither circumcision nor uncircumcision means anything" (Gal. 6:15; cf. 2:3; 5:2–6; 1 Cor. 7:19), he recognized in this case that to leave Timothy uncircumcised would impede the progress of the gospel in Asia Minor. Paul was conceding to a particular social, cultural, and religious situation, not establishing a moral precedent for circumcision. He was willing to do whatever was necessary to advance the gospel: "To those under the law I became like one under the law (though I myself am not under the law), so as to win those under the law" (1 Cor. 9:20).

The classic issue with reference to this criterion is slavery. Paul's failure to call for the full emancipation of slaves is disturbing to most modern readers. Although neither Paul nor any other biblical writer advocates or affirms the institution of slavery, they also do not explicitly condemn it or call for Christians to free their slaves. This silence, however, must be judged within a cultural context where a call for emancipation would have resulted in immediate arrest and execution. The Roman Empire was built on the backs of slaves, and the Romans did not look kindly on those who opposed their institution. Slave revolts were ruthlessly suppressed. While Paul repeatedly hints at the discrepancy between the redemption provided by Christ and the institution of slavery (1 Cor. 7:22; Gal. 3:28; Eph. 6:9; Col. 3:24; Philem. 16–17), he evidently viewed it as counterproductive to the progress of the gospel to actively work toward emancipation.

Someone might argue against this conclusion that Paul was certainly ready to give his life for the faith, so why would he not speak out against slavery? But Paul had a specific commission from Jesus Christ, which was to take the gospel to the ends of the earth, and, more specifically, to serve as apostle to the Gentiles. The inevitable consequences of working for the emancipation of the slaves would have sidetracked Paul from this divine commission. Furthermore, Paul expected the return of Christ in the near future, even during his lifetime (1 Thess. 4:17). A transitory earthly institution like slavery was of little consequence in light of the coming radical transformation that would come with the kingdom of God. Looking back from two thousand years later, especially in light of the horrors of African slavery in America, we wish Paul and others would have spoken more strongly against this evil institution. But we can better understand their reluctance when we see the strong cultural and social factors against which they were working. Just as countercultural statements in Scripture are likely to transcend specific situations, so statements that appear to be concessions to culture are *less likely* to have universal application.

6. *Criterion of Creation Principle*

This criterion asserts that "a component of a text may be transcultural if its basis is rooted in the original-creation material."[37] The rationale here is that all of God's created order prior to the fall was "very good" (Gen. 1:31), so patterns established in Eden transcend cultural norms. Klein, Blomberg, and Hubbard assert, "Creation ordinances refer to principles for how people should live that God established prior to the Fall of humanity into sin. Presumably, such principles remain part of the redemptive ideal for Christians as they are progressively renewed in God's image after their salvation."[38] One example of this is in the role relationship between men and women, which Paul appears to link to the order of creation in 1 Timothy 2:13–14. (We will take up this issue below in a case study on the role of women and men in the church and the home.) Another example for this criterion is heterosexual monogamy, which is the pre-fall standard for human sexuality (Gen. 2:24). Both Jesus (Matt. 19:5) and Paul (Eph. 5:31) appeal to Genesis 2:24 when discussing marital and sexual ethics. The implication is that all other sexual behaviors (such as polygamy, homosexuality, adultery, pederasty, and bestiality) fall outside of God's will. Although divorce (Matt. 19:8; Deut. 24:1) and polygamy (Gen. 29:15–30) are tolerated in certain cultural contexts, neither represents God's original intention for human relationships. (We will discuss homosexuality in a case study below.)

7. Criterion of the Character of God

This criterion asserts that the fundamental attributes of God—such as holiness, mercy, love, and justice—adjudicate in disputed contexts, or when the cultural background is obscure. In Leviticus 19:2, the Lord commands all Israelites to "be holy because I, the LORD your God, am holy."[39] As children of God, our lives should reflect the holiness that is inherent in God's nature and character.

In 1 Corinthians 13, Paul pauses in the midst of his long and complex discussion related to spiritual gifts in the church to affirm the priority of love in all things. Throughout chapters 12–14 the apostle seeks to strike an appropriate balance, affirming the Corinthians' use of spiritual gifts while warning against the pride, elitism, and confusion characteristic of their use of spiritual gifts. In the midst of this, he says, "And yet I will show you the most excellent way" (1 Cor. 12:31). This better way is the way of self-sacrificial love for others, the fundamental character of God that should control all behavior. Paul says something similar in his discussion of food sacrificed to idols a few chapters earlier (chaps. 8–10). "We all possess knowledge," he says, "but knowledge puffs up while love builds up" (8:1). Again, God's fundamental attribute of love becomes the adjudicating principle for disputed issues.

8. Criterion of Redemptive Priority

Throughout this book I have stressed the nature of the Bible as the story of God's redemptive action in restoring creation. This last criterion states that commands directly related to God's historical-redemptive purpose take priority over lesser issues, such as those related to church order and function. Suppose, for example, that the doctrinal position of a particular church states that believers' baptism by immersion is the proper method of baptism established in the New Testament. Another church approaches them about joining together in an evangelistic outreach in the community. This second church, however, practices infant baptism by sprinkling. Should the first church partner in such a case? All other things being equal, this

233

criterion would assert that the fundamental command to make and baptize disciples of all nations should take precedence over an issue such as the nature or mode of baptism (a disputed doctrine among evangelicals). On the other hand, suppose the second church affirmed the doctrine of baptismal regeneration, the claim that the baptismal waters actually accomplish the spiritual cleansing of salvation. In this case, the first church might choose not to participate, since the issue has now become one of redemptive priority, concerning the actual means of salvation.

Three Test Cases: Sabbath Observance, Homosexuality, and Women in Church Leadership

Here we will apply our criteria to three theological and ethical issues of pressing concern for the church.

The Sabbath Commandment

The relevance of the command to abstain from all work on the Sabbath (Exod. 20:8; Deut. 5:12) is a disputed issue in the church, and there is a range of views on the command's validity. Seventh-Day Adventists, for example, consider the command to be valid, and, like Jews, observe the Sabbath from Friday evening through Saturday evening. Many other Christians consider the Sabbath to have continuing validity but view Sunday as the new "Christian Sabbath," since this was the day of Christ's resurrection. Yet others consider the Sabbath day to have been fulfilled in Christ, though the principle of a Sabbath rest still applies today. Christians, they say, should therefore set aside regular times for rest, reflection, and worship.

The criterion of canonical consistency would appear to favor this third option. The Sabbath command is the only one of the Ten Commandments not repeated in the New Testament, and there is evidence that New Testament writers considered the command to be fulfilled in Christ. Jesus claims to be "Lord of the Sabbath" (Matt. 12:8; Mark 2:28; Luke 6:5), presumably with the authority to overrule it, and Paul tells the church at Colossae that they should "not let anyone judge you" with reference to Jewish festivals or a "Sabbath day" (Col. 2:16). Even more explicitly, in Romans 14:5 Paul writes,

"One person considers one day more sacred than another; another considers every day alike. Each of them should be fully convinced in their own mind." This lack of canonical consistency suggests that Old Testament commands to abstain from work on the seventh day (Saturday) are no longer binding for Christians.

At the same time, the criterion of creation principle favors some sense of continuing validity for a Sabbath rest. After the six days of creation, God rested on the seventh day, setting it off as holy. Genesis 2:3 reads, "Then God blessed the seventh day and made it holy, because on it he rested from all the work of creating that he had done." No command is given here for humans to avoid work on the Sabbath, however, and only in the law given to Israel at Mount Sinai do we find a specific command to cease all labor on the Sabbath (= the seventh day). While the principle of rest is a part of God's nature and so should be practiced by his human subjects, the specific command to rest on the seventh day was part of Israel's ceremonial law. The early Christians, as far as we can tell, did not consider the Sabbath commandment to be binding, gathering instead to worship on "the first day of the week" (1 Cor. 16:2), "the Lord's Day" (Rev. 1:10)—that is, the day of the resurrection.

While the questions of whether and how Christians should keep the Sabbath continue to be debated,[40] our criteria suggest that while the principle of Sabbath rest may be binding for all time, the specific application of how and when that rest is practiced is governed by our freedom in Christ.

Homosexuality

Homosexuality is likely the most divisive ethical issue facing the modern church. Hardly a week goes by when there is not a news story about a church or denomination making some statement or taking some action either supporting or opposing homosexual behavior. I tell my students that if the role of women in leadership was the most contentious question for my generation (Christians in their forties and fifties), the issue of homosexuality will surely be the most controversial one for theirs. It is essential to approach this issue with sensitivity, balance, and fairness. Because many heterosexuals find homosexual behavior repulsive, they tend to assume that biblical

235

injunctions against homosexuality must certainly be binding today. Yet we must approach this issue with the same hermeneutical care and balance that we use with other cultural and theological issues, recognizing that the Bible was given within a particular cultural context and that not everything it says is necessarily binding for us now (e.g., the holy kiss, head coverings, footwashing, etc.).

Nevertheless, when we apply our criteria, it seems evident that the Bible's commands against homosexual behavior go beyond mere cultural norms. In contrast to the Bible's teaching on issues like food laws, tithing, and the Sabbath, the perspective on homosexuality remains consistent throughout Scripture.[41] Applying the criterion of creation principle, we see that Genesis 2 establishes monogamous heterosexual relationships as the pre-fall standard for human sexuality: "a man leaves his father and mother and is united to his wife, and they become one flesh" (Gen. 2:24). Any form of sexual behavior outside the marriage relationship—whether premarital, extramarital, or homosexual—lies outside the bounds of God's purpose for human sexuality. While the teaching in Genesis 2 is implicit, the Old Testament law explicitly condemns homosexual behavior: "Do not have sexual relations with a man as one does with a woman; that is detestable" (Lev. 18:22; cf. 20:13; 1 Cor. 6:9).

The New Testament continues this canonical consistency. In Romans 1, Paul identifies homosexual behavior as one example of the depravity that results from humanity's rejection of God. Because human beings exchanged the truth of God for a lie and worshiped and served created things rather than the Creator, "God gave them over to shameful lusts. Even their women exchanged natural sexual relations for unnatural ones. In the same way the men also abandoned natural relations with women and were inflamed with lust for one another. Men committed shameful acts with other men, and received in themselves the due penalty for their error" (Rom. 1:26–27). The phrase "God gave them over," repeated three times in the passage (vv. 24, 26, 28), indicates that human beings received the natural consequences of their rejection of God and idolatry, which in this case was a distortion of their human sexuality.

Pro-homosexual advocates often use the criterion of cultural correspondence to argue that Paul's teaching against homosexuality has nothing to do with loving, monogamous, homosexual relationships.

Paul knew nothing of such relationships, and he is only condemning abusive sexual relationships like pederasty and slave prostitution. Similarly, it is often argued that Romans 1 only condemns "perversion" (acting contrary to one's natural sexual orientation) not "inversion" (acting in line with one's natural sexual orientation, whether heterosexual or homosexual).[42]

But this cannot be Paul's meaning. First, Paul's Jewish background rules out any such interpretation, since Judaism unequivocally condemned homosexual behavior. Second, as Douglas Moo points out, Paul's use of the antonyms "male" and "female" (v. 27), rather than "man" and "woman," "stresses the element of sexual distinctiveness and throws into relief the perversity of homosexuality by implicitly juxtaposing its confusion of the sexes with the divine 'male and female he created them' [Gen. 1:27]."[43] Third, in context Paul explicitly identifies heterosexuality as that which is "natural" (*physikos*) and homosexual as "unnatural" (*para physin*). Since homosexuality was widely practiced and accepted in the Greco-Roman world, he cannot mean that it is "contrary to custom." He must mean that it is contrary to God's created order for human sexuality. C. E. B. Cranfield, in his widely acclaimed commentary on Romans, notes that by *physikos* and *para physin*, "Paul clearly means 'in accordance with the intention of the Creator' and 'contrary to the intention of the Creator,' respectively."[44] Like premarital sex, adultery, or pederasty, homosexual sex is ruled to be wrong by virtue of God's design. Other New Testament passages also identify homosexual behavior as contrary to God's will (1 Cor. 6:9–10; 1 Tim. 1:9–10).

Several cautions and clarifications are necessary at this point. First, lest homosexual behavior be viewed as somehow unique or the greatest of all sins, it should be noted that Paul goes on to list many other sins that result from our fallen state, including envy, murder, strife, deceit, malice, gossip, slander, God hating, insolence, and arrogance (Rom. 1:29–31). Second, while the Bible condemns homosexual *behavior*, it does not condemn homosexual *inclination*. Many young people experience enormous anxiety and guilt because of homosexual feelings. Like all other temptations, homosexual desires become sin only when they are acted upon (James 1:14–15). James says the key is not to let that desire give birth to sin but to deal with it in a constructive manner.

The church needs to play a constructive role in supporting and helping those with homosexual inclinations, developing an attitude of "welcoming but not affirming."[45] Too often the church has been a place of guilt and judgment instead of a community of education, support, guidance, counseling, and, most of all, grace.

Women in Leadership in the Church and the Home

While the testimony of Scripture toward homosexuality seems to be univocal, other controversial issues present a more complicated picture. This is true, for example, concerning the role of women in leadership. Massive tomes have been devoted to this controversial issue, and we certainly will not resolve it here.[46] By discussing the application of various criteria, however, we can better understand the process of cultural analysis.

Ancient Israel was a patriarchal society, and women generally did not serve in leadership roles. Male leadership was not so much mandated as assumed. This was true in both the religious and political spheres. Only men served as priests in the tabernacle and temple, and the legitimate king of Israel was the male heir from David's line. The patriarch of a household or clan had absolute authority over that clan. In the New Testament, too, patriarchy was the order of the day. Jesus—though countercultural in many ways—chose twelve men to be his apostles. As far as we can tell, elders and overseers in New Testament churches were all men (Titus 1:6; 1 Tim. 3:2). Paul writes to Timothy that he does not allow a woman to teach or to assume authority over a man (1 Tim. 2:11–15), and wives are encouraged by both Peter and Paul to submit to their husbands (Eph. 5:22; Col. 3:18; 1 Pet. 3:1).

At the same time, there are some notable exceptions to this male leadership in both the Old and New Testaments. Miriam served in a leadership role as a prophet beside her brothers Moses and Aaron (Exod. 15:20; Num. 12:1–2). Huldah was a prophet (2 Kings 22:14; 2 Chron. 34:22). Deborah was a prophet and a judge, the latter being a position of both judicial and political authority (Judges 4–5). In the New Testament, Priscilla was a gifted teacher and one of Paul's "co-workers in Christ Jesus" (Rom. 16:3). She is generally named before her husband Aquila, suggesting that she had the more prominent role (Acts 18:26). Phoebe is identified as a "deacon" and "patron" of the church at Cenchreae (Rom. 16:1). Junia is referred to as "outstanding among the apostles" (Rom. 16:7), a disputed phrase that may identify her as having apostolic authority. Two women, Euodia and Syntyche, are referred to as "co-workers" who have contended at Paul's side in the cause of the gospel (Phil. 4:2–3). While the precise nature of each of these roles is debated (endlessly), and some interpreters deny that any of these women actually assumed leadership over men, the preponderance of evidence suggests there were occasional exceptions to the general rule of male leadership. It seems to be special pleading, for example, to claim that Deborah was only a private counselor rather than a ruling judge.

The criterion of creation principle also comes into play on this issue. This is not because of the creation account itself, which does not (explicitly) refer to male leadership. Although Eve is referred to as Adam's "helper" (Hebrew: 'ezer; Gen. 2:18, 20), this term does not necessarily carry any sense of subordination. The same word is frequently used of God as the one who helps his human subjects (Exod. 18:4; Deut. 33:29; Hosea 13:9; Ps. 70:5; etc.). While God's judgment against the woman says that her husband "will rule over" her (Gen. 3:16), this is not part of God's perfect creation but part of the fallen world. The argument from the order of creation does appear, however, in the letter of 1 Timothy. In discussing order in worship, Paul writes, "A woman should learn in quietness and full submission. I do not permit a woman to teach or to assume authority over a man; she must be quiet. For Adam was formed first, then Eve. And Adam was not the one deceived; it was the woman who was deceived and became a sinner. But women will be saved through childbearing—if they continue in faith, love and holiness with propriety" (1 Tim. 2:11–15).

Paul apparently identifies Adam's priority in creation as the reason he does not allow a woman to teach or assume authority over a man.[47] As with 1 Corinthians 11, this text has many difficult exegetical questions. Is this passage about men and women generally, or about husbands and wives? In what way does the deception of Eve disqualify a woman from teaching or having authority over a man? Is Paul saying that women are more easily deceived than men and so should not be allowed to teach? If this is the case, why do churches forbid women to teach men (who should not be deceived) but allow them to teach children (who are easily deceived)? The answer I think most complementarians would give is that we are referring here to *authoritative teaching in a position of senior leadership*, which is reserved for men. But then the question becomes, When, who, and under what circumstances are women allowed to teach?

Even more perplexing in this passage is Paul's statement that woman will be "saved through childbearing" (1 Tim. 2:15). This can hardly mean that she will be saved by having children. Some interpret it to mean that women should "work out [their] salvation" (Phil. 2:12) through the traditional role of bearing and raising children. Others, that "childbearing" should be translated "the childbirth," a reference to the coming of Jesus the Messiah.[48] None of these views seem very convincing.

A storm of controversy surrounds this passage, especially related to our first two criteria (purpose and cultural correspondence). What is the purpose of Paul's command, and how does this purpose relate to the unique social and cultural situation in the church at Ephesus in which Timothy is ministering? Complementarians claim that the appeal to creation means Paul is establishing universal standards related to men and women in the church. Egalitarians counter that Paul is addressing a unique situation in the church at Ephesus and so the passage does not apply to the church in our own day and age. They argue that the women at Ephesus were likely uneducated and in need of instruction before they could teach or exercise authority over others.

The two sides of this issue have reached something of an exegetical impasse, and it is unlikely to be resolved any time soon. It will likely be worked out for each individual, church, or denomination in the trenches of pastoral ministry rather than in the ivory towers of academia. Here, however, are a few points to consider.

First, there is no doubt that the biblical world was strongly patriarchal and that this worldview had an impact on the early church. Not everything we see happening in the Bible with reference to men and women necessarily applies to the church of all time. Most everyone would agree that this is true with issues like women and men praying with heads covered or uncovered (1 Cor. 11:4–5), men lifting hands in prayer (1 Tim. 2:8), and women not wearing gold, pearls, or certain hairstyles (1 Tim. 2:9; 1 Pet. 3:3; 1 Cor. 11:15). But might it also be true for leadership roles in the church? From a cultural standpoint, it is likely that elders and overseers in the first-century church were all men, but this does not necessarily rule out women in such leadership positions today. The occasional exceptions in Scripture should caution against too rigid a stance.

Second, despite these cautions, some of the biblical imperatives related to men and women appear to go beyond merely first-century cultural norms. This seems to be the case with Paul's argument from the order of creation in 1 Timothy 2:13, which is hard to explain away culturally. It is also likely true for his statements about male "headship" in 1 Corinthians 11:3, and the leadership role he affirms for husbands in the home (Eph. 5:22; Col. 3:18; cf. 1 Pet. 3:1). We must, of course, qualify these statements with the biblical nature of leadership. True Christian leaders, Jesus says, serve rather than rule, and they sacrifice themselves for others (Mark 9:35; 10:42–45). The husband's role is not to rule his wife but to love her sacrificially, "just as Christ loved the church and gave himself up for her" (Eph. 5:25). If men were exercising the kind of self-sacrificial leadership Jesus taught, I suspect this issue would be much less volatile.

Third, in a disputed case like this, the greatest need is for mutual respect and charity. Paul's constant appeals for unity in the church have a much more prominent place in his letters than the relatively isolated discussions of the role of women in leadership (see Rom. 15:5; 1 Cor. 1:10; 11:18; 2 Cor. 13:11; Eph. 4:3; Phil. 2:2; Col. 3:14; cf. 1 Pet. 3:8). While this does not make these gender passages unimportant, it would be a terrible thing for the cause of Christ if we allowed this issue to divide the church and so compromise its fundamental mission.

Finally, if the criterion of redemptive priority is a valid one, it is certainly applicable here. The progress of the gospel should assume a higher priority than an issue of church order and function. Even very conservative churches have often affirmed the leadership roles of women in particular contexts, especially cross-cultural ones, where men are unable, unwilling, or unavailable to go.[49] It is sad and ironic that in some cases women are allowed to assume leadership roles "over there" but receive little respect in their home churches.

Perhaps it would be best to adopt a principle of exceptionalism, in which women whose gifts and calling are evident to the church are encouraged to pursue those gifts without constraint, but where it is assumed that God primarily equips men for such roles. This appears to be the biblical model, where occasional exceptions appear in a broader context of male leadership. I am fully aware that such a compromise solution will not be received favorably by those who stand firmly on either side of this issue. Complementarians will no doubt warn that this is opening Pandora's box and will result in a collapse of male leadership in the church. Egalitarians will object that this is a denial of the most fundamental truth of their position: that in Christ there is no longer any distinction between Jew or Gentile, slave or free, male or female. We are all one in Christ (Gal. 3:28). As I noted at the beginning of this section, we are unlikely to resolve this issue any time soon. But hopefully the discussion will continue with a spirit of love and gracious respect for the views of others.

Conclusion

This chapter has discussed models or analogies for conceptualizing the process of cultural analysis, whereby we seek to discern the heart of God in the culturally embedded texts of the Bible. Three models have been discussed.

The first model is a *hermeneutical bridge* spanning the chasm between two distinct cultural and historical contexts: the world of the text and the contemporary world. The strength of this model is that it highlights the distance between two worlds. We must hear the text on its own terms before we can apply it to our life. A weakness is that, by stressing discontinuity, we may too easily dismiss the Bible as for another time and place and so miss the immediacy and power of God's Word to speak directly to us. The Bible should challenge our worldviews and shake up our preconceptions.

The second model is a *pyramid* or *ladder of abstraction* moving from the top down—from general truths to specific, culturally unique applications. The strength of this view is that it provides a practical tool to evaluate somewhat objectively the degree to which biblical commands are culturally relative. A weakness is that by flattening application to merely finding principles, we risk giving priority to certain literary forms (laws, instruction, proverbs, etc.) over other, equally important ones (narrative, parables, prophecy, etc.).

The third model is a *trajectory of the Spirit*, where biblical commands are seen to lie somewhere along the path between God's condescension to human culture and the absolute ethic to which the Holy Spirit is leading God's people. This model has the strength of recognizing that all the imperatives of God's Word, even the New Testament ones, are embedded in human culture and must be recontextualized for the world in which we live. The potential weakness is that we will impose contemporary cultural standards on the text, rather than hearing and heeding *God's* standards of righteousness.

Models like these help us conceptualize a task but don't provide methods or rules for accomplishing that task. So next were introduced eight criteria by which we can analyze culturally embedded texts. The first three are primary, while the remaining five adjudicate in more ambiguous or disputed cases. These eight include: (1) purpose: the goal or intention behind the command allows us to find a contemporary application that will accomplish the same purpose; (2) cultural correspondence: biblical imperatives apply today if their social or cultural significance remains the same in modern times; (3) canonical consistency: commands or models of behavior that are consistent throughout Scripture most likely reflect the heart of God; (4) countercultural witness: statements that run counter to social or cultural values of their day are more likely to be transcultural; (5) cultural limitations: statements that appear to condescend to strong cultural constraints are less likely to be transcultural; (6) creation principle: the pre-fall situation is assumed to represent God's ideal standards; (7) character of God: fundamental attributes of God, like love, justice, holiness, and mercy, may be used to adjudicate in disputed cases; (8) redemptive priority: when criteria appear to conflict, priority may be given to those standards that align most closely with God's redemptive purpose.

Finally, these criteria were brought to bear on three theological and ethical test cases: the relevance of the Sabbath command, the morality of homosexual behavior, and commands and instructions related to women in leadership roles. Though we can never fully transcend our personal prejudices and theological blinders, the goal is to read the Bible as Scripture, to hear God speak to us today with as much clarity and conviction as he spoke to our spiritual ancestors in the past.

Discussion and Reflection Questions

1. Why is it not possible or appropriate to apply every command or promise in Scripture directly to our lives?

2. What are the three models or analogies for cultural analysis introduced in this chapter? How does each envision the process of taking a message in one cultural context and transferring it to another? Which model do you find most helpful?

3. What is the criterion of purpose? How does it enable us to discern transcultural truth?

4. What is the criterion of cultural correspondence, and how does it enable us to discern transcultural truth?

5. What is the criterion of canonical consistency, and how does it enable us to discern transcultural truth?

6. Which of the five remaining criteria do you find most helpful? Do you see problems or difficulties with any of these?

9

Conclusion

O N JULY 7, 2005, A. J. JACOBS SET OUT ON A ONE-YEAR odyssey. His goal: to live out the Bible as literally as possible. Jewish by ancestry and an agnostic by belief, Jacobs was motivated by a desire to reconnect with his Jewish roots (and to write a book about his experiences). His daily journal was eventually published as *The Year of Living Biblically: One Man's Humble Quest to Follow the Bible as Literally as Possible.*[1] The germ of the idea, Jacobs says, came from his eccentric Uncle Gil, "quite possibly, the most religious man in the world," a "religious omnivore," who at some point along his spiritual journey decided to take everything in the Bible literally.[2] The Bible says to bind money to your hand (Deut. 14:25 KJV), so Gil withdrew three hundred dollars from an ATM and tied the money to his palm with a thread. Following the command to wear fringes on your garments (Num. 15:38; Deut. 22:12), he bought yarn and tied blue tassels to his collar and sleeves. Since the Bible says to give money to widows and orphans, he walked the streets asking people if they were widows or orphans so that he could give them cash.

Jacobs modeled his year after this pattern. He read the Bible voraciously and took on a variety of spiritual advisors, including rabbis, ministers, and priests. He visited diverse communities of faith, each claiming to take the Bible literally—from fundamentalist Christians, to ultra-Orthodox Jews, to the Amish of Pennsylvania, to an ancient community of Samaritans.

The book describes Jacobs's humorous and often bizarre attempts at biblical literalism. He grows a wild and woolly beard, dresses like Moses, eats only kosher food, ties tassels to his clothing and stops wearing garments made of different kinds of material. The Bible commands the stoning of Sabbath breakers and adulterers, so Jacobs prowls Central Park looking for offenders. Not wanting to be arrested for assault, he pelts them secretly from behind with pebbles instead of rocks.

The book is entertaining and at times very funny. Jacobs learns a great deal about himself, about the Bible, and about a variety of religious traditions. He also experiences the impossibility of replicating the biblical world within the complexity of modern life. Indeed, this is where the book is heading all along—a parody of biblical literalism. Jacobs writes,

> Millions of people say they take the Bible literally. According to a 2005 Gallup poll, the number hovers near 33 percent; a 2004 *Newsweek* poll put it at 55 percent. . . . But my suspicion was that almost everyone's literalism consisted of picking and choosing. People plucked out the parts that fit their agenda, whether that agenda was to the right or left. Not me, I thought, with some naïveté. I would peel away the layers of interpretation and find the true Bible underneath. I would do this by being the ultimate fundamentalist. I'd be fearless. I would do exactly what the Bible said, and in so doing, I'd discover what's great and timeless in the Bible and what is outdated.[3]

This last statement is made with tongue firmly in cheek. Jacobs knows full well that taking the Bible "literally" will become an exercise in futility. In the end his noble experiment is a grand failure. It is a failure, however, not just because of the absurdity and "righteous idiocy" of biblical literalism.[4] It is a failure because Jacobs never really discovers what the Bible is about. It remains for him an often baffling, sometimes contradictory, list of rules to follow, a recipe book for finding a way in life.

But as we have seen, living "biblically" isn't about trying to figure out how to stone an adulterer without getting caught, or how to go shopping without being "defiled" by all the nonkosher food, or how to avoid touching women on the subway because they might be menstruating. It is about learning the ways and purpose of God in the world and walking with him on a day-to-day basis.

Finding the Heart of God in Scripture

In this book we have explored the nature of the Bible and how to apply its message to our lives in a constantly changing world. We began with the question of whether the Bible can ever be heard as the authentic voice of God, or whether its ancient message will forever be shaped by the competing agendas and personal motives of its diverse readers. To explore this question, we have to understand what the Bible is not: It is not a magic-answer book, a list of commands to obey, or a collection of promises to claim. Nor is it a textbook of systematic theology or a Help menu for Christian living. I proposed, rather, that the Bible is the drama of redemption, an authoritative and inspired narrative of the creation and fall of humanity, and God's plan to bring people, and all of creation, back into a right relationship with himself.

The key to reading the Bible well is recognizing its unity and diversity, the divine-human convergence that makes it both the words of humans and the Word of God. By diversity I mean it is a library of diverse works, written by many authors over many centuries in different cultures, contexts, and languages. To comprehend its message, we must enter the world of the text and seek to hear its message as it was originally heard. Exploring this diversity is the task of exegesis, which is utilizing our knowledge of the genre, language, historical setting, and literary context to determine the author's intended meaning.

While the diversity of the Bible illustrates its human side, the Bible's unity reminds us that Scripture is not just a collection of human reflections on religious themes. It is the Word of God, an authoritative message from God, revealing his purpose and plan for the world. We hear God speak to us today by finding our place in the Story and learning to walk with him. Applying Scripture begins by immersing ourselves in the ways of God in the past so that we can anticipate his will for the future.

I have called this immersion into the Bible's story a "heart-of-God" hermeneutic. Whichever analogy we use—living in light of God's story, improvising the drama of redemption, or walking with God along the journey of life—our goal is to bring our attitudes and actions in line with God's purpose and will. We should ask four key questions of any text of Scripture: (1) Where is this passage in the larger story of Scripture? (2) What is the author's purpose in light of the passage's genre and historical and literary context? (3) How does this passage inform our understanding of the nature of God and his purpose for the world? and (4) What does this passage teach us about who we ought to be (attitudes and character) and what we ought to do (goals and actions) as those seeking to reflect the nature and purpose of God? These questions allow us to find our place in the Story and gradually shape our heart, soul, mind, and strength according to the heart of God and the image of Christ.

This journey is never merely cognitive but always involves our whole person. Nor does this spiritual insight happen in isolation. God's voice is amplified and sharpened through our dialogue partners: the traditions of the church, the worldwide community of faith, and the guidance of the Holy Spirit. While none of these are infallible, neither is our private reading of the text. These partners therefore provide the checks and balances necessary to confirm the voice of God, which can otherwise be distorted through our lack of knowledge, spiritual blind spots, personal prejudice, or sin. The three partners are ultimately one, since each is a channel through which the Holy Spirit communicates his will to the people of God. Just as multiple instruments become one great symphony when played together in harmony, so these multiple channels bring clarity and consistency to our reading of the Word.

Finally, we addressed the pressing question of how to discern God's truth in the culturally embedded texts of the Bible. Three models or metaphors for cultural analysis were examined. The first was a bridge spanning the chasm of time, culture, and language; this bridge must be crossed to enter the world of the text and then to bring its abiding principles back to our world. The second was a pyramid, or ladder of abstraction, whereby we discern transcultural principles by moving up the pyramid from concrete, culturally specific commands to abstract truths applicable to every time and place. The third was a trajectory of the Spirit, through which we determine in Scripture the direction that the Holy Spirit is pointing his people and then follow this "redemptive movement" to God's ultimate ethic. Like all models, each of these has strengths as well as shortcomings.

Since models like these can conceptualize a goal but don't necessarily provide a method for achieving it, we proposed eight criteria for cultural analysis. These help us evaluate individual texts and themes of Scripture to determine what is culturally specific and what is transcultural. In this way we can discern the values, attitudes, and actions that God would have us adopt in new and different situations. In using the criteria, it is essential to keep in mind that what is at the core of the redemptive story should be kept at the center of our lives and ministries.

When the Story Is Silent: How to Read the Bible in Changing Times

Throughout this book we've discussed how to read the Bible and interpret its many literary forms. We've discussed how to discern eternal truth in culturally embedded texts. We've proposed how to apply these divine-human words in the rapidly changing world around us.

But what about those issues in contemporary culture about which the Bible is silent? What about abortion, or euthanasia, or stem-cell research, or pornography, or drug abuse, or the medical use of marijuana, or illegal immigration, or environmental care?[5] In fact, a heart-of-God hermeneutic is ideal for dealing with these kinds of new and changing circumstances. This is because the ultimate goal of this approach is not to determine which biblical commands to obey and which to safely ignore. The goal is, rather, to so immerse ourselves in the nature, purpose, and plan of God that we can think his thoughts after him and so discern his will in the changing circumstances of life.

Let me illustrate this. I've been married to my beautiful wife, Roxanne, for twenty-six years. In that time I've come to know her pretty well. Being a guy, I'm sure it has taken me longer than it should

249

have. Nevertheless, if I arrive first at a restaurant and she is running late, I could order for her and probably get it right (a nice chicken and pasta dish, generally). If some friends invited us to join them on vacation, I would know without asking whether she would want to go (a weekend in Las Vegas? no, thanks; a trip to the mountains for skiing or hiking? you bet!). If a time share company called and offered us a free weekend somewhere exotic if we would listen to their sales pitch, I know exactly what she would say (over her dead body . . . or possibly *my* dead body if I said yes). I have walked with her long enough and far enough to know her well. We usually can tell what the other is thinking. We've seen each other at our best, and at our worst.

Living our lives in relationship with God means walking long enough and far enough with him to be able to anticipate his will in our lives, to make good and godly decisions that correspond with his larger purpose for the world. This does not happen overnight but comes from drinking deeply from God's Word, the water of life. It comes through lessons learned and mistakes that we've made. It comes through growing through failure as well as success. It comes as we nurture a heart that desires to grow, rather than one stuck in old prejudices and old patterns. It is a willingness to hear the message afresh and listen to the promptings of the Holy Spirit.

Consider some of the issues mentioned above. How do we discern God's will on a topic like abortion? Obviously, the fundamental biblical value that all human beings are created in the image of God is an important factor (Gen. 1:26–27; 9:6). So also is the fact that God knew and cared about us before we were born (Ps. 139:13). Contrary to some views of personhood, our bodies are not our own, to do with as we please. They are God's, to be used for his glory (1 Cor. 6:19). These things should move us toward a position supporting life—whether that life is preborn, aged, disabled, or mentally challenged. At the same time we must not neglect the many commands related to God's love for the sinner and the outcast, and the damage done to the poor by society's injustices. Young girls who become pregnant need the church's love and support, not judgment and condemnation. The church is a family, and a family must care for its own. We have no right to oppose abortion unless we are ready to reach out and help those who have made mistakes in life, providing

250

encouragement, support, and viable options like prenatal care and adoption services.

Or consider the issue of illegal immigration, a volatile issue where I live in Southern California.[6] The Bible certainly calls us to obey the laws of the land (Rom. 13:1–7), and Christians who support immigration rights must take care lest they engage in illegal activities. At the same time, the Old Testament frequently calls on Israel to care for the poor, the alien, and the foreigner living among them, remembering that they themselves were once aliens oppressed in a foreign land (Exod. 22:21; 23:9; Deut. 24:17–20; 26:12–13; 27:19). In the New Testament, Christians are referred to as exiles and aliens living in a world that is not their true home (1 Pet. 1:1, 17; 2:11; Heb. 11:13–14).

Even if someone considers illegal immigrants to be "enemies" who take away resources and jobs, we must not forget that Jesus calls his people to love their enemies, to give to anyone who asks, and to pray for those who persecute them (Matt. 5:38–48). I once preached a sermon on the Good Samaritan (Luke 10) and mentioned the immigrant question as one area where Christians sometimes fail to love their neighbors. That week I received an angry letter attacking me for supporting "those people" who were stealing our resources and robbing our country. While I can understand the political and social concerns of this person, absent was any concern for the second of the two greatest commandments: to love your neighbor as yourself (Matt. 22:36–40).

Finding the heart of God in contemporary issues like these is not about plugging in a magic formula. It is about gradually growing into the likeness of Christ. Just as a successful marriage takes an investment of time and effort, a willingness to learn and grow, and an attitude of humility, so discerning the heart of God in Scripture means an openness to set aside our personal agendas and learn daily what it means to walk with him.

Walking with God in His World

Throughout this book concrete steps and criteria have been introduced to help the reader discover the meaning of the Bible and its application for today. Reading Scripture involves both exegetical skills to discern the author's meaning in its original context and cultural awareness to determine its significance for modern times. Yet our ultimate goal is not to become better Bible readers. Our goal is to know and love God, to bring our lives into conformity with his will, and to walk with him every day. While knowing and applying God's Word can be hard work, the rewards are great, as we see our lives gradually transformed into the image of his Son, Jesus Christ.

At the beginning of the Psalter, the Psalmist celebrates the joys and blessings that come from knowing and meditating on God's Word. I can think of no better way to end this book than to reflect on these words.

> Blessed is the one
>   who does not walk in step with the wicked
> or stand in the way that sinners take
>   or sit in the company of mockers,
> but whose delight is in the law of the LORD,
>   and who meditates on his law day and night.
> That person is like a tree planted by streams of water,
>   which yields its fruit in season
> and whose leaf does not wither—
>   whatever they do prospers. (Ps. 1:1–3)

May you be richly blessed as you drink deeply from the life-giving streams of the Word of God.

Notes

Chapter 1 Introduction

1. Alvin J. Schmidt, *How Christianity Changed the World* (Grand Rapids: Zondervan, 2004); see also Jonathan Hill, *What Has Christianity Ever Done for Us? How It Shaped the Modern World* (Downers Grove, IL: InterVarsity, 2005).

2. For more on Miller and the Millerites, see George R. Knight, *Millennial Fever and the End of the World* (Boise, ID: Pacific, 1993).

3. See Kenneth Samples, *Prophets of the Apocalypse: David Koresh and Other American Messiahs* (Grand Rapids: Baker, 1994). For more on millennial movements, see Richard Kyle, *The Last Days Are Here Again: A History of the End Times* (Grand Rapids: Baker, 1998); Robert G. Clouse, Robert N. Hosack, and Richard V. Pierard, *The New Millennium Manual: A Once and Future Guide* (Grand Rapids: Baker, 1999).

4. Cited by James Sire, *Scripture Twisting: 20 Ways the Cults Misread the Bible* (Downers Grove, IL: InterVarsity, 1980), 7.

5. Sire, *Scripture Twisting*, 70–74, 84–88.

6. Susannah Heschel, *The Aryan Jesus: Christian Theologians and the Bible in Nazi Germany* (Princeton: Princeton University Press, 2008), esp. 26–66.

7. Heschel, *Aryan Jesus*, 27.

8. See Stephen R. Haynes, *Noah's Curse: The Biblical Justification of American Slavery* (New York: Oxford University Press, 2002); David M. Goldenberg, *The Curse of Ham: Race and Slavery in Early Judaism, Christianity, and Islam* (Princeton: Princeton University Press, 2003).

9. Benjamin M. Palmer, *Our Historic Mission: An Address Delivered before the Eunomian and Phi-Mu Societies of the La Grange Synodical College, July 7, 1858* (New Orleans: True Witness Office, 1859); cited by Haynes, *Noah's Curse*, 129. See also the 1841 essay by Thornton Stringfellow, available at http://docsouth.unc.edu/church/stringfellow/stringfellow.html.

10. Hill, *What Has Christianity Ever Done*, 176–80; Schmidt, *How Christianity Changed the World*, 271–91.

11. This letter has appeared in different forms on the internet, with various changes and additions. The version of the letter printed here is the original, as written by J. Kent Ashcraft, with corrections to a couple of Scripture references. Used by permission of the

253

author. A discussion of the letter's history (by Barbara Mikkelson) can be found at http://www.snopes.com/politics/religion/drlaura.asp.

Chapter 2 What the Bible Is Not

1. Beza's Latin Bible of 1555 was the first full Bible to have verses. The first English version with such divisions was the Geneva Bible of 1560. See Gordon D. Fee and Mark L. Strauss, *How to Choose a Translation for All Its Worth* (Grand Rapids: Zondervan, 2007), 123.

2. Henry T. Blackaby and Claude V. King, *Experiencing God* (Nashville: Thomas Nelson, 1994), 1. The book's subtitle is *How to Live the Full Adventure of Knowing and Doing the Will of God.*

3. Blackaby and King, *Experiencing God*, 4.

4. Blackaby and King, *Experiencing God*, 106.

5. Gordon D. Fee and Douglas Stuart, *How to Read the Bible for All Its Worth*, 3rd ed. (Grand Rapids: Zondervan, 2003), 30 (italics original).

6. Written by John H. Sammis (1846–1919) and Daniel B. Towner (1850–1919).

7. See Fee and Stuart, *How to Read the Bible*, 69: "In many cases the reason the texts are so difficult for us is that, frankly, they were not written to us."

8. R. Laird Harris, "Leviticus," in *Expositor's Bible Commentary*, vol. 2, ed. Frank E. Gaebelein (Grand Rapids: Zondervan, 1990), 606.

9. See Richard L. Pratt Jr., "Historical Contingencies and Biblical Predictions," in *The Way of Wisdom: Essays in Honor of Bruce K. Waltke*, ed. J. I. Packer and Sven K. Soderlund (Grand Rapids: Zondervan, 2000), 180–203; cf. Robert Chisholm, "When Prophecy Appears to Fail, Check Your Hermeneutic," *Journal of the Evangelical Theological Society* 53.3 (2010), 561–77; Bruce K. Waltke, "The Phenomenon of Conditionality within Unconditional Covenants," in Israel's Apostasy and Restoration: Essays in Honor of Roland K. Harrison, ed. Avraham Gileadi (Grand Rapids: Baker, 1988), 123–39.

10. Chisholm, "When Prophecy Appears to Fail," 561.

11. Pratt, "Historical Contingencies," 183.

12. Chisholm, "When Prophecy Appears to Fail," 562–63.

13. There is a major scholarly debate today concerning which of these Paul is opposing and what he means by the "works of the law." The traditional Reformation view is that he is opposing those who say that salvation comes through works—that is, that a person can earn their salvation through meritorious actions. The "New Perspective" on Paul argues instead that Paul is opposing those who claim that one's identification with the old covenant people of God brings salvation. He is opposing those who say a person must first become a Jew (through circumcision and law keeping) in order to become a follower of the Messiah. In either case, Paul asserts that it is faith alone in Jesus that brings salvation.

14. For various views on this issue see Mark L. Strauss, ed., *Remarriage after Divorce in Today's Church: Three Views* (Grand Rapids: Zondervan, 2006). The three perspectives are provided by Gordon Wenham, William Heth, and Craig Keener.

Chapter 3 What the Bible Is

1. Anthony C. Thiselton, *The Two Horizons: New Testament Hermeneutics and Philosophical Description with Special Reference to Heidegger, Bultmann, Gadamer, and Wittgenstein* (Grand Rapids: Eerdmans; Exeter: Paternoster, 1980).

2. See Gordon D. Fee and Mark L. Strauss, *How to Choose a Translation for All Its Worth* (Grand Rapids: Zondervan, 2007), esp. 25–41.

3. Fee and Strauss, *How to Choose a Translation*, 147–57.

4. Like *Chuck E. Cheese*, or *Dave and Buster's* (an adult version of *Chuck E. Cheese*), in the ancient world pagan temples served as venues for social events and parties.

5. See G. C. Chirichigno, *Debt-Slavery in Israel and the Ancient Near East*, Journal for the Study of the Old Testament: Supplement Series 141 (Sheffield: Sheffield Academic Press, 1993).

6. Bruce Wells, "Exodus," in *Zondervan Illustrated Bible Background Commentary*, ed. John H. Walton (Grand Rapids: Zondervan, 2009), 1:237.

7. See Christopher J. H. Wright, *Old Testament Ethics for the People of God* (Downers Grove, IL: InterVarsity, 2004), 325–37. Referring to polygamy, divorce, and slavery, Wright points out that "Some customs and practices common in the ancient world were tolerated within Israel, without explicit divine command or sanction, but with a developing theological critique that regarded them as falling short of God's highest standards" (329–30).

8. One of the first great challenges to the idea of a metanarrative came from French philosopher Jean-François Lyotard in *The Postmodern Condition: A Report on Knowledge* (Manchester: Manchester University Press, 1984). For a critique of this aspect of postmodernism, see Richard J. Middleton and Brian Walsh, *Truth Is Stranger Than It Used To Be: Biblical Faith in a Postmodern Age* (Downers Grove, IL: InterVarsity, 1995), 71–79.

9. See, for example, Gabriel Fackre, *The Christian Story: A Narrative Interpretation of Basic Christian Doctrine* (Grand Rapids: Eerdmans, 1984); Bernhard W. Anderson, *The Unfolding Drama of the Bible*, 3rd ed. (Philadelphia: Fortress, 1988); Christopher J. H. Wright, *The Mission of God: Unlocking the Bible's Grand Narrative* (Downers Grove, IL: IVP Academic, 2006); Preben Vang and Terry G. Carter, *Telling God's Story: The Biblical Narrative from Beginning to End* (Nashville: Broadman & Holman, 2006).

10. N. T. Wright, "How Can the Bible Be Authoritative?" *Vox Evangelica* 21 (1991): 7–32; N. T. Wright, *The New Testament and the People of God* (Minneapolis: Fortress, 1992), 141–43.

11. Craig G. Bartholomew and Michael W. Goheen, *The Drama of Scripture* (Grand Rapids: Baker Academic, 2004).

12. C. S. Lewis develops this idea in *Perelandra* (1943), the second volume of his space trilogy: a new Adam and Eve are on the planet Venus and eventually pass the test God has given them.

13. Brian J. Walsh and J. Richard Middleton, *The Transforming Vision: Shaping a Christian World View* (Downers Grove, IL: InterVarsity, 1984), 35; cf. Middleton and Walsh, *Truth Is Stranger*. Many others have adopted and adapted their questions, including N. T. Wright, *New Testament and the People of God*, 122–24; C. J. H. Wright, *Old Testament Ethics*, 17–19.

Chapter 4 A Heart-of-God Hermeneutic

1. N. T. Wright points out that "the phrase 'authority of scripture' can make Christian sense only if it is a shorthand for 'the authority of the triune God,' exercised somehow *through* scripture" (*The Last Word: Beyond the Bible Wars to a New Understanding of the Authority of Scripture* [New York: HarperCollins, 2005], 23).

2. The hymn was written by Mary A. Lathbury in 1877. "Beyond the Sacred Page," from this verse in the hymn, was the original title proposed for the book eventually called *Four Views on Moving beyond the Bible to Theology* (ed. Gary T. Meadors [Grand Rapids: Zondervan, 2009]).

3. The recent resurgence apparently began in the 1990s when Janie Tinklenberg, youth group leader at Calvary Reformed Church in Holland, Michigan, found a copy of the book and began promoting the idea with her youth. For the full story, see Sandy Sheppard, "What Would Jesus Do?" http://www.christianity.com/ChristianLiving/Features/11622298/.

4. Thomas à Kempis, *Imitation of Christ*, trans. E. M. Blaiklock, Hodder Christian Classics (London: Hodder and Stoughton, 1979); E. J. Tinsley, *The Imitation of God in Christ: An Essay on the Biblical Basis of Christian Spirituality* (Philadelphia: Westminster, 1960); Michael Griffiths, *The Example of Jesus*, The Jesus Library (Downers Grove, IL: InterVarsity, 1985).

5. Some theologians distinguish between "communicable" and "incommunicable" attributes of God. The communicable attributes are those we share, in part, with God, while the incommunicable are unique to him. The problem with this distinction is that with most characteristics, it is a matter of degree rather than complete difference. Human beings have power, knowledge, and presence, but we are not all-powerful, all knowing, or present everywhere at once. In the same way, humans can be loving, but we are not all loving, as God is. Truly incommunicable traits of God are things like his eternality, immutability, and self-existence, which would be impossible to imitate even if we tried. See Louis Berkhof, *Systematic Theology* (Grand Rapids: Eerdmans, 1941), 55–56, for more on these distinctions.

6. E. J. Tinsley, "Some Principles for Reconstructing a Doctrine of the Imitation of Christ," *Scottish Journal of Theology* 25 (1972): 45–57 (quote from p. 45). Tinsley notes that "Luther was critical of the ideal of the *imitatio Christi*, partly because he was repelled by the excesses of the sects where it was being interpreted in a crudely liberal [*sic*] way (e.g. among the Anabaptists) and partly because he became convinced that the 'imitation' of Christ conflicted with the essence of the Christian Gospel as he had come to interpret it. He found himself unable to reconcile the presuppositions of the practice . . . with his doctrine of justification by faith" (p. 45).

7. Robert Coleman, *The Master Plan of Evangelism* (Old Tappan, NJ: Revell, 1963), 38.

8. Hans Urs von Balthasar, *Theo-drama: Theological Dramatic Theory*, vols. 1–5 (San Francisco: Ignatius Press, 1988–98); Kevin Vanhoozer, *The Drama of Doctrine: A Canonical Linguistic Approach to Christian Theology* (Louisville: Westminster John Knox, 2005).

9. Kevin Vanhoozer, "A Drama-of-Redemption Model," in Meadors, *Moving beyond the Bible*, 156.

10. Vanhoozer, *Drama of Doctrine*, 102.

11. Samuel Wells, *Improvisation: The Drama of Christian Ethics* (Grand Rapids: Brazos, 2004), 65.

12. Vanhoozer, "Drama-of-Redemption Model," 173.

13. Vanhoozer, "Drama-of-Redemption Model," 175.

14. Vanhoozer, "Drama-of-Redemption Model," 170.

15. The material that follows was first developed in my essay, "Reflections on Moving beyond the Bible to Theology," in Meadors, *Moving beyond the Bible*, 271–98, esp. 290–93.

16. See J. I. Packer, *"Fundamentalism" and the Word of God* (Grand Rapids: Eerdmans, 1958), 101–14.

17. A "call-out" in publishing is a portion of text pulled out and placed in the margin to highlight an important point. Most magazine articles and many textbooks contain call-outs.

18. See Gordon D. Fee and Douglas Stuart, *How to Read the Bible for All Its Worth*, 3rd ed. (Grand Rapids: Zondervan, 2003), 30.

19. This is especially true of the "new hermeneutic" as well as some forms of reader-response criticism. On the new hermeneutic, see J. M. Robinson and J. B. Cobb, eds., *The New Hermeneutic* (New York: Harper & Row, 1964), and H. G. Gadamer, *Truth and Method* (London: Sheed and Ward, 1975). On reader-response criticism, see J. P. Tomkins, ed., *Reader-Response Criticism* (Baltimore: Johns Hopkins University Press, 1980). A good summary of the issues (and suggested solutions) can be found in Grant Osborne, *The Hermeneutical*

Spiral: A Comprehensive Introduction to Biblical Interpretation, 2nd ed. (Downers Grove, IL: IVP Academic, 2006), 465–521 (Appendixes 1, 2).

20. See Ben F. Meyer, *Critical Realism and the New Testament*, Princeton Theological Monograph Series 17 (Allison Park, PA: Pickwick, 1989); N. T. Wright, *The New Testament and the People of God* (Minneapolis: Fortress, 1992), 32–37.

21. Especially important in this regard are speech-act theory, developed by J. L. Austin and John Searle, and relevance theory, developed by Dan Sperber and Deirdre Wilson.

22. See Gordon Fee, *New Testament Exegesis: A Handbook for Students and Pastors*, 3rd ed. (Louisville: Westminster John Knox, 2002); John H. Hayes and Carl R. Holladay, *Biblical Exegesis: A Beginner's Handbook*, 3rd ed. (Louisville: Westminster John Knox, 2007); Osborne, *Hermeneutical Spiral*, esp. 35–175; William W. Klein, Craig L. Blomberg, and Robert L. Hubbard Jr., *Introduction to Biblical Interpretation* (Nashville: Thomas Nelson, 2004); J. Scott Duvall and J. Daniel Hayes, *Grasping God's Word* (Grand Rapids: Zondervan, 2005).

23. Mark L. Strauss, *Four Portraits, One Jesus: A Survey of Jesus and the Gospels* (Grand Rapids: Zondervan, 2007), 29.

24. Mormons practice baptism for the dead, based in part on this passage.

25. See the discussion of this text in chapter 8.

26. "Evaluative point of view" is a narrative category that describes the perspective the reader is expected to take when reading a narrative text. For details, see Mark Allen Powell, *What Is Narrative Criticism?* (Minneapolis: Fortress, 1990); Strauss, *Four Portraits, One Jesus*, 70. See also the discussion of Old Testament narrative in chapter 6, below.

Chapter 5 Seeking the Heart of God in Dialogue

1. See, for example, InterVarsity Press's highly successful series *The Ancient Christian Commentary on Scripture* and Eerdmans' *The Church's Bible*. McKnight points to three important monographs to illustrate this resurgence: Thomas Oden, *The Rebirth of Orthodoxy* (San Francisco: HarperSanFrancisco, 2003); J. I. Packer and Thomas Oden, *One Faith: The Evangelical Consensus* (Downers Grove, IL: InterVarsity, 2004); Chuck Colson, *The Faith* (Grand Rapids: Zondervan, 2008).

2. Scot McKnight, *The Blue Parakeet: Rethinking How You Read the Bible* (Grand Rapids: Zondervan, 2008), 30 (italics original).

3. McKnight, *Blue Parakeet*, 31.

4. William A. Dyrness & Veli-Matti Kärkkäinen, *Global Dictionary of Theology* (Downers Grove, IL: IVP Academic, 2008); Timothy C. Tennent, *Theology in the Context of World Christianity: How the Global Church Is Influencing the Way We Think about and Discuss Theology* (Grand Rapids: Zondervan, 2007); William A. Dyrness, *Emerging Voices in Global Theology* (Grand Rapids: Zondervan, 1994); Tokunboh Adeyemo, ed., *African Bible Commentary* (Grand Rapids: Zondervan, 2010).

5. See, for example, the works of Samuel Escobar, Rene Padilla, Simon Chan, Kwame Bediako, and Tite Tienou.

Chapter 6 Finding the Heart of God in the Diverse Genres of the Old Testament

1. Charles Dickens, *A Tale of Two Cities*, ed. Richard Maxwell (London: Penguin Classics, 2003). According to a Wikipedia article on the book, the novel has sold well over 200 million copies.

2. For more details on the nature of these genres, see the comprehensive introductions to hermeneutics, such as William W. Klein, Craig L. Blomberg, and Robert L. Hubbard Jr.,

Introduction to Biblical Interpretation (Nashville: Thomas Nelson, 2004); J. Scott Duvall and J. Daniel Hayes, *Grasping God's Word* (Grand Rapids: Zondervan, 2005); Grant Osborne, *The Hermeneutical Spiral: A Comprehensive Introduction to Biblical Interpretation*, 2nd ed. (Downers Grove, IL: IVP Academic, 2006); Gordon Fee and Douglas Stuart, *How to Read the Bible for All Its Worth*, 3rd ed. (Grand Rapids: Zondervan, 2003); Robert H. Stein, *A Basic Guide to Interpreting the Bible: Playing by the Rules*, 2nd ed. (Grand Rapids: Baker Academic, 2011); Bruce Corley, Steve W. Lemke, and Grant I. Lovejoy, eds., *Biblical Hermeneutics: A Comprehensive Introduction to Interpreting Scripture*, 2nd ed. (Nashville: Broadman & Holman, 2002).

3. The Hebrew text has three divisions: the Law (*Torah*; Genesis–Deuteronomy), the Prophets (*Nevi'im*), and the Writings (*Kethuvim*). Together they are called the *Tanak*, an acronym formed from the first letter of the three Hebrew divisions (*TNK*).

4. For more detailed discussion, see Robert Alter, *The Art of Biblical Narrative* (New York: Basic Books, 1981); Mark Allen Powell, *What Is Narrative Criticism?* (Minneapolis: Fortress, 1990); Leland Ryken, *Words of Delight: A Literary Introduction to the Bible* (Grand Rapids: Baker, 1987); David M. Howard, *Introduction to the Old Testament Historical Literature* (Chicago: Moody, 1993); V. Philips Long, *The Art of Biblical History* (Grand Rapids: Zondervan, 1994).

5. See Fee and Stuart, *How to Read the Bible*, 91–92.

6. Fee and Stuart, *How to Read the Bible*, 98.

7. See Anthony Thiselton, *The First Epistle to the Corinthians: A Commentary on the Greek Text*, New International Greek Testament Commentary (Grand Rapids: Eerdmans, 2000), 725–28.

8. See, for example, G. K. Beale and D. A. Carson, *Commentary on the New Testament use of the Old Testament* (Grand Rapids: Baker Academic, 2007); Kenneth Berding and Jonathan Lunde, eds., *Three Views on the New Testament Use of the Old Testament* (Grand Rapids: Zondervan, 2008), presenting views by Walter C. Kaiser, Darrell L. Bock, and Peter Enns; G. K. Beale, ed., *The Right Doctrine from the Wrong Texts? Essays on the Use of the Old Testament in the New* (Grand Rapids: Baker, 1994); Steve Moyise, *Evoking Scripture: Seeing the Old Testament in the New* (London/New York: T&T Clark, 2008).

9. See J. Daniel Hays, "Applying the Old Testament Law Today," *Bibliotheca Sacra* 158 (2001): 21–35; Elmer A. Martens, "How Is the Christian to Construe Old Testament Law?" *Bulletin for Biblical Research* 12 (2002): 199–216.

10. Peter T. Vogt, *Interpreting the Pentateuch: An Exegetical Handbook* (Grand Rapids: Kregel, 2009), 42–48.

11. See Christopher J. H. Wright, *Old Testament Ethics for the People of God* (Downers Grove, IL: InterVarsity, 2004), esp. 62–74; C. J. H. Wright, *Walking in the Ways of the Lord* (Downers Grove, IL: InterVarsity, 1995), esp. 113–14.

12. C. J. H. Wright, *Old Testament Ethics*, 63.

13. C. J. H. Wright, *Old Testament Ethics*, 64–65; Vogt, *Interpreting the Pentateuch*, 45.

14. *NIV Study Bible*, ed. Kenneth L. Barker (Grand Rapids: Zondervan, 2008), 1840–41.

15. For a survey of the best commentaries on Amos, see Tremper Longman III, *Old Testament Commentary Survey*, 4th ed. (Grand Rapids: Baker Academic, 2007).

16. For key issues in reading and interpreting the Psalms, see Walter Brueggemann, *The Message of the Psalms* (Minneapolis: Augsburg, 1984); Tremper Longman III, *How to Read the Psalms* (Downers Grove, IL: InterVarsity, 1988); Mark D. Futato and David M. Howard, *Interpreting the Psalms: An Exegetical Handbook* (Grand Rapids: Kregel, 2007).

17. While most modern English Bibles have 150 psalms, other versions of the Psalter have existed throughout the centuries. The numbering of the Psalms is slightly different in

the Greek Septuagint than in the Hebrew Bible, and most Septuagint manuscripts contain Psalm 151 (included in Eastern Orthodox translations as well). Also, the Syriac Bible (the Peshitta) contains 155 psalms.

18. The Hebrew says *ledavid*, which could mean "by David," "for David," "to David," or something else. So the nature of the connection to David is not clear.

19. For these identifications of psalms of disorientation, orientation, and new or reorientation, see Brueggemann, *Message of the Psalms*, 18–23.

20. For surveys of wisdom literature, see Roland E. Murphy, *The Tree of Life: An Exploration of Biblical Wisdom Literature* (Grand Rapids: Eerdmans, 2005); Daniel J. Estes, *Handbook on the Wisdom Books and Psalms* (Grand Rapids: Baker Academic, 2005); Derek Kidner, *The Wisdom of Proverbs, Job, and Ecclesiastes: An Introduction to Wisdom Literature* (Downers Grove, IL: InterVarsity, 1985).

21. Most commentators consider Elihu to be an arrogant and angry upstart whose words are an advance on the counsel of the three friends, but who still falls far short of God's final word.

22. See Craig Bartholomew, *Ecclesiastes*, ed. Tremper Longman III, Baker Commentary on the Old Testament Wisdom and Psalms (Grand Rapids: Baker Academic, 2009), 93–94.

23. *The Message* (Colorado Springs: NavPress, 2002).

Chapter 7 Finding the Heart of God in the Diverse Genres of the New Testament

1. Dummar's story was eventually made into an Academy Award–winning film, *Melvin and Howard* (1980). See Richard Hack, *Hughes: The Private Diaries, Memos and Letters; The Definitive Biography of the First American Billionaire* (Beverly Hills: New Millennium Press, 2001). A summary of the story, with recent news reports claiming that Dummar's story may, in fact, check out, can be found at http://en.wikipedia.org/wiki/Melvin_Dummar.

2. For details on the nature and function of the Gospels, see Mark L. Strauss, *Four Portraits, One Jesus: A Survey of Jesus and the Gospels* (Grand Rapids: Zondervan, 2007); Craig Blomberg, *Jesus and the Gospels: An Introduction and Survey*, 2nd ed. (Nashville: Broadman & Holman, 2009).

3. For the development of this idea, see Richard Bauckham, ed., *The Gospels for All Christians: Rethinking the Gospel Audiences* (Grand Rapids: Eerdmans, 1998).

4. Strauss, *Four Portraits, One Jesus*, 25–29.

5. Craig Blomberg, *The Historical Reliability of the Gospels*, 2nd ed. (Downers Grove, IL: IVP Academic, 2007).

6. Darrell L. Bock and Robert L. Webb, eds., *Key Events in the Life of the Historical Jesus: A Collaborative Exploration of Context and Coherence* (Grand Rapids: Eerdmans, 2010).

7. See, for example, Kurt Aland, ed., *Synopsis of the Four Gospels: Greek-English Edition of the Synopsis Quattuor Evangeliorum with the Text of the Revised Standard Version* (Munster: United Bible Societies, 1964).

8. The destinations of the Gospels are uncertain, but Rome (Mark), Antioch (Matthew), and Ephesus (John) are among the most widely accepted for these three Gospels. Luke's destination is anyone's guess.

9. See the summary of the drama of redemption in chapter 3, above.

10. J. Scott Duvall and J. Daniel Hays, *Grasping God's Word: A Hands-On Approach to Reading, Interpreting and Applying the Bible*, 2nd ed. (Grand Rapids: Zondervan, 2005), 278.

11. The indisputable Pauline letters are Romans, 1 and 2 Corinthians, Galatians, Philippians, 1 Thessalonians, and Philemon. Some scholars question the Pauline authorship of

Colossians, Ephesians, and 2 Thessalonians. Most disputed are the Pastoral Epistles (1 & 2 Timothy and Titus).

12. See E. Randolph Richards, *Paul and First-Century Letter Writing: Secretaries, Composition, and Collection* (Downers Grove, IL: InterVarsity, 2004).

13. Stanley Stowers, *Letter Writing in Greco-Roman Antiquity* (Philadelphia: Westminster, 1986), 28.

14. Paul uses first-person singular Greek verbs 681 times in his New Testament letters. While he also uses first-person plural verbs 380 times, many of these are the editorial "we."

15. This distinction was popularized by Adolf Deissmann (*Light from the Ancient East* [New York: Harper & Brothers, 1922]).

16. For examples of this from the Greco-Roman world, see Gordon D. Fee, *The First Epistle to the Corinthians*, New International Commentary on the New Testament (Grand Rapids: Eerdmans, 1987), 542n55.

17. See Gordon D. Fee and Mark L. Strauss, *How to Choose a Translation for All Its Worth* (Grand Rapids: Zondervan, 2007), 56.

18. See Daniel B. Wallace, *Greek Grammar beyond the Basics* (Grand Rapids: Zondervan, 1996), 119–20.

19. This identification is rendered more likely by the fact that Babylon the prostitute is identified as sitting on "seven hills" (Rev. 17:9)—the city of Rome was built on seven hills.

Chapter 8 When Cultures Collide

1. J. Scott Duvall and J. Daniel Hays, *Grasping God's Word: A Hands-On Approach to Reading, Interpreting and Applying the Bible*, 2nd ed. (Grand Rapids: Zondervan, 2005), 21–25.

2. Joel B. Green, *Seized by Truth: Reading the Bible as Scripture* (Nashville: Abingdon, 2007), 56 (italics are mine).

3. Green, *Seized by Truth*, 54–55.

4. Green, *Seized by Truth*, 61.

5. Jack Kuhatschek, *Taking the Guesswork out of Applying the Bible* (Downers Grove, IL: InterVarsity, 1990), 54–57.

6. Walter Kaiser, *Toward Rediscovering the Old Testament* (Grand Rapids: Zondervan, 1987), 164–66. Kaiser acknowledges his debt to Michael Schluter and Roy Clements for developing this model of the ladder of abstraction from the area of jurisprudence. The ladder of abstraction with reference to literature seems to have been first developed by S. I. Hayakawa in *Language in Thought and Action*, 5th ed. (San Diego: Harvest Original, 1991), first published in 1939.

7. Walter Kaiser, "A Principlizing Model," in *Four Views on Moving beyond the Bible to Theology*, ed. Gary T. Meadors (Grand Rapids: Zondervan, 2009), 25; Kaiser, *Rediscovering the Old Testament*, 165–66 (see the diagram on p. 166).

8. Kuhatschek, *Applying the Bible*, 58–60.

9. Daniel Doriani, "A Response to Walter C. Kaiser Jr.," in Meadors, *Moving beyond the Bible*, 54. See further Daniel Doriani, *Putting Truth to Work: The Theory and Practice of Biblical Application* (Phillipsburg, NJ: P&R, 2001), 161–212.

10. David K. Clark, *To Know and Love God: Method for Theology* (Wheaton: Crossway, 2003), 112. Jeannine K. Brown raises a similar concern, pointing out that the transcultural principle in fact reflects the culture of the interpreter (*Scripture as Communication: Introducing Biblical Hermeneutics* [Grand Rapids: Baker Academic, 2007], 261–64).

11. William J. Webb, *Slaves, Women & Homosexuals: Exploring the Hermeneutics of Cultural Analysis* (Downers Grove, IL: InterVarsity, 2001). A similar method is developed in the earlier work of Richard Longenecker, *New Testament Social Ethics for Today* (Grand Rapids: Eerdmans, 1984); Longenecker, *New Wine into Fresh Wineskins: Contextualizing the Early Christian Confessions* (Peabody, MA: Hendrickson, 1999); and more recently in volumes by I. H. Marshall, *Beyond the Bible: Moving from Scripture to Theology* (Grand Rapids: Baker Academic, 2004); Glen Scorgie, *The Journey Back to Eden* (Grand Rapids: Zondervan, 2005).

12. See William J. Webb, *Corporal Punishment in the Bible: A Redemptive-Movement Hermeneutic for Troubling Texts* (Downers Grove, IL: InterVarsity, forthcoming); Webb, "A Redemptive-Movement Model," in Meadors, *Moving beyond the Bible*, 228–36.

13. Webb, "Redemptive-Movement Model," 233. Webb acknowledges that some of these texts relate to slaves and "fools," but he sees parallel language used for children and teens.

14. Webb, "Redemptive-Movement Model," 244.

15. Webb, "Redemptive-Movement Model," 246. I. H. Marshall makes a similar point when he notes that "*The closing of the canon is not incompatible with the nonclosing of the interpretation of that canon. . . .* The closing of the canon did not bring the process of doctrinal development to an end" (*Beyond the Bible*, 54; italics original).

16. Webb, "Redemptive-Movement Model," 226.

17. See the review by Thomas R. Schreiner, "Review of *Slaves, Women & Homosexuals*," in *The Southern Baptist Journal of Theology* 6/1 (2002): 46–64.

18. Daniel M. Doriani, "A Response to William J. Webb," in Meadors, *Moving beyond the Bible*, 258.

19. An interesting parallel to this appears in a recent book by Stephen Tomkins on the Clapham Sect, the British social reformers led by abolitionist William Wilberforce. Although the group founded the Sierra Leone colony to abolish the slave trade, a system of indentured apprenticeship was eventually established, a system almost as cruel as slavery itself. When Lt. Thomas Thompson, the colony's crown governor, objected to the practice and abolished the apprenticeships, Sierra Leone Company chairman Henry Thornton reinstituted the apprenticeships, a decision approved by Wilberforce himself. Under pressure from his peers, Wilberforce had surprisingly settled for a compromise solution rather than full emancipation of slaves (Stephen Tomkins, *The Clapham Sect: How Wilberforce's Circle Transformed Britain* [Oxford: Lion, 2010]). See Ted Olsen, "The Abolitionists' Scandal," *Christianity Today* 54.1 (October 2010): 46–49.

20. See, for example, Duvall and Hays, *Grasping God's Word*, 22–25. A similar four-step method appears in William W. Klein, Craig L. Blomberg, and Robert L. Hubbard Jr., *Introduction to Biblical Interpretation* (Nashville: Thomas Nelson, 2004), 485.

21. Grant Osborne, *The Hermeneutical Spiral: A Comprehensive Introduction to Biblical Interpretation*, 2nd ed. (Downers Grove, IL: IVP Academic, 2006), 422–26. Osborne actually refers to these as "three basic steps" or "criteria," followed by "five principles." But I see no difference in kind between his "criteria" and his "principles."

22. Charles Cosgrove, *Appealing to Scripture in Moral Debate: Five Hermeneutical Rules* (Grand Rapids: Eerdmans, 2002).

23. Walter C. Kaiser and Moisés Silva, *Introduction to Biblical Hermeneutics*, rev. ed. (Grand Rapids: Zondervan, 2007), 234–37.

24. Webb, *Slaves*, 73–235.

25. Gordon Fee and Douglas Stuart, *How to Read the Bible for All Its Worth*, 3rd ed. (Grand Rapids: Zondervan, 2003), 74–87.

26. "Ten questions for evaluating the level of specificity of the original application" in Klein, Blomberg, and Hubbard, *Introduction to Biblical Interpretation,* 485–98.

27. These criteria are an expansion and development of those proposed in my essay "Reflections on Moving beyond the Bible to Theology," in Meadors, *Moving beyond the Bible,* 293–98.

28. Cosgrove, *Appealing to Scripture,* 12; cf. Webb, *Slaves,* 105–10.

29. Fee and Stuart, *How to Read the Bible,* 75.

30. Osborne, *Hermeneutical Spiral,* 423.

31. Cosgrove, *Appealing to Scripture,* 51; see James M. Gustafson, "The Place of Scripture in Christian Ethics: A Methodological Study," in *Theology and Ethics* (Philadelphia: United Church Press, 1974), 121–45 (quote from p. 133).

32. In her important work on hermeneutics and the communicative function of Scripture, Jeannine Brown, while reluctant to develop lists of guidelines, identifies *purpose* and *coherence* as two key questions to ask when recontextualizing biblical passages (*Scripture as Communication,* 246–51).

33. See Fee and Stuart, *How to Read the Bible,* 82–83.

34. Osborne, *Hermeneutical Spiral,* 424. Cf. Cosgrove, *Appealing to Scripture,* 90–115; Klein, Blomberg, and Hubbard, *Introduction to Biblical Interpretation,* 494–95.

35. The Jewish community that produced the Dead Sea Scrolls also taught hatred for enemies. For example, the scroll known as the "Rule of the Community" says that God's people are to "love all the sons of light . . . and to detest the sons of darkness" (1QS 1:10).

36. Fee and Stuart, *How to Read the Bible,* 83–84.

37. Webb, *Slaves,* 123–45. Cf. Klein, Blomberg, and Hubbard, *Introduction to Biblical Interpretation,* 493. Webb has separate discussions of creation patterns and the principle of primogeniture.

38. Klein, Blomberg, and Hubbard, *Introduction to Biblical Interpretation,* 493.

39. Klein, Blomberg, and Hubbard, *Introduction to Biblical Interpretation,* 493–94.

40. See, for example, D. A. Carson, ed., *From Sabbath to Lord's Day: A Biblical, Historical, and Theological Investigation* (Grand Rapids: Zondervan, 1982).

41. See especially Robert A. J. Gagnon, *The Bible and Homosexual Practice: Texts and Hermeneutics* (Nashville: Abingdon, 2001). For a more popular treatment, see Mark Strauss and Peter Vogt, "A Biblical Perspective on Homosexuality," *Heart and Mind* (Spring 2006), available through Bethel University's Office of Communication and Marketing.

42. See, for example, John Boswell, *Christianity, Social Tolerance, and Homosexuality* (Chicago/London: University of Chicago Press, 1980), 109, 112; R. Scroggs, *The New Testament and Homosexuality: Contextual Background for Contemporary Debate* (Philadelphia: Fortress, 1983).

43. Douglas J. Moo, *The Epistle to the Romans,* The New International Commentary on the New Testament (Grand Rapids: Eerdmans, 1996), 114.

44. C. E. B. Cranfield, *A Critical and Exegetical Commentary on the Epistle to the Romans,* International Critical Commentary (Edinburgh: T&T Clark, 1975), 1:125. Cf. J. D. G. Dunn: "Paul's attitude to homosexual practice is unambiguous. . . . [It is] of a piece with and direct result of the basic corruption of the glory and truth of God in idolatry" (*Romans 1–8,* Word Biblical Commentary 38A [Dallas: Word, 1988], 74).

45. Stanley J. Grenz, *Welcoming but Not Affirming* (Louisville: Westminster, 1998). See also Timothy Bradshaw, ed., *The Way Forward? Christian Voices on Homosexuality and the Church,* 2nd ed. (Grand Rapids: Eerdmans, 2003); Thomas E. Schmidt, *Straight and Narrow? Compassion & Clarity in the Homosexuality Debate* (Downers Grove, IL: InterVarsity, 1995).

46. For the egalitarianism perspective, see Ronald W. Pierce, Rebecca Merrill Groothuis, and Gordon D. Fee, eds., *Discovering Biblical Equality: Complementarity without Hierarchy* (Downers Grove, IL: InterVarsity, 2004). For complementarianism, see John Piper and Wayne Grudem, eds., *Recovering Biblical Manhood and Womanhood* (Wheaton: Crossway, 1991). A good balanced presentation of both views is James R. Beck, ed., *Two Views on Women in Ministry* (Grand Rapids: Zondervan, 2005).

47. For cautions and a contrary view, see Webb, *Slaves*, 134–45.

48. For a detailed discussion of these issues, see William D. Mounce, *Pastoral Epistles*, Word Biblical Commentary 46 (Nashville: Thomas Nelson, 2000), 117–49.

49. Consider, for example, the work of Elisabeth Elliot and Rachel Saint among the Auca Indians after the murder of their husband (Jim Elliot) and brother (Nate Saint). See Elisabeth Elliot, *The Savage My Kinsman* (New York: Harper, 1961).

Chapter 9 Conclusion

1. A. J. Jacobs, *The Year of Living Biblically: One Man's Humble Quest to Follow the Bible as Literally as Possible* (New York: Simon and Schuster, 2007).

2. Jacobs, *Year of Living Biblically*, 5.

3. Jacobs, *Year of Living Biblically*, 7.

4. Jacobs, *Year of Living Biblically*, 119.

5. For a good discussion of Christian ethics related to many of these issues, see John R. W. Stott, *Decisive Issues Facing Christians Today* (Old Tappan, NJ: Revell, 1990).

6. On this issue, see M. Daniel Carroll R., *Christian at the Border: Immigration, the Church and the Bible* (Grand Rapids: Baker Academic, 2008).

Scripture Index

266

270

271

1:17 251
2:11 251
2:18 6
2:21 74
2:21–25 99
3:1 238, 241
3:1–6 8
3:3 241
3:8 241
3:12–18 99
4:12–19 99
5:12 184
5:13 200
5:14 10, 23, 223

2 Peter

1:2 182
1:21 45

1 John

2:6 74
2:18 203
2:22 203
3:2 60
3:16 74
4:3 203

2 John

7 203

Revelation

1 195, 203
1:1 194
1:1–3 196
1:3 197
1:4 182, 196
1:8 64
1:9–19 196
1:10 235
1:12–20 194
1:17 64
2–3 195, 196
2:8 64
2:10 196
2:13 196
4 203
4–5 195
5:5–6 112, 194
5:6 198
5:9–12 64
6–8 4
6–16 195
6:2–8 201
7 202, 204
7:3–8 5
7:4–8 198
7:9 202
7:14 202
7:15–17 202
12:9 203
13 204, 209

13:8 204
13:18 198
8:7 201
13 202
13:1 201
13:11 203
14:1–4 5
17–18 195
17–19 200
19 195
19–22 64
20 195
20–22 80, 204
20:1–7 198
20:2 203
20:7–8 201
21–22 167, 195, 196, 204
21:1 64, 195
21:3–4 64–65
21:6 64
21:27 204
22:7 197
22:10 197
22:13 64
22:16 112
22:18 197
22:18–21 196
22:19 197

Mark L. Strauss (PhD, Aberdeen) is professor of New Testament at Bethel Seminary San Diego, where he has served for seventeen years. He has a passion for connecting God's Word to real life and preaches and teaches regularly at churches, conferences, and college campuses. He lives in San Diego with his wife, Roxanne, and their three children, ages eighteen, sixteen, and twelve.

Strauss is the author of many books and articles, including: "Mark," in the revised *Expositor's Bible Commentary* (2010); *Four Portraits, One Jesus: An Introduction to Jesus and the Gospels* (2007); *How to Choose a Translation for All Its Worth* (with Gordon D. Fee; 2007); *The Essential Bible Companion* (with John Walton; 2006); "Luke" in the *Zondervan Illustrated Bible Background Commentary* (2002); *Distorting Scripture? The Challenge of Bible Translation and Gender Accuracy* (1998); and *The Davidic Messiah in Luke-Acts* (1996). He was co-editor of and contributor to *The Challenge of Bible Translation: Communicating God's Word to the World* (2003).

Strauss also serves as vice chairman on the Committee for Bible Translation for the New International Version, as an associate editor for the *NIV Study Bible* (2008), and as New Testament editor for the *Expanded Bible* (2011) and the Teach the Text Commentary Series (Baker Books, forthcoming). He is a member of the Society of Biblical Literature (SBL), the Institute for Biblical Research (IBR), and the Evangelical Theological Society (ETS).